# Representing God
# at the Statehouse

# Representing God at the Statehouse

## Religion and Politics in the American States

Edited by Edward L. Cleary
& Allen D. Hertzke

ROWMAN & LITTLEFIELD PUBLISHERS, INC.
*Lanham • Boulder • New York • Toronto • Oxford*

ROWMAN & LITTLEFIELD PUBLISHERS, INC.

Published in the United States of America
by Rowman & Littlefield Publishers, Inc.
A wholly owned subsidiary of The Rowman & Littlefield Publishing Group, Inc.
4501 Forbes Boulevard, Suite 200, Lanham, Maryland 20706
www.rowmanlittlefield.com

PO Box 317
Oxford
OX2 9RU, UK

British Library Cataloguing in Publication Information Available

**Library of Congress Cataloging-in-Publication Data**

Representing God at the statehouse : religion and politics in the American states /
  edited by Edward L. Cleary and Allen D. Hertzke.
    p. cm.
  Includes bibliographical references and index.
  ISBN 0-7425-3437-5 (cloth : alk. paper)—ISBN 0-7425-3438-3 (pbk. : alk. paper)
  1. Religion and politics—United States. I. Cleary, Edward L. II. Hertzke, Allen D.,
  1950–
BL2525.R4717 2006
322'.1'0973—dc22                                                              2005017365

Printed in the United States of America

∞™ The paper used in this publication meets the minimum requirements of American
National Standard for Information Sciences—Permanence of Paper for Printed Library
Materials, ANSI/NISO Z39.48-1992.

# Contents

# Introduction

## Edward L. Cleary and Allen D. Hertzke

**W**hile a great surge of interest in religion and politics has occurred at the national level in the past three decades, extensive activity has gone on largely unnoticed at the state level. Systematic studies of politics and religion at the state level[1] are virtually unknown except for a few attempts to analyze hot issues, such as abortion.[2]

Yet churches and other religious organizations focus significant lobbying efforts at the state level. It is here that policy decisions strongly affect the allocation of government resources, monetary and symbolic, often through religious organizations. State government has expanded exponentially in the past thirty years, and state interest groups have similarly increased in number and diversity.[3]

## EMERGENCE OF RELIGION AND POLITICS AT THE STATE LEVEL

This volume provides the first systematic view of religion and politics at the state level. It explores the lobbying efforts of churches and other religious organizations. Several factors have entered into the extensive growth of religion and politics at the state level, opening up a relatively new field of activity for religious groups. First, state budgets have grown exponentially, including billions of dollars now available for appropriation through devolution of monies from federal programs. Second and more fundamental, American federalism has changed. Efforts have been made to grant more power to states in areas such as welfare policy. There is good reason to believe that this change has led to greater religious advocacy in the states.

Third, the composition of the lobbying enterprise has rapidly changed. For good reason—at least in many western states—lobbyists in the past presented a sinister appearance. Lobbyists typically represented gambling interests, rapacious logging groups, and employers of underpaid migrant workers. Now many other interests have representatives in state capitals. Evidence for this widening activity can be found in the initiatives placed on state ballots. Lobbying firms handle the whole package of gathering signatures and whatever else is needed for passage of initiatives.

Moreover, states have become venues for major contentious issues in ways that are relatively new and likely to continue. Abortion, for one, became a great issue fought out in many states and is monitored carefully by state watchdog groups. Gay marriage looms ahead in state-by-state battles following Vermont's opening the door to recognizing gay marriage and the Massachusetts Supreme Court decision striking down the exclusion of homosexuals to marriage. However much controversy surrounds faith-based social services and school vouchers, discussion of legislative initiatives began at the state level, with interest groups playing a decisive role in framing the policy debates.

Changes in the larger political and religious environment have also taken place. The black church's role in the civil rights movement changed expectations of largely excluded groups. Significant civil rights victories acted as a spur to a variety of religious interest groups. Then, too, major churches have altered their theological resistance to entering into the public sphere. President George W. Bush, of course, has made religion and the cooperation of religious groups in government programs a major theme of his presidency. His faith-based initiatives have carried religion into the public domain in ways that few predicted. Finally and perhaps most important, a new willingness on the part of the American public has allowed religion to enter what was considered a secular domain.[4]

Thus, a much broader array of contentious issues is being fought out in the statehouses, very large resources are at stake, and many more actors have entered the fray. What makes observation of religion and politics at the state level particularly fascinating are the differences between the states. One needs a guide here for an increasingly important field. Why is religion and politics in some states seemingly important only on an episodic basis? Is there something about the political culture of the state? Then there are those differences between churches. What impels the Catholic Church into politics? What holds the Baptists back? The differences illuminate questions of religion and democratic participation, political culture, and themes that aid significantly in understanding the current state of affairs of religion within American democracy.

## CONTRIBUTIONS OF THIS VOLUME

The comparison of religious advocacy across states shows readers the vibrant enterprise of religious lobbying and contentious issues in differing contexts. Further, the authors will pursue their studies with a view toward contributing to the larger field of interest group politics, believing that democracy in a large society such as the United States could not exist without them.

Great changes have taken place in many states. Whereas previously interest groups largely meant a few powerful groups at the state capital blocking progressive legislation, the number and diversity of interests represented at the state level has exploded. The potential for undue influence has also been recognized as many states created stringent regulations about lobbying. The regulations now fill several bookshelves. Professionalization of the corps of persons utilized as lobbyists has also been a major development.

Further, lobbying has increased as a business enterprise in itself, with large firms managing a host of political activities beyond the state capital. Their reach extends to employing canvassers to stand at supermarkets and shopping malls to obtain hundreds of thousands of signatures to allow initiatives to be placed on state ballots. Nonetheless, there is still space for small and active voices to reach into legislators' or governors' offices. This wide range calls attention to the usefulness of the comparative approach this volume takes.

In this regard, the authors bring special strength to the project. Clyde Wilcox has published widely read studies of American interest groups, including his coauthored 1999 *Interest Groups in American Campaigns*. Besides many other works, Professor Wilcox contributed "Interest Groups at the Dawn of the New Millennium" to *The Interest Group Connection*, a 1998 work that summarized a good deal of current research on interest groups. Similarly, David Magleby has researched interest groups as a form of direct government as well as state–local connections in a variety of states.

The volume is further enhanced by having Allen Hertzke, a recognized authority on religion and politics, as coeditor and coauthor of the conclusion to the book along with Kevin den Dulk. Hertzke and den Dulk examine the findings of the individual chapters with an eye to advancing a thematic understanding of this first systematic view from the state level.

The authors in the state chapters and in the concluding chapter aim to make a contribution to political science though the comparative nature of the project. One question addressed is, What does the comparison of religious advocacy across states tell us about factors that shape interest group tactics and effectiveness? We presume that other illuminating questions will emerge as experienced observers of interest group politics reflect on the findings from the states.

## AUTHORS AND NEW SCHOLARSHIP

The authors enter this field with a broad array of scholarship. The more senior—Clyde Wilcox, Allen Hertzke, Charles Bullock III, David Magleby, Edward Cleary, and Mary Segers—have been looking at religion and politics for some years both in the United States and from a comparative perspective. Their widely cited works are contained in the author biographies at the end of this book.

Younger scholars bring new views to the field. Through lengthy graduate research, continued through their early teaching careers, they have investigated underlying historical and philosophical causes for political involvement by religious groups. Kevin den Dulk looked into how a religious tradition's particular ideas have an independent effect on whether and how it will mobilize to advance a rights agenda. He looked at the two largest religious traditions in the United States: Roman Catholic and evangelical Protestantism. He showed that despite their agreement on certain policy issues, Catholic and evangelical groups took different paths over rights advocacy over the past thirty years. He was able to show the relative effects of their political and legal ideas on mobilization.

Kevin den Dulk's scholarship added to the conventional political understanding that groups mobilize as a rational response to their political environment or the availability of resources. Similarly, David Yamane took on previous explanations about religion and politics. His target was the social science paradigm of secularization theory. This widely held view predicted a long-term decline in the scope of religious authority vis-à-vis secular authority. Yamane showed both the resurgence of religious authorities in political institutions and the reasons behind the religious impulse toward prophetic advocacy. His study of religious advocacy at the Wisconsin legislature adds theoretically and empirically to the ever-widening field of religion and politics.

Elizabeth Oldmixon showed how morality issues will become increasingly important to legislators in a postindustrial era. She focused on morality issues faced over a six-year period by the House of Representatives. Her extensive investigation through roll-call analyses and in-depth qualitative interviews showed that legislators do in fact draw heavily on religion and ideology as they address moral issues. Her and her colleagues' investigation of Texas religion and politics will extend this previous work.

Professor Anne Marie Cammisa's dissertation research at Georgetown gained a wide audience in her *Governments as Interest Groups* (1995), in which she examined three issues—child care, welfare reform, and housing—noting how governors and mayors acted as interest group advocates. Her next work on the comparative history and politics of welfare reform received an even wider audience in *From Rhetoric to Reform? Welfare Policy in American Politics* (1998). Her current research over the past few years focuses on women in the Massachusetts statehouse, affording her a sustained view of state politics.

Den Dulk, Yamane, Oldmixon, and Cammisa have added depth to a specialization especially salient to this volume: religious advocacy. This area of scholarship, virtually unknown thirty years ago, grew especially in the past ten years. Seventy-six dissertations on religious advocacy have been published since 1991, adding to our theoretical understanding of what facilitates or retards activism and providing empirical evidence of religious groups' successes and failures.

Newer scholarship in religion and politics has drawn both younger scholars into the field and students into the classroom because scholars and students have seen that religion is a versatile fuel, sometimes an explosive one. Unlike a previous generation that saw religion as a private affair, they have absorbed images of Martin Luther King Jr., Cesar Chavez, or Archbishop Romero. In their minds, religion not only has entered the public square but is presumed to be entitled to be there as well. Nonetheless, they recognize this mix as possibly hurtful to both religion and politics. New scholars and students have a keen interest, along with some reservations, in faith-based government programs. Thus, the study of religion and politics at the state level occurs at a time when both interest in religious advocacy is high and when recent scholarly work has added analytical depth to the field.

## STATES FEATURED

As coeditors, we chose a variety of criteria to determine the selection of states to be investigated. These criteria included Daniel Elazar's classification of the political culture of states along moralistic, individualistic, or traditionalistic lines. We also sought regional diversity, different institutional settings, and different political contexts.

We also chose the states where disputes are most illustrative of major issues being addressed in state politics. Major issues, such as textbook adoption, teaching evolution, abortion, school vouchers, and similar issues, are being fought out most strongly in some states and are more muted in others. Thus, Texas is included here because of the classic wars over textbook selection that are fought out in Austin and throughout the state.

The choice of states to be included in itself is fascinating, as we found in numerous discussions among the proposed authors. In early stages, we conferred with political scientists with long experience in investigating state politics. These colleagues—such as Ronald Hrebenar, Mark Hyde, Ted Jelen, and Mary

Anne Borelli—in effect served as an advisory committee for state selection. The process was refined by reviewing research in state interest groups. The study of interest group politics at the state level has advanced strongly in the past two decades, and our selection benefited from these studies.[5]

We view this work as a pioneering study, one that helps to open an important field. It does not pretend to be exhaustive of the possible ways of viewing state religion and politics. We have chosen religious interest groups as the main way to view religious influence operating within states. The authors recognize the strengths and weaknesses to this approach. One hopes that further studies will look into religious ideas operative in legislators' decisions, the effect of dominant religious groups within and among states, and a host of other themes. We believe that the present study will illuminate issues of religion and democratic participation, political culture, and other larger themes that aid significantly in understanding the current state of affairs of religion within American democracy.

## NOTES

1. David Yamane's 1998 dissertation is an exception. See his "A Religious Advocacy in Secular Society: A Neo-Secularization Perspective" (Ph.D. diss., University of Wisconsin–Madison, 1998). He investigated the role of religious advocacy organizations at the Wisconsin state legislature.

2. Timothy A. Brynes and Mary C. Segers, eds., *The Catholic Church and Abortion: A View from the States* (Boulder, Colo.: Westview, 1992), and Mary C. Segers and Timothy A. Brynes, eds., *Abortion Politics in the States* (Armonk, N.Y.: M. E. Sharpe, 1995). See also Mark Rozell and Clyde Wilcox, eds., *God at the Grassroots: The Christian Rights in the 1994 Elections* (Lanham, Md.: Rowman & Littlefield, 1995), with chapters on selected states.

3. Clive S. Thomas and Ronald J. Hrebenar, "Who's Got Clout," *State Legislatures* 25, no. 4 (April 1999): 30–34.

4. For this last point, see Felicia R. Lee, "The Secular Society Gets Religion," *New York Times*, August 24, 2002.

5. Illustrative of overviews and studies are Virginia Gray, Russell L. Hanson, and Herbert Jacob, eds., *Politics in the American States: A Comparative Analysis*, 7th ed. (Washington, D.C.: Congressional Quarterly Books, 1999), and the four volumes on interest group politics in individual states edited by Ronald J. Hrebenar and Clive S. Thomas: *Interest Group Politics in the American West* (Salt Lake City: University of Utah Press, 1987); *Interest Group Politics in the Midwestern States* (Ames: Iowa State University Press, 1993); *Interest Group Politics in the Northeastern States* (University Park: Pennsylvania State University Press, 1993); and *Interest Group Politics in the Southern States* (Tuscaloosa: University of Alabama Press, 1992).

# 1

## Religious Advocacy in New Jersey

*Mary C. Segers*

New Jersey is in many ways an odd and quirky state. It is full of anomalies and paradoxes, apparent contradictions and unexpected contrasts. Although it is the most densely populated state in the United States, it has a virtually untouched expanse of one million acres—the Pinelands—in the southern part of the state.

The Garden State has no sales tax on clothes or groceries but is known for excessive reliance on property taxes that are the highest per capita in the United States. New Jersey is one of only two states where it's a crime to pump your own gas and the only state where you have to pay for a tag to use a public beach. People who live in New Jersey have, on average, the longest commutes to work in the nation. Finally, the state is home to some of the most affluent communities in the country as well as some of the most impoverished.[1]

The paradoxes persist in the area of religion and politics. Despite its reputation as a liberal northeastern state, New Jersey was the first state in the nation to enact a faith-based initiative funding social services provided by religious groups.[2] Moreover, New Jersey is the third-largest Catholic state in the nation, and seven of its last nine governors have been Roman Catholic. Yet under their leadership, the state enacted a domestic partnership law, passed legislation supporting embryonic stem cell research, and is one of a handful of states that provides Medicaid funding of poor women's abortions.

Legally, New Jersey's was the first state constitution to explicitly outlaw racial discrimination and to establish rights for women. Yet today the schools in only three other states are more segregated, and New Jersey ranks dead last when it comes to political participation by women.[3] Finally, New Jerseyans are proud of their identity as the home of both the TV family "The Sopranos" and Tom Kean, the former New Jersey Republican governor who cochaired the 9/11 Commission.

Why these paradoxes and anomalies? To begin to understand the Garden State, its political organization, its religious culture, and its religious advocates, we need to pay attention to historical and structural factors in New Jersey and especially to its individualistic political culture. These factors set the context within which religious lobbyists function.

## HISTORICAL BACKGROUND AND CONTEXT

New Jersey is one of the thirteen original colonies that fought the Revolutionary War, formed the new nation in 1783, and wrote and later ratified the 1787 Constitution. Because of its key location connecting New England and New York with Pennsylvania and the South, New Jersey felt the full force of the independence struggle and was the site of four major battles—Trenton, New Brunswick, Monmouth, and Princeton—as well as ninety minor skirmishes.

Economically, the state was largely agricultural in its early history, although the coming of the railroad and industry in the nineteenth century led to early twentieth-century urban-industrial areas predicated on electric and steam power. Paterson with its silk mills was a major manufacturing center, and Newark, the state's largest city, was known for its leather industry, beer breweries, insurance companies, and shipping port. The southern part of the Garden State was known for truck farming, Jersey tomatoes, Campbell's soup, blueberries, and cranberry bogs.

The continuing transformation that began in the 1960s moved the state from a manufacturing economy to a high-tech service economy tied to computer, communications, and information technology as well as to financial and pharmaceutical industries. These newer sectors gave the state a high-income, high-education workforce, and in 2000, New Jersey had the nation's highest median household incomes. This transformation has also led to the decline of the old industrial centers (Jersey City, Newark, Elizabeth, Paterson, Trenton, and Camden) and to the emergence of a suburban state with its office parks, edge cities, high-tech centers, and shopping malls.

The state's population, according to the 2000 census, is 8,414,350—an increase of 8.6 percent over the 1990 census figure (7,748,000). Of the total population, 13.6 percent are African American, 5.7 percent are Asian, and 13.3 percent are Hispanic (with large numbers of Mexicans, Puerto Ricans, and Cubans).[4] In the 1990s, the state's Asian and Arab populations grew, meaning that there has been an increase in the number of Muslims and Hindus in the state. There are also significant populations of earlier immigrant groups: Italians, Irish, Polish, and other eastern European nationalities. These statistics indicate the tremendous diversity of the state.[5]

## POLITICAL STRUCTURE

Among the American states, New Jersey is known as a political system with a strong governor, a commuter legislature, an innovative supreme court, and a competitive party system. The governor is New Jersey's only statewide elected official; there is no lieutenant governor and no elected attorney general or treasurer. If he or she leaves office before the end of the four-year term (as Christine Todd Whitman did in 2001 and James E. McGreevey did in 2004), the senate president becomes acting governor while remaining senate president. This succession pattern threatens institutional separation of powers, and there is a current movement to amend the constitution to create a lieutenant governor.

New Jersey's governor has formidable policy and administrative powers. He sets the agenda and has wide latitude to initiate by issuing executive orders (a prerogative of only nine of the nation's fifty governors). He also has broad powers to reject legislation: a total veto, a line-item veto, and a conditional veto that enables him to reject portions of a bill and suggest new language. The governor also has wide-ranging administrative powers. He appoints and may remove all cabinet members. He is party leader and chief executive. He appoints all judges and county prosecutors as well as the state police superintendent and the president of the state university. The position carries tremendous patronage powers; each year, the governor dispenses about 500 appointments to boards and commissions. With routine access to the state's media, the governor serves as public spokesman for New Jersey. Little wonder that this governor has been likened to "a little president" or "an American Caesar."[6]

The state legislature is bicameral, with a forty-member senate and an eighty-member general assembly. New Jersey's is a part-time legislature and a commuter legislature. The state is sufficiently small that representatives can drive to Trenton in the morning and return home in the evening. The capital community is small and easily navigable. The statehouse is home to the 120 legislators; nearby are the offices of the governor and of department heads (called commissioners) as well as the headquarters of statewide associations and the offices of various interest groups and lobbyists.[7]

State senators and assembly members earn $49,000 per year and are also allocated $110,000 annually to set up offices and hire staff.[8] New Jersey is one of a few states that allow legislators to hold dual public offices; thus, State Senator Sharpe James is also mayor of Newark, State Senator Joseph Doria is also mayor of Bayonne, State Senator Rodney Rice is also deputy mayor of Newark, and so on. Such double-dipping may contribute to conflict-of-interest situations; it does underscore the fact that the legislature is part time since a legislator must devote considerable time to local as well as state duties.[9]

The New Jersey Supreme Court is known nationally as one of the most innovative state supreme courts in the country. It has issued pioneering rulings in matters of public education funding, land use and exclusionary zoning, end-of-life bioethical decisions, Medicaid financing of abortions, and racial profiling. "Its opinions are widely cited and followed, both by federal and other state courts."[10] Many citizens and political leaders recognize the central importance of a strong and independent judiciary and are justifiably proud of their highest court. Others worry about judicial activism, especially on social issues such as same-sex marriage and disparities in state funding of public schools.

In his typology of political culture, Elazar characterized New Jersey as "one of the strongest bastions of the individualistic political culture among American states."[11] In an individualistic political culture, politics is perceived as utilitarian, centered on individual advancement rather than on public spirit-edness and devotion to realizing the common good. Political parties and the dispensation of patronage are very important as keys to individual advancement. Politics is left to professional practitioners who allocate individual and group rewards through negotiation and compromise. A certain amount of public corruption is tolerated. Forming a state of immigrants from its inception, New Jersey residents have been concerned with individual opportunity and advancement.

The Garden State has a competitive political party system. Party leaders at the county level are old-fashioned political bosses who wield significant power in their home counties. They control their county party organizations and decide which candidates get the party line on the ballot, that is, the endorsement of the regular party organization. Candidates for governor and for U.S. senator must court the twenty-one county party leaders in the party nomination process.

Political access to the media is problematic because the state is sandwiched between New York and Philadelphia. New Jersey has no statewide affiliate TV or radio station and no statewide newspaper either. The fact that New Jersey political campaigns must buy TV ad time in New York and Philadelphia, two of the most expensive media markets in the country, underscores the need of candidates for funds to gain public visibility and become known to voters.

Thus, money matters in New Jersey politics. The election in 2000 of Senator Jon Corzine, a former chief executive officer of Goldman Sachs, a Wall Street investment firm, was greatly facilitated by his spending a record $62 million in courting county party leaders and developing a campaign organization in both the primary and the general election. This is why issues such as campaign finance and "pay-to-play" (the idea that you need to contribute to political campaigns to win government contracts) are perennial issues in New Jersey politics

Finally, independent local government is one of the strongest themes in the state's political culture; as former Governor Brendan Byrne once observed, "Home rule is a religion in New Jersey."[12] "Home rule" was enshrined by the legislature in 1917 with the declaration that municipalities should have "the fullest and most complete powers possible" over their internal affairs.[13] New Jersey currently has 566 municipalities and 611 school districts. Some criticize this as inefficient, given the costs of operating hundreds of tiny school districts, tiny police departments, and overlapping municipal governments. However, attempts at consolidating or eliminating these separate units have been largely unsuccessful, given the strength of the home rule principle.

## RELIGIOUS CULTURE

Religious pluralism has been a fact of life in New Jersey since the colonial period. Dutch Calvinists, Lutherans, Quakers, Anglicans, and Presbyterians were present from the seventeenth century on. Methodists, Catholics, and Jews came later, in the mid-nineteenth century. More recently, changes in immigration laws in the 1960s have brought "new" religions to New Jersey, including Buddhists, Muslims, and Hindus. New Jersey has the largest percentage of Hindus outside New York and also the highest percentage of Jews as well as Muslims outside New York.[14] The current demographic picture of religion in New Jersey reveals the state's continuing diversity. New Jersey is the third-largest Catholic state (after Rhode Island and Massachusetts). The state's religious pattern is 46 percent Catholic, 26 percent Protestant, 6 percent Jewish, 1 percent Muslim, 5 percent atheist/agnostic, and 16 percent other.[15]

New Jersey's 1947 constitution, considered a model of sound governmental structure and of civil liberties, guarantees religious freedom and forbids both religious establishment and the use of religious or racial tests for public office.[16] Moreover, it prohibits public funding of houses of worship, stating that no person shall "be obliged to pay tithes, taxes, or other rates for building or repairing any church or churches, place or places of worship, or for the maintenance of any minister or ministry, contrary to what he believes to be right or has deliberately and voluntarily engaged to perform." This language, carried over from the 1776 constitution, is pertinent to whether public funds can be granted to faith-based organizations under New Jersey law. The current constitution also contains a nondiscrimination clause forbidding discrimination "because of religious principles, race, color, ancestry or national origin." On the basis of this constitutional provision, New Jersey requires that faith-based organizations receiving public funds not discriminate in hiring on the basis of faith or creed.

From this brief review, it is clear that religious pluralism is an enduring fact of life in New Jersey and that religious freedom and church–state separation are enshrined firmly in New Jersey's constitution. While racial and ethnic tensions are present, church–state relations are generally calm in the Garden State. In the past fifteen years, the only noteworthy controversy has centered on the use of holiday displays (crèches and menorahs) on public land (Jersey City, Harrison, and Milburn).[17] Religious groups have taken sides on the abortion issue, but it could be argued that this is not, strictly speaking, a religious issue.

The more salient and controversial issues in New Jersey politics concern the environment, the economy, suburban sprawl and traffic congestion, affordable housing, poverty, political corruption, homeland security after the attack on the World Trade Center, racial justice, education (the New Jersey Supreme Court ordered assistance to thirty-one poor, largely inner-city school districts), and—the paramount issue for most New Jerseyans—taxes (local government relies very heavily on property taxes, and the state reluctantly instituted an income tax in the 1970s). Social issues such as same-sex marriage and state funding of stem cell research are also high on the public agenda because of recent lawsuits and gubernatorial initiatives.

## THE INTEREST GROUP UNIVERSE

In the 1930s, there were about twenty lobbyists in Trenton. In 2003, more than 1,200 business, industries, and associations employed 584 registered lobbyists.[18] This increase in the number of lobbyists reflects several long-term trends in twentieth-century Jersey politics: the passage of a state sales tax in the 1960s and a state income tax in the 1970s, growing state identity and government activism, and the increasing complexity of issues legislators must face.

Like most other states, New Jersey has organized pressure groups representing business, real estate, builders, developers, insurance, banks, labor unions, pharmaceutical and chemical companies, and regulated occupations (such as beauticians and morticians). Some of the most powerful organizations are the New Jersey Educational Association, the New Jersey Business and Industry Association, and the New Jersey League of Municipalities. Professionals associated with health care (doctors, dentists, nurses, and hospital associations) constitute some 10 percent of lobbyists in the state.[19] Analysts of New Jersey politics have generally paid little attention to religious lobbyists who seldom command the resources of these traditionally powerful pressure groups.

Although New Jersey was one of the last states to regulate lobbyists, it has some of the strictest regulations. The 1964 Legislative Activities Disclosure Act, amended in 1971, 1983, and 1990, requires lobbyists to file annual financial reports and quarterly reports of lobbying activities with the New Jersey Election Law Enforcement Commission (ELEC). Lobbyists must pay an annual registration fee of $425 and are required to wear photo-ID badges when lobbying the legislature. In recognition of the scope of modern interest group strategies, laws passed in 2004 require lobbyists to report monies spent on grassroots lobbying (lobbying conducted through advertisements and direct mail to the general public) in addition to their efforts to influence legislation and state regulations. They must also report efforts to influence governmental processes, such as promulgating executive orders, rate setting, public contracting, and bidding procedures.[20]

## RELIGIOUS LOBBYING IN NEW JERSEY

Religious lobbying is extensive in the Garden State. In a 1985 essay, Alice Edelman described the work of lobbyists representing the New Jersey Council of Churches, the Association of Jewish Federations, the New Jersey Catholic Conference, and religious Right groups such as the Eagle Forum or Morality in Media.[21] Twenty years ago, these advocates worked to influence policy on issues ranging from school prayer, casino gambling, abortion, and sex education to "right to die" legislation, hunger, homelessness, the rights of migrant workers, and divestiture from apartheid South Africa. A generation later, the issues have changed somewhat, and the cast of characters is different. But religious lobbyists continue to have an impact on decision making in New Jersey and are respected and consulted for their moral and factual insights.

In New Jersey, there are, generally speaking, two types of religious lobbyists. The first are religious groups having governmental relations offices in Trenton, such as the Lutheran Office for Governmental Relations, the New Jersey Catholic Conference, or the Black Ministers Council of New Jersey.

The second are paradenominational groups that are not church affiliated but whose work stems from a sectarian religious perspective, such as New Jersey Right to Life or the New Jersey Family Policy Council (a group opposing same-sex marriage). In addition, there are secular organizations and social justice groups, such as the Coalition for Peace Action or GreenFaith; these are pacifist or environmental activists who belong, as Edelman noted, to a sizable category of altruistic persuaders: "They engage in the political fray not for material gain, but to voice a particular vision of the way society should function."[22] All these advocates "lobby," that is, use a variety of tactics and strategies to influence public opinion, public officials, and public policy.

Only a handful of these religious advocates are registered lobbyists with the ELEC. Most do the same job—attempting to put into social action principles of justice derived from a faith tradition—without registering formally as lobbyists or "legislative agents" (to use the quaint language of New Jersey's law). A few refuse to register as a matter of principle; they contend that the state should not interfere in or otherwise regulate a religious group's public ministry or expression of religious beliefs. In an example cited by Edelman, Rev. Dudley Sarfaty, then director of public issues for the New Jersey Council of Churches, explained his refusal to register in these terms: "There is a fine line of independence between the church and the state. It would be reporting to the state on what we believe is an integral part of our religious ministry."[23]

Whether registered or not, these religious lobbyists do not see themselves as representing a special interest group, the way a public relations firm might lobby for a corporate or industrial group. Like the Hebrew prophets, they call for justice for the poor, the marginalized, and the voiceless. Marlene Lao-Collins, associate director of the New Jersey Catholic Conference, flatly rejects the term "religious lobbyist" and sees herself as an advocate for the poor and underprivileged in accordance with Catholic social teaching.[24] As Edelman notes, Jewish leaders cite "the emphasis in Jewish tradition on community and *tzedakah* (charity, most broadly construed, or 'human services' in bureaucratese) as the impetus for their lobbying efforts."[25]

To be sure, these religious advocates occasionally engage in self-interested lobbying to protect the legitimate institutional interests of their religious group. The New Jersey Catholic Conference, for example, is deeply concerned about potential changes in the state's charitable immunity law, which, if enacted, would make the Catholic Church liable for sex-abuse violations by its clergy. Given the recent sex-abuse scandal, this could involve significant financial liability. The New Jersey Catholic Conference is also very interested in state legislation to pay hospital expenses of those without health insurance—primarily because many Catholic hospitals are located in urban areas and are therefore likely to have many charity care patients. These examples illustrate that not all religious lobbying is altruistic; some advocates must look after their own community's interests when they are threatened by potentially adverse legislative or administrative action.

To assess the influence of religious lobbyists in New Jersey, this chapter examines several prominent religious advocacy organizations to see what issues are important to them and whether their lobbying efforts have been at least partly successful. These organizations are the Anti-Poverty Network, the New Jersey Catholic Conference, the Lutheran Office of Immigration and Refugee Services, the United Jewish Communities of MetroWest New Jersey, the Black Ministers' Council of New Jersey, and various groups making up the religious Right in the Garden State.

## THE ANTI-POVERTY NETWORK

Poverty in New Jersey is an enduring problem, a persistent source of concern through Republican and Democratic gubernatorial administrations. The state houses some of the nation's most affluent communities and some of the poorest areas. As the state's median income rises, the percentage of New Jersey residents in poverty is rising, too. In New Jersey, the cost of living is fully one-third greater than the national average. For example, the average rent for a two-bedroom apartment is now $1,058 per month, putting rental housing in the Garden State far beyond the means of low-income households.[26] However, in this suburban state of "McMansions" and affluent communities, many New Jerseyans are unaware of this problem.

The Anti-Poverty Network (APN) is a loosely structured information network that champions poverty-related issues often ignored in the political arena. "Getting poverty clearly on the radar screen of our political leaders is a challenge," according to Rev. Bruce Davidson, director of the Lutheran Office of Governmental Ministry in New Jersey and a leader of the APN.[27] Through grassroots mobilization and information sharing among advocates for the poor, the APN keeps the focus on issues of affordable housing, increasing the minimum wage, providing universal health care, ending hunger by supporting community food banks, and protecting the rights of immigrants and refugees.

Founded in 1999, the APN includes churches, temples, mosques, and other faith-based groups; labor unions; community food banks and soup kitchens; housing advocates; neighborhood groups; and people living in poverty. Over 300 organizations have participated in at least one APN event. The APN meets monthly and has a steering committee to develop its agenda. Each December,

APN holds an annual conference bringing together several hundred people to discuss issues and strategies related to poverty in New Jersey. The conference also provides an opportunity to lobby state legislators and department commissioners on legislation and regulations affecting poor people.

I attended APN's Fifth Annual Conference on December 14, 2004. The conference was impressive in sharing information about current legislative initiatives in Trenton as well as federal policies regarding poverty, welfare, and immigration. Two Democratic legislators were present: Assemblyman Louis Greenwald (D-Camden), chair of the Budget Committee, who pressed attendees to provide creative solutions to poverty as well as identify the problems, and State Senator Joseph Vitale (D-Middlesex), chair of the Senate Health, Human Services and Senior Citizens Committee, who appealed to APN members to support his proposed "radical reform in health care," which he was to announce in January 2005. Senator Vitale had worked with members of the APN to develop his proposal (some 1.2 million New Jerseyans have no health insurance).

When asked what successes could be attributed to the work of the APN, Bruce Davidson cited several victories. In 2004, the legislature established a rental assistance program thanks to the collaborative efforts of APN and housing advocates. The APN was also instrumental in getting legislators to reverse then-Governor McGreevey's proposed cuts in housing and family care (health care for poor people) in the 2004 budget. Finally, in his 2005 State of the State Address, Acting Governor Richard Codey proposed increasing the minimum wage from $5.15 to $7.15 an hour over two years—a high-priority item on APN's agenda.[28]

Davidson is recognized as a key figure in religious advocacy in Trenton. As one Presbyterian minister said, "He is tireless in his efforts; he is everywhere."[29] Davidson himself is more realistic. Although he directs the Lutheran Office of Governmental Ministry in New Jersey, he acknowledges that only 1 percent of New Jersey's population is Lutheran. He has therefore chosen to work with other religious and secular advocates and counts as a victory the creation and establishment of the APN. The APN succeeds in keeping poverty issues on the public agenda in New Jersey.[30]

## THE NEW JERSEY CATHOLIC CONFERENCE

Marlene Lao-Collins, associate director of social concerns at the New Jersey Catholic Conference (NJCC), is another major leader of the APN. Energetic, charismatic, and extremely hardworking, Lao-Collins is a facilitator and organizer whose advocacy for the poor and underprivileged is inspired by

Catholic social teaching. Because of its opposition to same-sex marriage, abortion, and embryonic stem cell research, the NJCC is often perceived as part of the religious Right (alongside conservative evangelicals). In reality, the NJCC, representing the five dioceses of New Jersey (Camden, Trenton, Metuchen, Newark, and Paterson) tends to be conservative on issues of individual morality and bioethics but liberal on matters of social justice. Marlene Lao-Collins's work with APN represents the social justice thrust of the NJCC's work.

The NJCC is part of the institutional structure of American Catholicism. The official Catholic Church in the United States is represented by the United States Conference of Catholic Bishops in Washington, D.C. At the state level, there are currently thirty-four state Catholic conferences, including the New Jersey Catholic Conference headquartered in Trenton. A state Catholic conference is a church agency composed of the dioceses within a state; its purpose is to serve as government liaison for the state's bishops and also to communicate with non-Catholic churches and secular agencies. The bishops of the state form the board of directors and set policy. Each state Catholic conference has a staff, is headed by a lay executive director, and is located in the state capital.[31] The New Jersey Catholic Conference has a staff of six: three support staff and Executive Director William F. Bolan, Associate Director Marlene Lao-Collins, and Associate Director George Corwell.

The NJCC's positions on policy issues before the New Jersey legislature illustrate the truism that "the politics of Catholic bishops are not easily categorized." On social welfare, immigration, civil rights, and labor policies, they tend to take a more liberal posture. On the other hand, the Church's positions on abortion, sexual ethics, and educational policy align it with conservatives. "The Church is thus strategically placed as a sort of bridge between evangelical and liberal Protestants."[32]

This is true in New Jersey as well as nationally. The NJCC opposes the death penalty, rejects racism in all its forms, supports health care as a basic human right, and advocates housing assistance such as increasing funding for rental housing. At the same time, NJCC opposes gay marriage, domestic partnership laws, and the legalization of abortion and of physician-assisted suicide and supports school choice, including such models as tuition tax credits and vouchers. The comments of William F. Bolan, executive director of NJCC, about New Jersey's 2004–2005 budget capture the complexity of the Catholic Church's perspective; Bolan gave the budget mixed reviews: "This budget is mixed, containing funding for some very important services to the poor and vulnerable, but also containing funding for a facility which we oppose on moral grounds."[33] He was referring to Governor James McGreevey's $6.5 million state grant for creation of a stem cell research institute in New Jersey.[34]

In general, NJCC has been successful on social welfare issues (such as housing, immigrants' rights, and child welfare), particularly when they join APN in advocating such measures. But the Catholic Conference has not had success in opposing domestic partnerships, stem cell research, and abortion restrictions in New Jersey. In January 2004, the state enacted a domestic partner law and authorized funding of a major stem cell research institute.[35]

In opposing domestic partnership legislation, NJCC lobbied state legislators, used articles and editorials in diocesan newspapers to criticize the bill,[36] and posted legislative alerts in parish bulletins to mobilize grassroots opposition. For example, the December 28, 2003, bulletin of St. Teresa of Avila Church in Summit, New Jersey, contained the following notice: "Contact your Senator immediately regarding the Domestic Partners Benefits legislation S2820/A3743 and urge him/her to vote NO."

Despite these efforts, Catholic Church lobbying proved unpersuasive. When the state senate met on January 8, 2004, to vote on the bill, five senators spoke in support of the bill, and none voiced opposition. State Senator Raymond J. Lesniak (D-Union), who spoke in favor of the bill, noted the NJCC's opposition and said he wanted to respond "because I love my church." "But," he continued, "on secular matters, in legal matters on relationships between two people, it is not infallible."[37]

Not only did New Jersey pass a domestic partnership law and enact legislation supporting stem cell research at the same time, the state legislature also reported out of committee a bill stripping churches and nonprofits of a charitable exemption from prosecution that these institutions had long enjoyed. Specifically, the bill would remove charitable immunity from prosecution in sex-abuse cases (only in cases involving the sexual molestation of a minor). Supporters of the bill, which cleared the Senate Judiciary Committee, where it had been bottled up for several years, say it was prompted by the clerical sex-abuse scandal in the Catholic Church. Senator Joseph Vitale, the bill's sponsor, stated flatly, "It is because of the church sex scandal that we're here today."[38]

While the senate has passed the bill (S540), the full assembly has not yet voted. Final passage is being held up largely over the issue of retroactivity. According to Senator Vitale, the Catholic Church offered to drop its opposition to his bill if he made it apply only to future cases. But he said he couldn't support that because it would have created "two standards of justice," with different rights for past and future victims.[39] Other legislators oppose retroactivity, saying it is unfair to permit lawsuits for offenses that occurred decades ago, suits of the type that have bankrupted Catholic dioceses in other states.[40]

On all three issues—domestic partnerships, stem cell research, and charitable immunity—New Jersey Catholic citizens and lawmakers did not take political cues from Church leaders, despite efforts of the bishops and the NJCC to exert political influence. The NJCC suffered these setbacks despite claiming nearly half the state's population as adherents. The priest sex-abuse scandal was directly relevant to one of these policy debates and may have been a background factor in the other two discussions. A second factor may be the diversity of New Jersey combined with its population density. The religious pluralism and ethnic diversity of the Garden State means that Jerseyans prize tolerance and recognize that they must learn to live together peacefully, to cooperate, and to respect others' religious beliefs. This general context or political culture tends to dilute the influence of any single religious denomination in New Jersey.

## THE LUTHERAN IMMIGRATION AND REFUGEE PROGRAM

Homeland security and immigration are also major issues in New Jersey. The state lost some 800 people in the attack on the World Trade Center. Middletown in Monmouth County lost thirty-four residents, the most of any community in the New York metropolitan area. Continuing threats to financial institutions in New York City and Newark keep Jerseyans on alert. The shipping depots at Port Newark and Port Elizabeth, the bridges and tunnels connecting New York and New Jersey, and Newark's Liberty International Airport also present major security concerns. After the September 11 attacks, Arab American and Muslim communities in Hudson, Bergen, and Passaic Counties were subject to heightened surveillance by law enforcement authorities, and undocumented aliens were detained and in some cases deported.

National security and the application of the USA Patriot Act have immediacy and relevance to the Garden State because New Jersey continues to be home to large numbers of immigrants. In 2000, 29 percent of its residents were born in another country or had a parent who was.[41] Of the total population, some 13.3 percent are Hispanic (of many different nationalities), and 5.7 percent are Asian (including many from Middle Eastern countries). Four years after the World Trade Center attacks, intense surveillance of immigrants continues. In 2004 and early 2005, agents from the Bureau of Immigration and Customs Enforcement—an arm of the Department of Homeland Security—carried out dozens of early morning raids in Mercer County (Princeton and Trenton areas) in which scores of illegal immigrants were seized and detained in federal facilities or county jails while awaiting deportation.[42]

Against the background of the "war on terror" and legitimate concerns about national security, advocates for immigrant groups struggle to protect the human rights of undocumented aliens who may be here illegally and therefore have few civil rights. They also work to provide necessary services for immigrants and refugees who are here legally. One such advocate is Rev. Stacy Martin, who directs the Office of Immigration and Refugee Services, part of Lutheran Social Ministries of New Jersey.[43]

Headquartered in Trenton, the Office of Immigration and Refugee Services has a staff of twelve, including an immigration attorney, representatives to assist with immigration appeals, and staff to conduct the refugee resettlement program. During a refugee's first days and months in the United States, Rev. Martin's office arranges provision of basic services, such as housing, counseling, interpreting, enrollment in ESL (English-as-a-second-language) classes, and assistance in getting a job. In many cases, the office works together with a sponsoring church or relative. In some cases, Lutheran Social Ministries of New Jersey and Rev. Martin's office alone sponsor a refugee. The resettlement program is funded primarily by the U.S. State Department and also by the Federal Office of Refugee Resettlement in the Department of Health and Human Services. The Office of Immigration and Refugee Services assists some 175 to 200 refugees annually; in 2004, recipients included refugees from Colombia, Cuba, Liberia, Sierra Leone, Burma, Sudan, and Ukraine.

The office also assists some 1,200 immigrants every year, helping them learn English, find jobs, apply for appropriate social security documents, locate housing, and file immigration appeals. Funding for this work comes from the State of New Jersey (ESL funding) and from individual donors and church congregations.

Originally from Kansas, Rev. Stacy Martin received her master of divinity degree from Princeton Theological Seminary and is an ordained minister in the Presbyterian Church USA.[44] Martin draws inspiration for religious advocacy from the reformed Calvinist tradition of her church. As she stated, "In this faith tradition, I am compelled to serve the needs of others, especially the poor and vulnerable, and to do the work of social justice."

The Office of Immigration and Refugee Services is part of the APN. From Rev. Martin's perspective, her office cannot serve immigrants and refugees without working with other social service providers and without advocating on their behalf. Since both her office and Lutheran Social Ministries receive federal and state funding and have 501[c][3] status as not-for-profit agencies, they cannot be partisan. They therefore rely on Rev. Bruce Davidson's Lutheran Office of Governmental Ministries for direct legislative advocacy.

Since policies affecting immigrants are mostly federal policies, Martin's office participates in once-a-year advocacy days in Washington. At the state level, her office may contact individual legislators regarding constituents, that is, individual cases of immigrants or refugees in a particular legislator's district. Also, her office has joined with other immigrant advocates to monitor the early morning raids on houses sheltering allegedly illegal immigrants in Mercer County. In particular, Tatiana Durbak, the immigration attorney on Rev. Martin's staff, notes that federal agents from the Bureau of Immigration and Customs Enforcement identify themselves as police in making these raids, thus blurring the distinction between local and federal authorities. This undermines long-standing efforts by immigrants' advocates to build up good community relations between local police departments and the local immigrant population. At stake here is immigrants' need for police protection and medical services if they are preyed on by criminals or simply need hospital care. Immigrant advocates and local police departments worry that the federal raids will have a chilling effect, that is, intimidate immigrants into not calling for services they need and deserve.[45]

When asked about victories and successes in working with immigrants and refugees, Rev. Martin cited the number of clients helped annually. She also spoke of the facilitating role played by her office. Speaking primarily about refugees, she said, "These are not our successes. Rather, we have helped them tell their individual stories, which in some cases are horrific." In their own way, she implied, these refugees and immigrants are bearing witness.

## UNITED JEWISH COMMUNITIES OF METROWEST NEW JERSEY

At 500,000, or 6 percent of the population, New Jersey has one of the largest Jewish populations in the nation. A secular organization, United Jewish Communities of MetroWest New Jersey (UJC) is the preeminent Jewish philanthropy in the Garden State. MetroWest encompasses the counties of Essex, Morris, and Sussex and part of Union, making it the largest federation in the state and one of the largest Jewish federations in North America. With the $23 million UJC raised in 2003 and again in 2004, MetroWest provides a network of services to meet the needs of Jews in New Jersey, in Israel, and in other parts of the world, such as Russia, Argentina, and Ethiopia.

Within New Jersey, UJC supports Jewish day schools and synagogue religious schools, summer camps, trips to Israel, Holocaust education and remembrance, as well as a variety of social services such as job training, domestic abuse shelters, programs for the developmentally disabled, residences for the elderly, and programs to help seniors remain in their own homes. MetroWest gives special emphasis to preserving Jewish identity and heritage—supporting college campus services through Hillel organizations at Drew University and Rutgers University. In addition, through its Community Relations Committee, its public affairs and public policy arm, UJC mobilizes communal support for issues important to the Jewish community, such as the environment and quality of life in the MetroWest area, Israel advocacy and education, support for public education, issues of church–state separation, discriminatory policies and legislation, and Bill of Rights issues.

In an interview with Max Kleinman, executive vice president, he identified three issues of concern to UJC: combating anti-Semitism, homeland security (for both the United States and Israel), and concern for the elderly.[46] To illustrate the continuing struggle against anti-Semitism, he cited the case of Amiri Baraka, former poet laureate of New Jersey. In September 2002, Baraka caused a scandal after a public reading of his poem "Who Blew Up America?" at the Dodge Poetry Festival at Waterloo Village in Stanhope, New Jersey. The poem, a commentary on the September 11, 2001, terrorist attacks, includes several stanzas in which Baraka raises rhetorical questions suggesting that some groups and individuals had prior knowledge of the attacks. Among the lines included in the poem are, "Who knew the World Trade Center was gonna get bombed/Who told 4,000 Israeli workers at the Twin Towers to stay home that day?/Why did Sharon stay away?"

In the ensuing controversy, Baraka was accused of anti-Semitism and was asked to resign. When Baraka refused, state government officials started looking for legal ways to oust the poet laureate. Unable to end his two-year term as poet laureate, the legislature ultimately passed and Governor Mc-Greevey signed into law a bill abolishing the position itself. The UJC played an active role in the campaign to eliminate the position of poet laureate. Baraka accused those demanding his resignation of threatening free speech and artistic expression. But Jews in New Jersey, according to Kleinman, did not think poetic license justified spreading untruths about who was responsible for the terrorist attacks on the World Trade Center.

Homeland security is clearly a major concern of New Jersey's Jewish community, as is evident from the now-mandatory presence of security guards at synagogue services, at Jewish day schools, and at the entrance to the Parsippany (Morris County) headquarters of MetroWest. In the aftermath of the September 11 attacks, the Jewish community feels very vulnerable to terrorist attacks, as do many New Jersey residents. Jerseyans also feel that the federal government (Department of Homeland Security) has not given enough funding to the state to prevent attacks and to improve the police and medical response capacity of local communities. MetroWest has actively lobbied state officials to remedy these deficiencies. According to Kleinman, "When Acting Governor Richard Codey took office in November 2004, we lobbied him to give priority to homeland security issues. And he turned around and lobbied us, asking us to send him a letter detailing how New Jersey has been shortchanged when it comes to federal funds for homeland security." Given the emphasis on homeland security in Governor Codey's subsequent State of the State Address, MetroWest could claim some degree of success in its efforts to influence public policy.

Concern for the elderly is a third priority of MetroWest; as Kleinman notes, the Jewish population in New Jersey is aging. The UJC strongly supports Social Security, Medicare, and Medicaid policies. The headquarters of MetroWest in Parsippany, New Jersey, is a sizable campus that houses, in addition to UJC offices, a large senior citizen housing complex. In addition to supporting nursing homes and assisted living communities, MetroWest has secured federal and state grants of some $400,000 to pilot an aging-in-place grant known as NORC (naturally occurring retirement communities). The basic idea is to support independent living of seniors and to provide services to enable people to stay in their own homes, a less expensive form of elder care.

While the United Jewish Federation of MetroWest is a secular organization, its social action is prompted and sustained by Jewish values. A plaque in the MetroWest lobby summarizes these traditions and values. Through *Tzedakah*, "We Jews are obliged to pursue righteousness and justice through acts of loving kindness and philanthropy." Through *Tikkun Olam* (often translated as the obligation to repair the world), "We Jews are to be active participants in the ongoing process of creating a more perfect world." And through *Klal Yisrael*, "We Jews are one people, each responsible for one another."

As Kleinman suggests, Jews are still civil libertarians and strong supporters of civil rights. Most Jews, for example, support abortion rights, although they are uncomfortable with late-term abortions. Most Jews advocate church–state separation and are strong supporters of public schools; an exception is the Orthodox Jewish community, which runs day schools and is interested in school vouchers. Under Governor Christie Whitman's faith-based initiative, MetroWest served as a secular intermediary organization to distribute funds to various groups, but it was very concerned that agencies receiving funds not engage in any proselytizing activities. None of this is surprising given the long history of American Jewry's concern for religious freedom and disestablishment. This writer was surprised, however, to hear Kleinman say, when asked about Jewish fears of other religious groups, that he was "not so much concerned about the Religious Right as the Religious Left." He was referring to the decision made by the Presbyterian Church USA in July 2004 to begin selective divestiture in multinational corporations operating in Israel — as a protest against businesses that bear particular responsibility for the suffering of Palestinians.[47] In response to such a divestiture movement, Kleinman emphasized the concern of American Jews to protect the homeland of Israel and the need for Israel advocacy and education by the American Jewish community in New Jersey and the United States.

## AFRICAN AMERICAN RELIGIOUS GROUPS AND RACIAL JUSTICE

Given the historically central role black churches have played in African American communities, it is not surprising to find numerous church-related advocacy groups in the Garden State. At 13.6 percent of the state's population, African Americans struggle to overcome the legacy of 1960s' racial turmoil in Newark, Plainfield, Paterson, Asbury Park, and other communities. Rev. Reginald T. Jackson is executive director of the Black Ministers' Council of New Jersey, a major statewide minority organization representing some 800 African American churches. He is respected by state legislators for his role in calling attention to racial profiling in traffic stops by the New Jersey State Police. Pastor of St. Matthew's A.M.E. Church in Orange, Jackson strongly advocates funding for the poor, charity care for the uninsured, child welfare reform, and legislation to end predatory lending. He has recently called for school vouchers in New Jersey (thus allying the Black Ministers' Council with Orthodox Jews and the NJCC), but this move is controversial within the African American community.[48] With an office in Trenton, Rev. Jackson and the Black Ministers' Council are widely regarded as major advocates on issues of concern to New Jersey's sizable African American community.

## THE RELIGIOUS RIGHT IN NEW JERSEY

The religious Right in New Jersey has a number of different organizations, such as the New Jersey Right to Life Committee, whose public relations director, Marie Tasy, has good media contacts and is quoted all over the place whenever issues of abortion and stem cell research arise. New Jersey Right to Life has a political action committee (PAC) and contributes money to pro-life congressmen and to state legislators. (So does New Jersey Pro-Choice.) Other religious Right organizations, such as the Christian Coalition and Concerned Women for America, are not very well organized at all; the Christian Coalition exists on paper, and Concerned Women for America used to have a state chapter but no longer does. There is a group called New Jersey Family Policy Council (NJFPC) (an offshoot of Focus on the Family and the Family Research Council), whose major issue is same-sex marriage. Together with the NJCC, the NJFPC has filed an amicus brief in *Lewis v. Harris*, an important lawsuit regarding the constitutionality in New Jersey of same-sex marriage. The lawsuit was filed by seven gay couples in 2002, ruled on in November 2003 at superior court, then argued before an appellate court in December 2004, and will probably be appealed to the New Jersey State Supreme Court. Since it challenges the state's interpretation of the New Jersey constitution, the state supreme court is the court of last resort. The only ruling in the case thus far is by the superior court judge, who essentially took a judicial restraint posture, saying she could not find warrant in the state constitution to justify changing New Jersey's law on marriage and deferring to the people's elected representatives in the state legislature as the proper institution to make any such changes in the law. As indicated earlier, New Jersey enacted domestic partner legislation in 2004.

## CONCLUSION

This chapter discusses New Jersey's political organization and culture and notes the religious and ethnic diversity of the Garden State. The chapter considers some major issues in New Jersey, how religious advocacy organizations have addressed them, and whether they are successful in their lobbying.

The record is mixed. Advocates such as APN and UJC can point to some specific victories, but there are also some setbacks. Thus far, for example, the NJCC has not been successful in its opposition to stem cell research, to domestic partner legislation, and to changes in the state's charitable immunity law.

What factors might explain such successes and setbacks? Clearly, there are many explanatory factors. The ability to form coalitions, energetic political organizing and grassroots mobilization, issues specific to a particular denomination, as well as general background issues such as the state's economy and New Jersey's political culture—these factors help explain partly the victories and defeats of religious advocacy groups.

First, the ability of religious advocates to work together in loosely organized coalitions or information networks such as the APN seems to be one ingredient of success. Since religious advocacy organizations seldom command sizable material resources, forming such alliances has been helpful.

Second, good old-fashioned political organizing and grassroots mobilization should not be discounted in the Garden State. This seems especially true for minorities such as the African American and Jewish communities, who are adept at highlighting issues important to them. Through political mobilization, the APN manages to keep poverty issues on the public agenda.

Third, sometimes religious advocacy groups tend to be successful on issues that apply specifically to an individual denomination. Examples include MetroWest's lobbying to eliminate the post of poet laureate and the emphasis of the Black Ministers' Council on racial profiling. At other times, specific issues may work against religious advocacy. The NJCC's political ineffectiveness on, for example, proposed changes in the state's charitable immunity law clearly flowed in part from the clergy sex-abuse scandal in New Jersey. A well-organized, vocal chapter of the Survivors Network of Those Abused by Priests (SNAP) in Morris County succeeded in getting the bill reported out of committee and won't let the issue go away.

Fourth, on some issues, the state's economic needs will trump other priorities. The stem cell research initiatives of Governor McGreevey and Acting Governor Codey (both Roman Catholics) have succeeded, in the face of opposition by the NJCC and right-to-life groups, largely because of the state's economic reliance on the pharmaceutical industry. Most of the major pharmaceutical corporations are headquartered in New Jersey, and there are biotechnology companies as well. Indeed, New Jersey sees itself in competition with California; both states have allocated considerable sums of money to this research. However, state legislators recognize the ethical complexity of stem cell research and will consider ethical precautions in any bill authorizing funding of such research—because of the lobbying of the NJCC, New Jersey Right to Life, and other religious advocates.

Finally, New Jersey's individualistic political culture may be an explanatory factor. By and large, the state is fairly liberal or tolerant; for example, the public has a live-and-let-live ethos and is fairly tolerant of same-sex couples (thus the domestic partner law). New Jersey's religious and ethnic diversity, coupled with population density—it is the most densely populated state in the nation—may also encourage tolerance or engender a desire to avoid racial, ethnic, and religious conflict. There is a libertarian streak in New Jersey's political culture—a stress on individualism and above all privacy; the Libertarian Party has always fielded candidates in the state's elections. The state also has a tradition of moderate Republicanism (for example, former Governors Tom Kean and Christie Whitman); the New Jersey Republican Party has not been taken over by conservative evangelicals as it has in some other states.

In general, the observations of Alice Chasan Edelman, the only author I have found who has discussed religious lobbying in New Jersey, still ring true. Writing twenty years ago about the subject, she concluded that (1) religious lobbyists have an impact on decision making in New Jersey and are respected and consulted by state legislators and state commissioners for their moral and factual insights; (2) by and large, religious advocates are instrumental in maintaining church–state separation (here Edelman cited Baptists, Jews, and the New Jersey Council of Churches); and (3) religious advocates are pragmatic and practical; they recognize there will be setbacks as well as victories, and they keep at it and are in it for the long haul. This third aspect sounds a bit like what David Yamane, in chapter 7, calls faithfulness or fidelity of religious advocates; despite setbacks, these advocates remain faithful to their calling as religious organizations. Although issues and personalities have changed since Edelman's 1985 article, I think that her conclusions are, by and large, still valid.

I conclude with two observations. First, the perennial problem of charismatic leaders—leadership change or transition—applies to religious groups as well as to secular organizations. In some cases, religious advocacy organizations are effective because they are led by capable, competent, charismatic leaders who know how to deal with the media and keep their issues before the public. (Some examples might be Rev. Bruce Davidson, Rev. Reginald Jackson of the Black Ministers' Council, and Marie Tasy of New Jersey Right to Life.) What happens when these leaders pass on may be problematic for the organizations with which they are associated.

Second, one wonders why these many religious advocates say nothing about the seriousness and the degree of political corruption in New Jersey. A certain amount of such corruption has always been tolerated (as Elazar notes in his discussion of individualistic political culture). But the situation has become rather serious in New Jersey. In 2004, there was a steady parade of appalling cases, culminating in the resignation of Governor McGreevey, who acknowledged that he was "a gay American" and that he had placed his partner in a series of high-paying government jobs. Both political parties have had their share of bribery and other scandals; recently, some eleven mayors and local officials in Monmouth County (many of whom were Republican) were arrested on charges of bribery. There are structural reasons for such corruption in New Jersey; with 566 municipalities and 611 school districts, there are too many small governments whose actions are largely hidden from public view and where deals can be made in secret. What is surprising is that religious advocates have not addressed these issues. After all, truthfulness and honesty are virtues encouraged by major religious traditions, and a strong case can be made that it is immoral as well as illegal to use public funds for private self-interest instead of the common welfare. But the religious advocacy organizations are strangely silent on this issue.

## NOTES

I am grateful to the religious advocates interviewed for this chapter and to other colleagues and advocates for their assistance: Rev. Bruce Davidson, Max Kleinman, Rev. Stacy Martin, Marlene Lao-Collins, Ingrid Reed, Norman Samuels, Elizabeth Strom, and Myra Terry.

1. Sources for these New Jersey paradoxes are Cliff Zukin, "Political Culture and Public Opinion," in *The Political State of New Jersey*, ed. Gerald M. Pomper (New Brunswick, N.J.: Rutgers University Press, 1986), 3–26, and Jon Shure, Remarks to

the Housing and Community Development Network of New Jersey, Membership Meeting, December 2, 2004, available at www.njpp.org. Shure is president of New Jersey Policy Perspective, a nonpartisan, nonprofit research organization founded in 1997.

2. For more on New Jersey's faith-based initiative, see Mary C. Segers, "Drawing on Tradition: New Jersey's Statewide Initiative," in *Sanctioning Religion: Politics, Law, and Faith-Based Public Services*, ed. David K. Ryden and Jeffrey Polet (Boulder, Colo.: Lynne Rienner, 2005). See also Jo Renee Formicola, Mary C. Segers, and Paul Weber, *Faith-Based Initiatives and the Bush Administration: The Good, the Bad, and the Ugly* (Lanham, Md.: Rowman & Littlefield, 2003).

3. See "The Status of Women in the States," prepared by the Institute for Women's Policy Research (Washington, D.C.), as reported in the *New York Times*, 28 November 2004, sec. 14, 3. See also the statistics prepared by the Center for American Woman and Politics, the Eagleton Institute, Rutgers University, at www.cawp .rutgers.edu.

4. U.S. Census Bureau, *Statistical Abstract of the United States: 2001*, 121st ed. (Washington, D.C.: U.S. Census Bureau, 2001), 26–27.

5. An indication of the state's diversity is the fact that *U.S. News & World Report* has named my home university, Rutgers University's campus in Newark, the most diverse university in the nation for the past six consecutive years.

6. Barbara Salmore and Stephen Salmore, *New Jersey Politics and Government: Suburban Politics Comes of Age*, 2nd ed. (Lincoln: University of Nebraska Press, 1998), 128.

7. See Alan Rosenthal, "The Legislature," in Pomper, *The Political State of New Jersey*, 119. The legislative session is annual, but it is not a continuous sixty-day or ninety-day session as in other states. It meets periodically; it is always in session, but there is little activity in July or August. The legislature works through a committee system; traditionally, committee meetings are held every Monday and most Thursdays. The legislature has broad policy and financial powers. Party caucuses are important, and party allegiance is a principal factor in decisions on legislative organization and operations.

8. Fitzgerald's *Legislative Manual of the State of New Jersey*, 211th Legislature, First Session (Newark, N.J.: Skinder-Strauss Associates, 2004).

9. Deborah Howlett, "Behind the Headlines: Double-Dipping," *Sunday Star-Ledger*, January 9, 2005, sec. 10, 1.

10. John C. Pittenger, "The Courts," in Pomper, *The Political State of New Jersey*, 160.

11. Daniel J. Elazar, "Introduction," in Salmore and Salmore, *New Jersey Politics and Government*, xxvi–xxix.

12. Salmore and Salmore, *New Jersey Politics and Government*, 201.

13. Richard J. Connors, "Government," in, *Encyclopedia of New Jersey*, ed. Maxine Lurie and Marc Mappen (New Brunswick, N.J.: Rutgers University Press, 2004), 325–27.

14. See Suzanne Geissler Bowles, "Religion," in Lurie and Mappen, *Encyclopedia of New Jersey*, 686–88.

15. These figures are from the *Star-Ledger*/Eagleton Poll, September 2001. I am indebted to Cliff Zukin of the Eagleton Institute of Politics, Rutgers University, for supplying this information. The category of "other" includes religious groups under 1 percent, such as Mormons, Hindus, and Bahai.

16. The preamble to the 1844 constitution, which is repeated verbatim in the current constitution adopted in 1947, states, "We the people of the State of New Jersey, grateful to Almighty God for the civil and religious liberty which He hath so permitted us to enjoy, and looking to Him for a blessing upon our endeavors to secure and transmit the same unimpaired to succeeding generations, do ordain and establish this constitution." This and subsequent quotations from the New Jersey constitution are from *New Jersey Statutes Annotated Constitution of the State of New Jersey* (St. Paul, Minn.: West Group, 1997).

17. In December 2004, a controversy developed over the decision of the South Orange–Maplewood School District to ban Christmas carols and instrumental music during the holiday season. This drew national attention and comment in the editorial and op-ed pages of regional and national newspapers. But it quieted down after the New Year.

18. State of New Jersey Election Law Enforcement Commission, "Lobbying in New Jersey 2003," publication prepared by Frederick M. Herrmann, executive director, New Jersey Election Law Enforcement Commission, August 2003. The earlier reference to numbers of lobbyists in the 1930s is from Salmore and Salmore, *New Jersey Politics and Government*, 88.

19. The Salmores note, "To explain oddities like New Jersey's status as the only state that until 1992 did not license physicians' assistants (although its state medical school trained them) or as one of the only two states still without self-service gas stations, one need look no further than the many nurses, physicians, and independent gas station owners who are all legislators' vocal and well-organized constituents." Salmore and Salmore, *New Jersey Politics and Government*, 104–5.

20. See www.elec.state.nj.us/changesinthelaw.htm.

21. Alice Chasan Edelman, "Church & State Street," *New Jersey Reporter* 15, no. 5 (November 1985): 18–25.

22. Edelman, "Church & State Street," 18. A fourth category of altruistic lobbyists are the good-government groups, such as Common Cause and the League of Women Voters.

23. Edelman, "Church & State Street," 21.

24. Conversation with Marlene Lao-Collins at the Fifth Annual Meeting of the Anti-Poverty Network, Trenton, 14 December 2004.

25. Edelman, "Church & State Street," 22. Through *Tzedakah*, Jews are obliged to pursue righteousness and justice through acts of loving-kindness and philanthropy. The emphasis is on being "obliged." In Jewish tradition, *Tzedakah* is an obligation, a command of God to be obeyed. The word "charity," which implies that giving is voluntary, optional, a choice, does not quite capture the obligatory character of *Tzedakah*. I am indebted to my colleague Norman Samuels for this clarification.

26. "Jersey Rents Keep Soaring Out of Reach for Many," *Star-Ledger*, 7 January 2005, 27.

27. Rev. Bruce Davidson, Remarks at the Fifth Annual Conference of the Anti-Poverty Network, Trenton, 14 December 2004.

28. Telephone interview with Rev. Bruce Davidson, 23 February 2005.

29. Telephone interview with Rev. Stacy Martin, director, Immigration and Refugee Program, Lutheran Social Ministries of New Jersey, 15 December 2004.

30. Davidson shares office space with the New Jersey Council of Churches in return for acting as their voice on poverty issues. The New Jersey Council of Churches was established in 1945 and is a member of the National Council of Churches. Sixteen Christian denominations of diverse theological traditions and some 3,000 local congregations are represented in this statewide body. See Lurie and Mappen, "New Jersey Council of Churches," in Lurie and Mappen, *Encyclopedia of New Jersey*, 571.

31. David Yamane, "The Bishops & Politics," *Commonweal* 130, no. 10 (23 May 2003): 17; see also William Bole, "What Do State Catholic Conferences Do?" in Margaret O'Brien Steinfels, ed., *American Catholics and Civic Engagement: A Distinctive Voice* (Lanham, Md.: Rowman & Littlefield, 2004), 92–109.

32. Robert Booth Fowler, Allen D. Hertzke, and Laura R. Olson, *Religion & Politics in America*, 2nd ed. (Boulder, Colo.: Westview, 1999), 46.

33. *The Catholic Advocate* (the official newspaper of the Newark Archdiocese) 53, no. 6 (24 March 2004): 30.

34. Embryonic stem cell research has been denounced as unethical by the NJCC and by antiabortion groups because it can involve destroying a human embryo. According to New Jersey's Catholic bishops, "We believe it is more important than ever to stand for the principle that government must not treat any living human being as research material, as a mere means for benefit to others." But the Church does support research on adult stem cells, which can be retrieved without harming the donor. See Editorial, "Stem Cell Research Proposal Draws Opposition of Bishops," *The Catholic Advocate* 53, no. 5 (10 March 2004): 22.

35. In January 2005, Acting Governor Richard Codey gave top priority to funding stem cell research in his State of the State Address. *Star-Ledger*, 12 January 2005, 1 and 15.

36. Editorial, "Domestic Partners Bill Defeat Sought by NJCC," *The Catholic Advocate* 52, no. 23 (3 December 2003): 20.

37. Laura Mansnerus, "New Jersey to Recognize Gay Couples," *New York Times*, 29 January 2004, B5. In addition to Senator Lesniak, Governor McGreevey and Acting Governor Richard Codey, both Catholic, have strongly supported both domestic partner legislation and public funding of stem cell research.

38. Robert Schwaneberg, "Bill Lifts Nonprofits' Shield against Child Sex Lawsuits," *Star-Ledger*, 20 March 2004, 24. Vitale's bill would not abolish charitable immunity, which would continue to protect a church against a lawsuit by a parishioner who, for example, slips on the church steps. But the bill would make an exception allowing charities to be sued if they are careless in hiring or retaining any employee who sexually abuses a minor.

39. Schwaneberg, "Bill Lifts Nonprofits' Shield against Child Sex Lawsuits." All Catholic dioceses in New Jersey have had cases of clergy sex abuse of minors, and the diocese of Paterson has had an especially difficult history with a serial offender

priest in Mendham (an affluent suburb of Morristown). Victims' support groups such as SNAP (Survivors Network of Those Abused by Priests) have been very active in New Jersey, calling for Church reform and lobbying the state legislature to change the Charitable Immunity Act. They were successful in the first phase, which was to break the logjam in the Senate Judiciary Committee and get the bill reported out.

40. Paul Mulshine, "Charity Starts at Home, Not in Court," *Star-Ledger*, 2 December 2004, 17. Mulshine, who writes a regular column for the *Star-Ledger*, correctly notes that even if the legislature does not modify charitable immunity, the state supreme court is considering ending charitable immunity on its own. On November 29, 2004, the court heard oral argument in *Hardwicke v. American Boychoir School* (Docket No. A-17-04) on the question of whether one charitable institution, the American Boychoir School in Princeton, can be sued by a former student who alleges that he was molested in the 1970–1971 school year. The legal question before the court is, Does the Charitable Immunity Act protect the defendant institution from this complaint under the Child Sexual Abuse Act?

41. Michael Barone, Richard Cohen, and Grant Ujifusa, "New Jersey," *The Almanac of American Politics* (Washington, D.C.: National Journal, 2004), 1017–22.

42. Terry Golway, "Back into the Shadows: Crackdown on Illegal Immigrants Sends a Chill through Hispanic Population," *New York Times*, 20 February 2005, sec. 14, 1 and 9.

43. Since 1904, Lutheran Social Ministries has offered hospitality and service to those in need across the Garden State. According to Rev. Martin, this is the only Protestant social service agency in the state. This one hundred-year-old, not-for-profit agency serves more than 1,800 people daily at more than thirty locations throughout the state, with 650 employees, operating on an annual budget of approximately $42 million. The services provided include special needs housing, adoption services, counseling, disaster relief, affordable housing for families and for senior citizens, and immigration services and refugee resettlement. Telephone interview with Rev. Stacy Martin, 15 December 2004.

44. As a Presbyterian minister, Rev. Martin works for Lutheran Social Ministries because, as she explained, the Presbyterian Church USA and the Evangelical Lutheran Church in America (ELCA) are in full covenant and recognize one another's clergy. Both are reformed churches; the ELCA comes from a reformed Lutheran tradition, while the Presbyterian Church USA comes from a reformed Calvinist tradition. Telephone interview with Rev. Stacy Martin, 15 December 2004.

45. Golway, "Back into the Shadows," 9.

46. Interview with Max Kleinman, executive vice president, United Jewish Communities of MetroWest, New Jersey, 9 February 2005. Subsequent quotations are from this interview.

47. Alan Cooperman, "Israel Divestiture Spurs Clash: Jewish Leaders Condemn Move by Presbyterian Church," *Washington Post*, 29 September 2004, A8.

48. John Mooney, "Black Cleric Pushes School Vouchers," *Star-Ledger*, 11 February 2005, 27.

# 2

## Massachusetts Political and Religious Culture

*Anne Marie Cammisa*

Crowds of people lined the streets, gathered in the Boston Common and packed into the corridors of the Massachusetts statehouse. Lesbian couples held hands, and their adoptive children held up placards. In the meantime, clusters of people prayed the rosary aloud, while other individuals quoted Bible passages to passersby. Television cameras panned the area, with reporters having a heyday trying to find outrageous quotes from one side or the other. It was either society coming to a crashing halt or another giddy first for the brave new world of modern-day Progressives. It was the beginning of the debate on a constitutional amendment to ban same-sex marriage.

Welcome to Massachusetts politics: a world filled with grand new ideas and solid old traditions, a world populated with staunch Irish Catholics and progressive-minded liberal academics, with proper Boston Brahmins and peace-loving, Birkenstock-wearing intellectuals. It is the cradle of democracy, where citizens take their right to be heard seriously. It is also the world of backroom deals and old-fashioned logrolling. "All politics is local," said Tip O'Neill of the life of a congressman. This time, local and state politics were being played out on a national stage.

Controversy is not new to Massachusetts. Its history is replete with conflicts among competing groups, starting with the Puritans who arrived on its shores seeking religious freedom—and then denied it to other groups. Massachusetts has had a history of being involved in the defining moments of America: the creation of democracy and the abolition of slavery. Throughout it all, the Puritan legacy of creating a shining city on a hill has provided a moral and religious backdrop to the conflicts and controversies of the commonwealth's politics. This chapter examines that religious backdrop both historically and

27

through the lens of current-day religious lobbying groups, which include Catholic, Jewish, African American, and mainline Protestant and evangelical groups. The chapter begins with a discussion of Massachusetts political and religious culture, starting with the influence of the Puritans and, later, the Boston Irish. It then moves to an examination of the state's political culture, legislative professionalism, and current political environment. Next, the chapter discusses the various types of religious interest groups in Massachusetts, classifying them and examining their issues, expertise, access, and tactics. Finally, it assesses the impact of religious groups in Massachusetts, with special attention to the same-sex marriage debate.

## MASSACHUSETTS POLITICAL AND RELIGIOUS CULTURE

### The Puritan Influence

The political culture of Massachusetts is deeply intertwined with its religious history. Massachusetts was founded by Puritan settlers who fled England for religious freedom. Once having arrived in Boston, however, the Puritans established their own religious codes that restricted other denominations, most notably the Roman Catholic, or, in Puritan phraseology, "Papish," Church. For much of its history, Massachusetts—and especially Boston—was ruled by a Yankee elite (the Boston "Brahmins") that held a particular antipathy for the Roman Catholic faith. The British background of these Brahmins also gave them a deep-seated aversion to and distrust of all things Irish (an aversion and distrust that was returned in kind). In the late nineteenth century, Massachusetts was homogeneous, Anglo-Saxon, anti-Irish, and anti-Catholic. It was into this environment that Roman Catholic refugees from the Irish potato famine streamed in the late nineteenth century. As Thomas O'Connor put it in *The Boston Irish*,

> If there had existed in the nineteenth century a computer able to digest all the appropriate data, it would have reported one city in the entire world where an Irish Catholic, under any circumstance, should never, *ever* set foot. That city was Boston, Massachusetts.[1]

And yet, set foot in Boston the Irish did, one after another. The great migration of the Irish to America changed the complexion of the entire nation, and nowhere was this more evident than in Boston. And, as Boston was the political center of Massachusetts, the political complexion of the state was greatly changed and influenced not only by the Irish but also by their unique, antagonistic relationship with the descendants of the original Anglo-Saxon settlers.

First, let us examine the religious and political traditions of the Anglo-Saxons who built the "City upon the Hill." The Puritans came to America to practice a new form of religion, a religion that would "purify," as the name implies, the excesses of both the Roman Catholic Church and the Anglican Church, which was becoming, at least in the eyes of some of its members, too similar to Catholicism in its trappings of pomp and circumstance. No grand cathedrals or ostentatious churches for the Puritans. No hierarchical organizational structure for them, either. Instead, the Puritans would worship as they lived, simply and austerely. They would focus on hard work and self-denial. And they would build a new world. This new world was described in John Winthrop's famous "City upon a Hill" speech, given as the Puritans embarked on their journey to Massachusetts, and based on Matthew's (5:14) description of the kingdom of God on earth, "You are a city upon a hill. A city built upon a hill cannot be hid."

> Now the onely way to avoyde this shipwracke and to provide for our posterity is to followe the Counsell of Micah, to doe Justly, to love mercy, to walke humbly with our God, for this end, wee must be knitt together in this worke as one man, wee must entertaine each other in brotherly Affeccion, wee must be willing to abridge our selves of our superfluities, for the supply of others necessities, wee must uphold a familiar Commerce together in all meekenes, gentlenes, patience and liberallity, wee must delight in eache other, make others Condicions our owne rejoyce together, mourne together, labour, and suffer together, allwayes haveing before our eyes our Commission and Community in the worke, our Community as members of the same body, soe shall wee keepe the unitie of the spirit in the bond of peace, the Lord will be our God and delight to dwell among us, as his owne people and will commaund a blessing upon us in all our wayes, soe that wee shall see much more of his wisdome power goodnes and truthe then formerly wee have beene acquainted with, wee shall finde that the God of Israell is among us, when tenn of us shall be able to resist a thousand of our enemies, when hee shall make us a prayse and glory, that men shall say of succeeding plantacions: the lord make it like that of New England: for wee must Consider that wee shall be as a Citty upon a Hill, the eies of all people are uppon us.[2]

The highest Puritan ideals are embodied in this passage: community, hard work, humility, austerity, unity, charity, and the blessings of God. These ideals translated into a political outlook as well: laws should be made that encourage hard work and moral living. It is only then that the city of God can be realized on earth. The Puritans saw the New World as a fresh start, a chance to create a shining city that would reflect God's will, eliminate the excesses of traditional religions, and demonstrate to the world how an upright and moral society could be built.

Imagine the shock and horror that the Puritans' descendants faced when boatloads of poverty-stricken Irish Catholic immigrants landed in their city on the hill. Not only did the Irish arouse their worst inbred bigotry and racism (and the English at that time really did consider the Irish to be another, inferior race), but the Irish immigrants *were* poor and dirty and, because of the lack of available jobs, could be called shiftless. The two groups each met the other's worst expectations. And the conflicting outlooks each group held toward politics and society created the political culture of the state. In fact, immigration and migration patterns of various ethnic and religious groups form the basis of state political cultures throughout the United States, at least according to a classic theory laid out by political scientist Daniel Elazar, discussed in the following section.

## State Political Culture

According to Daniel Elazar,[3] there are three political subcultures residing in the American states: *individualistic*, *moralistic*, and *traditionalistic*. The subcultures are the result of patterns of immigration whereby various ethnic groups, with differing political, religious, and economic orientations, left their mark on the states. Both the moralistic and the individualistic political cultures are present in Massachusetts. The moralistic culture is characterized by a positive view of the role of government in society. Politicians and citizens view their state as a commonwealth where all are working together to create the good society. Private interactions may be regulated by public laws in order to uphold the public good, and corruption in politics is not tolerated. This political subculture, evident in a number of states, began with the ideals of the Puritans who arrived in the Commonwealth of Massachusetts:

> The Puritans came to these shores intending to establish the best possible earthly version of the holy commonwealth. Their religious outlook was imbued with a high level of political concern, in the spirit of the ancient Israelites whose ideal commonwealth they wished to reproduce.[4]

The individualistic culture, on the other hand, is rooted in the marketplace. Citizens and politicians agree that economics and politics are best left to individual transactions, that private interactions should be regulated as little as possible, and "that politics is a dirty—if necessary—business, better left to those who are willing to soil themselves by engaging in it."[5] While the moralistic subculture is characterized by a sense of community, the individualistic subculture is characterized by personal interactions and relationships as well as mutual obligations. And, in the individualistic subculture, corruption in politics is accepted as a necessary evil.

The individualistic subculture is in many ways a reaction against the moralistic subculture. Imagine an immigrant group (or groups) who came into an existing "commonwealth," where society was organized around a particular conception of the common good. Imagine that that immigrant group felt itself to be so different in tradition, religion, and culture from the dominant group that it could not consider itself part of this commonwealth. The group or groups would likely subscribe to a different view of politics, one in which unity and common goals were not so important but in which individuals were. Thus, the moralistic culture—injected with Irish and southern European immigrants—spawned the individualistic culture, and the two were likely to be in perpetual conflict. Massachusetts has historically exemplified that conflict.

Massachusetts political culture can also be examined through a narrower lens, focusing not on political orientation but on social and work status. Edgar Litt did just that in 1965.[6] He identified four distinct social/cultural groups in Massachusetts: the patricians, the managers and the workers, and the yeomen. Of these, the patricians and workers mirror the groups making up the moralistic and individualistic subcultures described by Elazar.

The patricians are the Boston Brahmins, the Massachusetts blue bloods, the Puritan stock of Massachusetts. They are the subscribers to the belief in the city upon the hill, in good government, in the commonwealth, and in public service. As they evolved over the generations, this group became urbane and sophisticated and developed a strong sense of both superiority and noblesse oblige. At one time, they ran the government of Massachusetts. Now they play a background role, involving themselves in philanthropy rather than good government:

> Where once they dominated the political life of the Commonwealth, today they are more likely to satisfy their sense of social obligation by serving on boards of social, cultural and charitable organizations.[7]

The second culture in Massachusetts is the managers, who derive their position in society not from wealth or birth (like the patricians) but from skill and profession. They are the administrators, the ones who bring professionalism and business practices to government. While this group may have been born from the moralistic political culture, its emphasis is more on profession and less on commonwealth. Good government may be the goal for both the moralistic and the managers, but the managers evaluate it in terms of means (administrative efficiency, for example) rather than ends (creating a moral society). Thus, managers have included both the Progressives and newly emergent immigrant groups attempting to integrate into politics by establishing themselves as neutral professionals. A good example of a manager is former

Governor Michael Dukakis, "Zorba the clerk," who claimed that "his [presidential] campaign in 1988 was not about value but about management skill."[8]

The workers were once the backbone of the Massachusetts economy. Predominately Irish, Italian, or French Canadian, the workers were mostly Catholic, urban, and blue collar. They formed the basis of the Democratic Party in Massachusetts not because of political clout or a particular interest in good government but because there were enough of them to support a political machine. While the moralistic Yankee Puritans may have had a more powerful and well-articulated vision of good government, the individualistic Irish immigrants were plucky enough to realize that vision is less important in a democracy than numbers. By delivering jobs and economic benefits, Irish machine politicians gained and maintained votes and were able to eradicate the power of the elite, intellectual, and sophisticated ruling class.

The yeoman culture is now almost nonexistent in Massachusetts. Like the patricians (also almost nonexistent), the yeomen also derive from the moralistic political culture. Unlike the patricians, who were composed of elites, the yeomen were the gentlemen farmers who participated in local government and were strongly interested in civic affairs and the public good writ small. With the decline of agriculture, the rise of a service economy, and the reform of local governments from town meetings to town managers, the yeoman class dwindled.[9] These same factors, however, led to the rise of the managerial class.

Massachusetts political culture, then, has been characterized by a conflict between its Puritanical strain (moralistic culture) and the more politically expedient strain exemplified by the newer European immigrants and their individualistic culture. Descendants of both groups, however, could find common ground as managers, with the Puritanical strain emphasizing good government and the newer immigrants attempting to gain power and acceptance through neutral competence and administrative efficiency.

## State Legislative Professionalism

The Massachusetts Great and General Court was established by royal charter in 1629. The legislature, once a form of direct democracy, has evolved and been modified over the years of its history. Once one of the largest legislatures in the world, its size was capped and then reduced. Changes in qualifications of and electoral procedures for state senators and representatives mirror national changes. But the most significant reforms of the legislative process occurred first during the Progressive era and then during the 1960s, when a wave of professionalizing reform swept across state legislatures throughout the country.

The Progressive movement began in the states around the turn of the twentieth century and was a response to rapid changes, particularly in urban areas. Political machines, fed by burgeoning numbers of immigrants, were rife with corruption, even as they provided some, albeit incomplete, form of social services to the urban poor. The Progressives, in true moralistic form worthy of Puritan descendants, attempted to end corruption and bring about "good government." Much of their desire for reform came from an altruistic desire to better society, and some of it came from a disdain for the poor and ethnic classes who were running the political machines.

In Massachusetts, Progressive reforms of the legislative process included the popular referendum and popular initiative, passed in 1917. The popular referendum gives voters a chance to accept or reject laws that have been passed by the legislature. The popular initiative gives citizens the opportunity to propose state legislative statutes or amendments to the state constitution. In Massachusetts, the initiative and referendum are indirect; that is, they must go through the state legislature first. In fact, the initiative process was of vital importance in the homosexual marriage debate, discussed later in this chapter. The Supreme Judicial Court (the Massachusetts Supreme Court), in a landmark case, decided in November 2003 that denying homosexual and lesbian couples the right to marry was unconstitutional. Opponents of the decision turned to the initiative process to propose a constitutional amendment affirming marriage as a heterosexual union.

While in this particular instance, the initiative process was used to take power away from the courts, overall, one can argue that the initiative and referendum process usurps the power of the legislature and, perhaps more important, takes away its accountability. (The legislature cannot be held responsible for citizens who overrule or propose various statutes.)[10] Progressive reforms, in general, tended to disburse power, yielding to the moralistic notion that political power equals corruption. Of particular importance in this regard is the repeal of the system of patronage, depriving the executive of the power to appoint cronies to political positions and replacing those cronies with a merit-based civil service, encouraging a system of neutral competence. In Massachusetts, Progressive reforms also led to the rise of the manager class and a chance for Irish Catholic politicians to break into traditional politics and establish themselves as professionals. It is no mere coincidence that the first Irish Catholic elected to statewide office in Massachusetts was Democratic Governor David D. Walsh. Elected in 1915, Governor Walsh was instrumental in forming the Union for a Progressive Constitution, a union that was successful in spearheading the drive for a constitutional convention to consider several progressive reforms, not the least of which were the referendum and initiative.[11]

**Table 2.1. Red, White, and Blue Legislatures**

| Red | Red Lite | | White | Blue Lite | Blue |
|-----|----------|--|-------|-----------|------|
| California | Alaska | Alabama | Minnesota | Georgia | Montana |
| Michigan | Illinois | Arizona | Missouri | Idaho | New Hampshire |
| New York | Florida | Arkansas | Nebraska | Indiana | North Dakota |
| Pennsylvania | Ohio | Colorado | North Carolina | Kansas | South Dakota |
| | Massachusetts | Connecticut | Oklahoma | Maine | Utah |
| | New Jersey | Delaware | Oregon | Mississippi | Wyoming |
| | Wisconsin | Hawaii | South Carolina | Nevada | |
| | | Iowa | Tennessee | New Mexico | |
| | | Kentucky | Texas | Rhode Island | |
| | | Louisiana | Virginia | Vermont | |
| | | Maryland | Washington | West Virginia | |

Source: National Conference of State Legislatures, 2004.

Other reforms in the years following the Progressive movement encouraged legislative professionalism through administrative oversight, increasing personal staff, and establishing legislative committees and subcommittees.[12] These developments allowed for specialization on the part of legislators. Reforms in the 1960s further professionalized Massachusetts government. In 1964, the governor's term increased to four years, and in 1966, his executive power was extended to include reorganizing the executive branch.

The cumulative effect of reforms throughout the twentieth century was to create a professionalized, highly paid, well-staffed legislature. According to the National Conference of State Legislatures, full-time legislatures have large districts, long legislative sessions, high salaries, and large staffs. It classifies legislatures as red, white, or blue. Red legislatures are full time, or professional; blue legislatures are part time (also known as citizen or traditional legislatures); and white legislatures are in the middle. Massachusetts is classified as "red lite," meaning that it is full time but scores somewhat lower than red states on measures of district size, length of legislative session, and so on. There are four red states and seven red lite states, making eleven states altogether (just over 20 percent) that are considered to have full-time professional legislatures (see table 2.1 for a listing of all fifty states according to red, white, and blue categories). Massachusetts also falls into the top-ten list of highest-paid legislators in the United States, coming in at number seven with a legislative salary of $53,379.93 (see table 2.2).

Also important to the legislative process is the centralization of power in the statehouse. The speaker of the house and the senate president each have significant powers over the membership in their respective chambers: they determine who is on what committees, who will chair those committees, where office and even parking space will be, and which staff will be hired and fired.

**Table 2.2.   Salaries of Legislators:**
**Top Ten States**

| | | |
|---|---|---|
| 1. | California | $99,000 |
| 2. | New York | $79,500 |
| 3. | Michigan | $77,400 |
| 4. | Pennsylvania | $64,638 |
| 5. | Illinois | $55,788 |
| 6. | Ohio | $53,707 |
| 7. | Massachusetts | $53,380 |
| 8. | Wisconsin | $45,569 |
| 9. | Delaware | $34,800 |
| 10. | Hawaii | $32,000 |

Source: National Conference of State Legislatures, www.ncsl.org/programs/legman/
03-legcomp.htm.

Together, these powers give an almost irresistible leverage to the leader-ship in each chamber. Rather than depending on floor debate, party caucuses, and committee deliberation to win votes for desired policy outcomes, Massachusetts legislative leaders are able to assemble coalitions behind the scenes through the dispensing or withholding of privileges and benefits. Massachusetts is also the only state that has "joint" committees: each committee has membership including both senators and representatives.

## MASSACHUSETTS POLITICS AND CULTURE TODAY

Massachusetts is no longer predominantly Anglo-Saxon, nor is it dominated by a rivalry between the English settlers and Irish immigrants. The population of Massachusetts is now more heterogeneous, although that heterogeneity is within an overwhelmingly white population (see table 2.3). The population includes both older and newer immigrant groups: Irish, Italian, French, and other European immigrants from the previous two centuries and more recent Asian and Latino immigrants. Massachusetts is a moderate-size state, with 2.2 percent of the total U.S. population. It is more urban than the country as a whole, and its median income is higher than U.S. median income ($50,502 vs. $41,994). Both the poverty rate and the unemployment rate are lower than those of the United States. In terms of race, Massachusetts is more homogeneous than the country as a whole, with 84.5 percent of its population being white (compared to 75.1 percent of the U.S. population). Its African American and Hispanic/Latino populations are significantly lower than those of the country as a whole, but its Asian population is slightly above the national average.

**Table 2.3.    Massachusetts Demographic Statistics Compared to the United States**

| Characteristic | Massachusetts | United States |
|---|---|---|
| Population (2000) | 6,349,097 | 2.2% of total |
| Distribution | | |
| Metro | 99.6% | 83% |
| Nonmetro | 0.4% | 17% |
| Economics | | |
| Median household income | $50,502 | $41,994 |
| Poverty rate (1999) | 9.3 | 12.4 |
| Unemployment (2002) | 5.3 | 5.8 |
| Race (2000) | | |
| White | 84.5 | 75.1 |
| African American | 5.4 | 12.3 |
| Hispanic/Latino | 6.8 | 12.5 |
| Asian | 3.8 | 3.6 |
| Other (including multiracial) | 6.0 | 7.9 |
| Native American | 0.2 | 0.9 |

Sources: United States Department of Agriculture, www.ers.usda.gov/StateFacts/MA.htm; www.fedstats.gov/qf/states/25000.html.

The Massachusetts legislature has also changed. A part-time, Republican, patrician legislature in the early twentieth century, the legislature first became majority Democratic in 1958. For much of the second half of the twentieth century, the legislature was dominated by Irish Catholic Democrats who were economic liberals and social conservatives. Although this group is still very powerful in the legislature—which remains 67 percent Catholic—its influence is waning. The legislature remains solidly Democratic, but it is a more socially liberal Democratic Party that now exists in Massachusetts. On issues such as birth control, abortion, and homosexual marriage, Catholic and non-Catholic legislators alike can be expected to take the liberal position, often in direct conflict with Church teaching and lobbying.

Religions represented in Massachusetts today include mainline and other Protestant churches, Orthodox Christians, Catholics, Reform, Orthodox and Jewish denominations, Muslims, Buddhists, and others. In addition, Massachusetts is seeing a rise in evangelical Christian denominations, particularly in the central and western part of the state, and evangelical clout is rising in the commonwealth, as evidenced by the prominence of the Massachusetts Family Institute during the same-sex marriage debate. Although the state is becoming more heterogeneous in many ways, almost half its population remains Catholic, making it the state with the second-largest Catholic population in the country (see table 2.4).

The Massachusetts legislature is professionalized, as noted earlier, and is dominated by the Democratic Party, but despite its overwhelming majority status, the Democratic Party in Massachusetts is disorganized and individual-

Table 2.4.   Top Ten U.S.
States with Highest
Proportion of Catholics in
Population, 1990 (%)

| | |
|---|---|
| Rhode Island | 63.12 |
| Massachusetts | 49.22 |
| Connecticut | 41.82 |
| New Jersey | 41.26 |
| New York | 40.47 |
| Louisiana | 32.44 |
| Wisconsin | 31.77 |
| Illinois | 31.59 |
| Pennsylvania | 30.93 |
| New Mexico | 30.85 |

Source: www.adherents.com.

istic.[13] The strength of the party is based on numbers and voters, not on party organizations. Campaigns are run by and for individual candidates. Since Massachusetts is a one-party state, most of its electoral competition occurs in the party primaries, forcing candidates from the same party to differentiate themselves, further splintering what party unity there might have been. On the other hand, the Massachusetts legislature is also known for its strong and centralized leadership and, in recent years, its conflicts with Republican governors. Although the party organization in Massachusetts may not be strong, the individual party members who become senate president and house majority leader are themselves quite powerful. Since Massachusetts has no seniority system, privileges, perquisites of office, and committee assignments are all doled out by the leadership.[14] Obviously, going against a majority leader would have strong consequences. Thus, a party that is disorganized on the outside is highly centralized on the inside of the legislature.

## RELIGIOUS INTEREST GROUPS IN MASSACHUSETTS

Having examined the political culture of Massachusetts, let us now evaluate how religious interest groups may fit into it. First, let us attempt to classify these groups; then we shall examine their issues, expertise, access, tactics, and coalition building before evaluating their impact in Massachusetts.

### Classification and Membership

Religious interest groups are generally classified as public interest groups. Unlike private interest groups, which represent private individuals united by occupation (the American Bar Association) or demographic grouping (the AARP), public interest groups' membership is united by a common view of public policy. Public interest groups may be single-issue groups (National Abortion Rights Action League) or multi-issue groups (National Organization of Women). Either way, the groups' members share a common outlook on what constitutes the public interest and what policies may best achieve that interest.

Members of religious interest groups do share a common interest in public policy, and that interest comes as a direct result of their religious beliefs. In some ways, religious group members are more united than other public interest group membership in that their political beliefs are the direct result of shared religious and moral beliefs rather than shared ideological beliefs. In other ways, religious interest groups may be less united around a single issue because issues themselves are not as important as the moral reasoning behind them.

Religious interest groups also differ from other public interest groups in terms of their membership; such differences may make a new classification scheme necessary to describe religious groups. Unlike traditional public interest groups, religious interest groups may be occupational in nature. For example, the United States Catholic Conference of Bishops is an occupational group (membership is based on whether one's occupation is that of a bishop). But the lobbyists for the group (or its related organization in Massachusetts, the Massachusetts Catholic Conference) is not interested primarily in policies that would directly affect bishops themselves; rather, they are interested in policies that both affect their flock and are consistent with Church teachings. Thus, the Catholic bishops as a group are an *institutional* organization, representing the Church hierarchy.

Another type of occupational interest group is service based. Some religious groups set up and run their own charities and services (often paid for with government funds). These various charities and service organizations will form an interest group within their own faith. Groups representing religious-based service providers can be classified as *service-based occupational*. Examples include the Jewish Community Resource Council and Catholic Charities. The representation of service-based occupational groups is threefold: at the macrolevel, they represent their religious denomination, but they also represent their service providers (people hired by their denomination who may or may not share the faith) and their clientele (the recipients of social services who again may or may not belong to the same faith community).

A final type of religious interest group is more similar in membership to other public interest groups. Some groups represent church members themselves or broader coalitions of like-minded religious people. Unlike the institutional groups, these groups have a bottom-up, grassroots approach. An example of a *grassroots membership group* representing church members would be the Christian Coalition. In all cases they would have a public interest component. In the first two types, the interest groups represent individuals or institutions of the same denomination. In the latter category, the interest group may represent a broad range of denominations. For example, the primarily evangelical Massachusetts Family Institute (MFI) does not represent any one faith but rather classifies itself as broadly representing "Judeo-Christian values," and its membership includes Catholics as well as all stripes of Protestants.

In examining state and local government interest groups, Donald Haider made a distinction between spatial interests and functional interests. A group has a spatial interest in determining exactly who will implement policies (in the government groups' case, whether it is the federal, state, or local government that will actually run a particular program). A group can also have a functional interest in a particular policy. The group in this case is more interested in the policy itself than in who actually administers it. While most public interest groups are concerned primarily with their functional interests, Haider argues that government groups are more concerned with spatial interests.[15] The service-based occupational groups, as providers of services (particularly education, health care, and welfare), also have a spatial interest in addition to their functional interests. Many of the policies for which these groups lobby involve services that they provide. It is often difficult to separate the spatial from the functional interests, and religious groups may have particular difficulty in that they believe that both society at large and religious institutions have an obligation to provide charity.

There are several religious interest groups that lobby in Massachusetts. Table 2.5 lists some of them and categorizes them according to the classification system described earlier. For the most part, these groups operate in much the same way that other interest groups do: they identify issues and monitor legislation, they mobilize grassroots support, they provide testimony at hearings, and they have face-to-face meetings with legislators and staff. In general, the groups ask to be and for the most part are treated the same as nonreligious interest groups.

## Issues

Religious interest groups differ from other interest groups in two distinct ways. First, their membership is made up of individuals who not only have a common moral code but whose moral code is based on a particular conception of God's will on earth. In contrast, other interest groups are made up of

Table 2.5.   **Religious Interest Groups in Massachusetts**

Institutional
  Massachusetts Catholic Conference
  Massachusetts Council of Churches
  Black Ministerial Alliance of Greater Boston

Service-based occupational
  Jewish Community Relations Council
  Catholic Charities

Grassroots membership
  Massachusetts Family Institute

members with similar policy or ideological interests. Those members may also subscribe to a common moral code, but the code is articulated in secular rather than religious, or God-centered, terms. While some members of a nonreligious interest group may have a religious reason for their belief in the interest group's goals, the language the group uses to define those goals will certainly not contain references to divine will.

Second, religious interest groups make their policy choices on the basis of scriptural precepts. For example, a religious group may say its concern for the poor stems from biblical references to taking care of the less fortunate. A nonreligious group concerned with taking care of the less fortunate would probably justify its concern with a more neutral "human rights" explanation. Religious and nonreligious groups may come to the same conclusions about appropriate policy goals, but the reasoning behind those goals may be completely different. Religious groups identify issues that are of importance to them on the basis of a distinctive worldview. Their text is more likely to be the Bible than the Constitution. For example, a representative of the Jewish Community Relations Council (JCRC) brought up the Fourth Commandment ("Honor thy father and mother") in explaining his group's support of policies for the elderly. Of course, even going directly to scripture does not ensure that all religious groups will come to the same conclusions. Interpretations of the same scripture vary from group to group, and, particularly in the case of institutional groups, church doctrine is an essential component of scriptural interpretation.

Religious groups therefore defy categorization on a liberal–conservative continuum. Not only do religious groups differ from each other on how liberal they might be on any given issue, but the internal logic of religious groups is not concerned with liberalism or conservatism in the political sense. This is particularly true of Catholic interest groups who are "liberal" on social welfare issues but "conservative" on other social issues: abortion, birth control, and same-sex marriage. Religious groups with whom the Catholics might align on social welfare issues (mainline Protestants, for example) would part company with the Catholic groups on abortion and same-sex marriage, while evangelicals would likely do the opposite.

In general, the issues that religious groups are concerned with can be divided into two main types: social welfare policy issues and moral issues. Social welfare policy issues include housing, care for the elderly and disabled, immigration, poverty, and health care. Moral issues include the death penalty, abortion, contraception, stem cell research, and, most recently, homosexual marriage.

Social welfare issues bring together Catholics, mainline Protestants, black Protestants, and Jewish groups, who are, for the most part, in alignment with nonreligious liberal groups on these issues. Fundamentalists and evangelicals, on the other hand, align with conservatives on these issues. Catholics leave their liberal friends behind when it comes to moral issues, standing on the same side as fundamentalists, evangelicals (black and white), and Orthodox Jews on same-sex marriage.

Of course, saying that social welfare issues are different from moral issues is itself bringing a secular slant to the topic: for groups who identify policy goals on the basis of their perception of divine will and biblical precepts, every issue is a moral issue. But social welfare policy issues are perhaps more easily discussed in secular terms, and the religious divide on these issues coincides with the conservative–liberal divide. While an evangelical might agree with a social conservative that personal responsibility should be a hallmark of any social welfare program, the rationale would be different. Personal responsibility may be a way of encouraging individuals to respond to God's will, or it may be a libertarian reaction to governmental largesse. The evangelical and the social conservative might well part ways on the issue of same-sex marriage, with the former seeing it as an abomination of God's will and the latter seeing it as another issue best left to individual choice.

While its Puritan architects might be shocked, the current political climate in Massachusetts discourages religious-based discussion of moral issues. There are several reasons for this. First, in a state that has become relatively heterogeneous, it is easier to minimize religious differences by not discussing them or by phrasing policy debates in nonreligious terms. Thus, in discussing same-sex marriage, for example, many politicians and activists pointed to the "separation of church and state" as reason enough to leave religious arguments out of the debate. Second, unlike other states covered in this volume, Massachusetts has only recently begun to see large numbers of evangelicals residing in the state, participating in its political processes, and espousing religiously based conservative ideals. The evangelical-based MFI's participation in the same-sex marriage debate may well mark a turning point in evangelical participation in Massachusetts politics. Third, Catholic politicians, who have been dominant in the political process for decades, have themselves been reluctant to "wear their religion on their sleeves." Historically, Catholics in America have felt the need to prove that their allegiance to Rome does not impede their allegiance to the United States.[16] As Catholic politicians in Massachusetts have found themselves increasingly on the same side as mainline Protestants on many social issues, they have also increasingly identified themselves, politically at least, as liberals rather than Catholics. The Church's positions on welfare, social justice, and the death penalty are easy to defend; its positions on abortion, birth control, and same-sex marriage are not. Consistent with their focus on neutral competence and good management, modern Catholic Democrats use liberal ideology rather than Catholic social teaching to defend their position on issues, and using that ideology, they more often than not part with Catholic social teaching on moral issues.

## Expertise

One of the primary functions of interest groups is to provide information and expertise to legislators. In many but not all cases, the information religious groups provide comes in the form of moral suasion. Sometimes moral arguments are welcome; other times, especially when there are strong feelings on both sides, moral arguments can become problematic for legislators. Massachusetts Catholic legislators, for example, may be hesitant to appear to be following a religious mandate, preferring, like John F. Kennedy in 1960, to make decisions "without regard to outside religious pressures or dictates."[17]

But for the occupational/service provider groups, this concern may be somewhat muted. When these groups go to lobby for or against particular legislation, they lobby as expert service providers rather than as theologians. According to Allen D. Hertzke, who studied the role of religious groups in lobbying Congress,

> Liberal lobbies, whether Catholic or Protestant, find their greatest success when they report on the homeless shelters, soup kitchens and the work of their social service agencies with the poor and those of modest means.[18]

Expertise can come in other forms as well. For example, the MFI, a religious coalition that lobbied strongly against homosexual marriage, did not use overtly religious arguments. "We don't use religious arguments," says Evelyn Murphy of the MFI. Instead, "we turn to social science research supporting marriage and the concept that children need a mother and a father, that homosexuality is not genetic, but is harmful. We don't make any statements without documentation." There is an important distinction between making theological arguments and social science arguments. Turning to research studies is not the same as turning to church doctrine or biblical passages.

On the other hand, an understanding of moral and theological concepts is also a form of expertise. And the religious groups will use this understanding as the basis for their arguments. For example, in explaining his group's support of same-sex marriage, Brad Kramer turns to the Jewish tradition: "[The argument for same-sex marriage] relies on traditional values of social justice. It is very much within the Jewish tradition to support those values." Of course, an Orthodox Jew would heartily disagree, arguing that homosexual marriage is not a question of social justice.

## Access

No lobbying group can be successful unless it can make its voice heard. Access refers to the ability of interest groups to get a foot in the door: to meet with legislative staff and/or state legislators. If a group has no access, it has no voice. Like other interest groups, the access of the religious groups varies from policy to policy, from lobbyist to lobbyist, and from office to office. In general, religious lobbyists don't have a difficult time meeting with legislative staff. "Clergy from any faith represent organized groups in the community," says Norma Shapiro of the Massachusetts American Civil Liberties Union (ACLU). "It is always important for legislators to listen to them."[19]

Catholic interest groups have historically had a good deal of access to the legislature; it has been dominated by Catholic legislators since the mid-twentieth century. Access does not guarantee success, but for several decades, the Catholic Church had little difficulty both getting its voice heard and its issues acted on. In the days when the senate president was Billy Bulger and the house speaker was Tom McGee, "it was easy to lobby," according to Gerry D'Avolio, outgoing executive director of the Massachusetts Catholic Conference. "We had an automatic 90 votes in the house, 25 in Senate. There was a feeling that 'if the Church is supporting it, it must be good.'"[20] Those days are long gone. D'Avolio says that the legislature began to change in the early 1980s and that since then "the legislature has totally transformed. We need to do a lot more work on educating the legislators on the teachings and positions of the Church." Shapiro, of the ACLU, agrees: "The legislature represents a wide range of different views of Catholicism. The Massachusetts Catholic Conference has easy entrée into the legislature, but it does not have an easy time convincing legislators of its positions." D'Avolio credits the growing number of lobbying groups with the change in the legislature. As homosexual rights groups, the National Abortion Rights Action League (NARAL), the National Organization for Women (NOW), the ACLU, and other groups became more of a force, the Catholic groups' powers waned.

Of course, Catholic groups are not the only religious interest groups in Massachusetts, but they do have a special relationship with a predominantly Catholic legislature. And Gerry D'Avolio, lobbyist for the Massachusetts Catholic Conference for thirty years, is held with special regard by legislators and lobbyists alike:

> In lobbying circles, where personal relationships sometimes drive policy, D'Avolio takes pride in his friendships with Republicans and Democrats, liberals and conservatives. One day he sits with Norma Shapiro of the American Civil Liberties Union of Massachusetts to oppose the death penalty; the next he sits across the witness table from her on an abortion rights bill. Each time he is unfailingly cordial, never bitter, even as the issues become more and more contentious. "He's a wonderful, sweet guy," Shapiro said.[21]

Catholic lobbyists faced a difficult time during the period that the clergy sex-abuse scandal was coming to light. Public and elite opinion of the Catholic Church was particularly low. As D'Avolio put it, "It [the scandal] hurt us." However, it did not have a great deal of impact on the access that the Massachusetts Catholic Conference had to the legislature. D'Avolio continues, "Not once did I have any kind of repercussion. Anger was not directed at me or conference. It hurt Catholic legislators, but they were angry at the hierarchy. I had conversations with them about the scandal; I never ran from it or hid from it. It was indefensible; there are no excuses for it."

Other religious groups report little difficulty in gaining access to the legislature. "We have an excellent relationship with legislators," says Brad Kramer of JCRC. "Sure there are individuals who see it [religious group lobbying] as a violation of the separation of church and state, but overall it is a tremendous relationship."

Access is not the same thing as impact, as we shall see later; nonetheless, it is an important component of interest group success.

## Tactics

Interest groups rely on a variety of strategies to get their message across. Those strategies may be divided into two general types: *insider* and *outsider*. Insider strategies involve typical lobbying tactics: meetings with legislators and staffs, providing expertise on important legislative matters, testifying at committee hearings, and drafting and/or commenting on legislative language. Outsider strategies involve mobilizing the grassroots: organizing protests and marches, sending out mass mailings to constituents and urging them to contact their representatives, and, if funds allow, creating newspaper, radio, and television advertising.

Insider tactics are generally behind-the-scenes tactics and involve working with legislators and their staffs. They utilize an interest group's resource of expertise. Outsider tactics, on the other hand, work outside the system by mobilizing large numbers of voters to let their voices be heard in the system. The advantage of outsider tactics is obvious in a democracy: there is strength in numbers, and if large numbers of people can be motivated to protest on an issue, they can also be mobilized to vote against legislators who do not support their position. The risk of an outsider strategy is that it may alienate decision makers who may then be less inclined to provide access to interest groups who would like to utilize an insider strategy.

Which strategy a group might use depends on its strengths. Obviously, a group that represents large numbers of individuals who can easily be mobilized will be more likely to use an outsider strategy. Groups that cannot easily mobilize membership or that have expertise as their greatest asset would be more likely to use insider tactics. So grassroots membership organizations such as the MFI rely on grassroots strategies, while occupational/service providers tend to use insider strategies to share their expertise, as does the institutional/hierarchical group. This is not to say that strategies are monolithic. Grassroots organizations such as the MFI often have professional lobbying staff who engage in one-on-one lobbying in addition to organizing grassroots activities. And institutional and occupational/service provider interest groups will also exhort their membership to action should the need arise and may also write letters to the editor or use media (free media are more often used than paid) to bring attention to their issues. For example, the Massachusetts Catholic Conference issued a major mailing to Catholics in Massachusetts after the *Goodridge* ruling.

## Coalitions and Issue Networks

Interest groups often form coalitions with one another in order to present a united front on a given issue. Coalitions are useful to both interest groups and decision makers. They allow for compromises to be made outside of government, they encourage the exchange of information, and they broaden the groups' focus.[22] Coalitions are alliances of groups that enable them to broaden their base and increase their bargaining position. Coalitions often form around specific issues and are generally temporary in nature. "Coalitions are 'action sets,' temporary alliances for limited purposes."[23] Indeed, Hugh Heclo's concept of "issue networks" posits that interest group alliances are fluid and vary from issue to issue.[24]

Religious groups find coalitions useful, even though coalition building can involve vastly different actors, depending on the issue. "We don't formally join coalitions," says Gerry D'Avolio. "We will join in with other organizations. For example, we worked closely with the ACLU on the death penalty. We collaborate when other groups call for help." Like its national counterpart, the Massachusetts Catholic Conference will work with other groups on individual policy goals; it prefers, however, to issue its own statements and goals, distancing itself from other groups. First, even if the Catholic group has goals in common with other groups, the Catholic Conference wants to make clear that its rationale is based on Catholic social teaching. Second, given that it is difficult to classify the Catholic Conference as liberal or conservative, the group does not want to become too closely associated with other groups on one issue when it may be in opposition to them on others.

## IMPACT OF RELIGIOUS GROUPS IN MASSACHUSETTS

It is difficult to measure the success or failure of an interest group on any particular policy. One can examine the policy statements made by a group and compare them to the provisions of final legislation, or one can ask interest group and congressional actors to identify who had an impact on what provisions. Neither method is completely satisfactory. An issue a group claims as a success—and that is consistent with its policy positions at the beginning of the process—may have been resolved in the same manner even without the group's input. Nonetheless, an analysis of a particular policy, along with a general knowledge of resources, techniques, and other factors that are more likely to lead to success, can demonstrate whether and to what extent a group had an impact on a particular policy. In general, interest groups are more successful on incremental than on comprehensive change; on narrow issues than on broad, noncontroversial over conflictual changes; and on keeping the status quo rather than changing it. In addition, interest groups are more successful when they act in coalitions and when they have access to decision makers.

Let us examine some of the priorities of the religious interest groups in light of these factors. First, we shall examine several issues together and then treat the same-sex debate, which was of central concern to religious groups at the time of this writing, separately.

## Priority Issues

As noted earlier, religious interest groups have priorities that can be divided into social welfare or moral issues. Let us address social welfare issues first. In Massachusetts, the biggest recent concern is the budget. Because of a fiscal crisis, funding for many social programs has been slashed. Groups that support these programs are put in a defensive position: trying to restore money that has already been cut or keeping the cuts from going further. One priority for JCRC and the Massachusetts Catholic Conference has been maintaining spending on the state's Welfare-to-Work initiative, from which $18 million was cut in the most recent budget. The groups, along with others, worked to restore the spending. Eventually, $5 million of the cuts was restored to the program. Was this a success? It depends on how you define it. Obviously, the interest groups would have liked to maintain or even increase funding, an option that was not a possibility given the current state of the budget.

Given the factors for success discussed earlier, the spending restoration can be considered a win, if a qualified one. Success is more likely on incremental, narrow, noncontroversial issues. Rather than holding out for what they might have liked in an ideal world, the groups lobbied for something less than that. But their lobbying did make a difference. As several respondents noted, lobbying is often not about changing a legislator's mind but about making sure that particular issues are at the top of the list. By making sure that legislators know their groups' priorities, lobbyists give their issues a fighting chance. In the same way, these groups fought for affordable housing, and when housing legislation was reauthorized, their priority was to make sure that the law was not weakened by major changes. It was not. Again, group success, narrowly defined: lobbying for the status quo is easier than lobbying for major comprehensive change. The groups understand this and make sure they present legislators with reasonable options rather than best-case scenarios.

The groups are not always successful. Religious groups that are more progressive on social policies (Catholics, Jewish groups, and mainline Protestants) experienced recent losses primarily in the area of immigration. The Citizenship Access Program, which funded efforts of community-based organizations to help new immigrants gain citizenship, was the victim of budget cuts that eliminated the program. The funding has not been restored despite efforts by a coalition including religious groups. These same religious groups have also been in favor of restoring food stamp eligibility to immigrants; again this has not happened. Why were the groups less successful on these issues? It probably has less to do with effectiveness of lobbying than it does with timing and political milieu. Since September 11, 2001, and the new focus on national security, spending on new immigrants has become less popular. The groups have a hard time gaining support for such programs.

Moral issues are another area where religious groups have a difficult time. The Massachusetts Catholic Conference often stands alone in its opposition to issues involving morality: emergency contraception, stem cell research, and mandated insurance coverage of contraception. Mandated contraception coverage is a particularly interesting issue because it affects the Catholic organizations directly since they will be required to pay for a benefit that they find morally objectionable. Despite the best efforts of the Massachusetts Catholic Conference, they lost the legislative battle, and the coverage was mandated. On the other hand, the Massachusetts Catholic Conference was successful in its opposition to stem cell research. In November 2003, a measure expressing support for stem cell research (as a means of encouraging biotech companies to stay in Massachusetts) was defeated after extensive lobbying. "Both supporters and opponents laid the provision's demise at the feet of the Speaker, a devout Catholic. Finneran did not sit on the House-Senate panel, but he typically exerts tight control over his lieutenants."[25]

## Same-Sex Marriage

By far the biggest moral issue in recent history has been the debate over same-sex marriage. It pitted religious groups against each other, caused a great deal of contention and name-calling and massive protests on either side, and, to date, has not been resolved to the satisfaction of anybody.

It started with a Supreme Judicial Court ruling on November 18, 2003. In a 4 to 3 ruling in *Goodridge v. Department of Public Health*, the state supreme court upheld the right of eight homosexual and lesbian couples to marry in Massachusetts, saying that "barring an individual from the protections, benefits, and obligations of civil marriage solely because that person would marry a person of the same sex violates the Massachusetts Constitution." The court stayed the judgment for six months "to permit the Legislature to take such action as it may deem appropriate in light of this opinion."

Religious groups divided on the issue. More liberal, progressive-minded groups, particularly mainline Protestants, supported same-sex marriage on mostly political grounds. They stressed the separation of church and state, arguing that while the state could not interfere in churches' decisions as to whom to marry, neither should churches impose their definitions of marriage on the state. These groups argued that same-sex marriage was an issue of social justice and human rights. As the Religious Coalition for the Freedom to Marry said,

> The most fundamental human right, after the necessities of food, clothing and shelter, is the right to affection and the supportive love of other human beings. We become most fully human when we love another person. We can grow in our capacity to be human—to be loving—in a family unit. This right to love and to form a family is so fundamental that our Constitution takes it for granted in its dedication to "secure the blessings of liberty to ourselves and our posterity"; our Declaration of Independence likewise affirms the essential right of human beings to "life, liberty, and the pursuit of happiness."[26]

These groups also argued that same-sex marriage is a civil rights issue and that denying same-sex couples the right to marry would also deny them legal protections and economic benefits such as hospital visitation and health insurance coverage for employee spouses. Massachusetts NOW explains this position:

> This legislation endangers all current and potential state and private benefits for same-sex couples—benefits that are readily available to and taken for granted by opposite-sex couples. It therefore codifies blatant discrimination against gays and lesbians, and insures that they and their families are discriminated against and deprived of basic rights.[27]

Finally, proponents of same-sex marriage expressed fear that denying marriage to homosexuals would result in a backlash of hatred and bigotry.

On the other side, the conservative Massachusetts Family Institute opposed same-sex marriage, as did evangelicals, Catholics, and many black Protestants. Neither Catholics nor blacks can be neatly classified as conservative, given their position on social welfare and civil rights issues. But they agreed with the more conservative Christians on the traditional nature of marriage: that it is intended to support children and families, that it is foundational to society, that it has always been and always should be between a man and a woman. According to Archbishop Sean O'Malley,

> The nature of marriage as a lifelong union of man and a woman, who enter into a total sharing of themselves, for the sake of a family, is not simply a religious teaching. Marriage predates the founding of our government. Indeed, it predates the founding of our church. Marriage is not a creation of the state or of the church, and neither has the legitimate authority to change its nature. To dismiss people's legitimate concerns about the institution of marriage as simply unjust discrimination against homosexual persons is to dismiss the centrality of marriage for the well-being of society.[28]

Additionally, the groups argued that the union of a man and a woman is biblically based. According to Rev. Gregory G. Groover, pastor of the Charles Street African Methodist Episcopal Church in Boston,

> As black preachers, we are progressive in our social consciousness, and in our political ideology as an oppressed people we will often be against the status quo, but our first call is to hear the voice of God in our Scriptures, and where an issue clearly contradicts our understanding of Scripture, we have to apply that understanding.[29]

These religious groups also made the argument that homosexuality is unnatural and harmful both to the homosexuals themselves and to the children being raised by them.

The opposition to gay marriage mobilized in support of a constitutional amendment affirming marriage as the union of a man and a woman, thereby overruling the supreme court decision. The amendment was written by Representative Phillip Travers, a pro-family, evangelical Democrat representing Rehoboth in southern Massachusetts. A constitutional convention was called in the legislature to debate the amendment in March 2004. The amendment failed by one vote. A compromise amendment was proposed in which (1) marriage is defined as the union between a man and a woman and (2) civil unions between same-sex partners would be legalized, giving them the same legal benefits and rights as married couples. This amendment passed by a slim margin. According to Massachusetts constitutional procedures, the amendment needs to be voted on again in the legislature and will be presented to the public for a vote sometime after November 2006. In the meantime, town and city clerks began granting marriage licenses to homosexual and lesbian couples in May 2004.

It is hard to judge success or failure of the interest groups on this issue. The compromise amendment satisfies neither group. Those who favor same-sex marriage are upset that the amendment grants second-class status to same-sex unions, and those who oppose it are upset that the amendment legalizes civil unions and that the public will not get the opportunity to vote up or down solely on the definition of marriage as a union between a man and a woman.

Lobbying efforts on both sides were intense. The MFI sent out e-mail alerts to its membership, encouraging them to come to the statehouse for the debates; the Freedom to Marry Coalition of Massachusetts did the same. The Massachusetts Catholic Conference spent about $100,000 to send out a million mailings to Catholics in Massachusetts, encouraging them to support traditional marriage; the Freedom to Marry Coalition took out full-page advertisements in the *Boston Globe*. After the debate, the Massachusetts Catholic Conference sent letters to pastors and encouraged Catholics to vote against legislators who supported same-sex marriage in the November elections; the

Black Ministerial Alliance of Greater Boston also encouraged its faithful to hold their legislators accountable on the issue.

Much of the lobbying techniques were outsider tactics: mobilizing the grassroots to show massive public support. But the groups used insider techniques as well, talking to legislators one-on-one, especially those who might be on the fence. "We went to those who support traditional marriage, to give them the best argument for it," said Evelyn Murphy of the MFI. "We also went to the undecided, to those in the middle, those who might change their minds." They were not alone. The coalition supporting same-sex marriage identified legislators whose religious affiliation made them nervous about voting in favor of homosexual marriage and then had people of the same religious affiliation call them. "They weren't organized about it, but they had people who made calls to legislators who said their faith was what was troubling them about gay marriage," according to Norma Shapiro of the ACLU. "They made connections between people of faith and legislators of same faith," presumably connecting Catholic legislators hesitant about same-sex marriage with other Catholics who supported it.

Who won on the same-sex marriage issue? Although at this writing the jury is still out (the constitutional amendment has not yet worked its way through the unwieldy constitutional process to come to a public vote), some conclusions can be drawn. First, the supreme court decision validating same-sex marriage was a stunning victory for homosexual rights advocates. It was a nonincremental, radical change that overturned the status quo. Such changes do not happen frequently, and it is not surprising that the decision elicited such a massive response. Lobbyists tend to be more successful when they lobby for the status quo or for incremental changes to it. The supreme court decision changed the status quo. Rather than defending traditional marriage, its supporters were put in the position of creating comprehensive change (amending the constitution to overturn a Supreme Judicial Court ruling). The supreme court changed the lay of the land, making the lobbying efforts of traditional marriage supporters more difficult. Before *Goodridge*, lawmakers supporting traditional marriage could simply do nothing, passively agreeing with marriage as it existed. After *Goodridge*, and with the constitutional amendment vote, lawmakers had to take a stand one way or the other. The same-sex marriage lobby was successful in creating an environment in which it became politically dangerous to speak out against same-sex marriage. The traditional marriage lobby was successful in at least putting on the table the affirmation of marriage as the union of a man and a woman in this new environment. Perhaps in such a volatile, bifurcated environment as Massachusetts was in 2003–2004, the unpopular compromise, upholding both one-man/one-woman marriage and same-sex civil unions, is the best one could expect.

## CONCLUSION

Massachusetts politics is no longer dominated by animosity between the Puritans' descendants and their Irish-Catholic adversaries, nor is it completely controlled by a unified Irish Catholic political bloc. The cultural and political environment has changed in some significant ways. First, it is still true that the legislature is majority Catholic, and Catholic interest groups have easy access to legislators. But that access no longer translates into automatic votes for and support of Church positions and teachings. Second, the moralistic culture of the state has waned, leaving in its place an emphasis on more secular, civil issues and individual rights as opposed to a broader public good. And third, evangelical Protestants exercise new muscle in Massachusetts, allying themselves with Catholics on traditional definitions of marriage and including Catholics in their grassroots organization.

Where does this leave religious lobbyists? It gives them the opportunity to participate in debates along with other groups. It forces them to make both moral and social science or rights-based arguments for their issues. Can they be successful? Yes, but their success is not guaranteed. Religious groups, although some may have special access, have to compete in the marketplace of political ideas just like everybody else. And perhaps that's what the Framers (if not the Puritans) would have wanted.

## NOTES

1. Thomas H. O'Connor, *The Boston Irish* (Boston: Northeastern University Press, 1995), xv.

2. John Winthrop's "City upon the Hill" speech, 1630, www.mtholyoke.edu/acad/intrel/winthrop.htm.

3. Daniel J. Elazar, *American Federalism: A View from the States*, 3rd ed. (New York: Harper and Row, 1984).

4. Elazar, *American Federalism*, 127.

5. Elazar, *American Federalism*, 116.

6. Edgar Litt, *The Political Cultures of Massachusetts* (Boston: MIT Press, 1965).

7. Jeffrey Leigh Sedgwick, "The Massachusetts General Court and the Commonwealth's Political Crisis," in Eugene W. Hickok Jr., *The Reform of State Legislatures: The Changing Character of Representation* (Lanham, Md.: University Press of America, 1992), 80.

8. Sedgwick, "The Massachusetts General Court and the Commonwealth's Political Crisis," 81, note 30.

9. Sedgwick, "The Massachusetts General Court and the Commonwealth's Political Crisis," 82.

10. Sedgwick, "The Massachusetts General Court and the Commonwealth's Political Crisis," 71.

11. www.iandrinstitute.org/Massachusetts.htm. See also David Schmidt, *Citizen Lawmakers: The Ballot Initiative Revolution* (Philadelphia: Temple University Press, 1989).

12. Sedgwick, "The Massachusetts General Court and the Commonwealth's Political Crisis."

13. John Berg, "Massachusetts: Citizen Power and Corporate Power," in *Interest Group Politics in the Northeastern States*, ed. Ronald J. Hrebenar and Clive S. Thomas (University Park: Pennsylvania State University Press, 1993).

14. Berg, "Massachusetts."

15. Donald Haider, *When Governments Come to Washington: Governors, Mayors, and Intergovernmental Lobbying* (New York: Free Press, 1974), 223–24.

16. Timothy Byrnes, *Catholic Bishops in American Politics* (Princeton, N.J.: Princeton University Press, 1991).

17. Address of Senator John F. Kennedy to the Greater Houston Ministerial Association, Rice Hotel, Houston, Texas, September 12, 1960, John F. Kennedy Library, www.jfklibrary.org/j091260.htm.

18. Allen D. Hertzke, *Representing God in Washington: The Role of Religious Lobbies in the American Polity* (Knoxville: University of Tennessee Press, 1988), 143.

19. Telephone interview, August 5, 2004.

20. Interview, August 5, 2004.

21. Michael Levenson, "A Career Finding Common Ground," *Boston Globe*, July 20, 2004, B1.

22. David Truman, *The Governmental Process* (New York: Knopf, 1951), 366–67.

23. David Knoke, *Organizing for Collective Action: The Political Economies of Association* (New York: Aldine de Gruyter, 1990), 19.

24. Hugh Heclo, "Issue Networks and the Executive Establishment," in *The New American Political System*, ed. Anthony King (Washington, D.C.: American Enterprise Institute for Public Policy Research, 1990).

25. Scott Greenberger, "Legislature Drops Stem Cell Support; Action Is a Victory for Catholic Church," *Boston Globe*, November 24, 2003.

26. The Religious Coalition for the Freedom to Marry, "Massachusetts Declaration of Religious Support for the Freedom of Same-Gender Couples to Marry," www.ftmc.org/rcfm/declare.htm.

27. Testimony submitted by National Organization of Women to the Judiciary Committee of the Massachusetts Great and General Court, April 28, 2003.

28. "What's at Stake," Address of Archbishop Sean P. O'Malley, O.F.M. Cap., Archdiocese of Boston, Summit of October to Save (SOS) Marriage, Celebration International Church, Wayland, Massachusetts, October 2, 2003.

29. Quoted in Michael Paulson, "Black Clergy Rejection Stirs Gay Marriage Backers," *Boston Globe*, February 10, 2004.

# 3

# Religious Lobbying in Virginia: How Institutions Can Quiet Prophetic Voices

## Carin Larson, David Madland, and Clyde Wilcox

The 2004 legislative session in Virginia was a tense one. A string of fiscally conservative governors from both parties had cut spending on higher education, transportation, and social services, and still the state faced a huge projected budget deficit. Republicans in the assembly refused to support a tax increase, although they could not propose a budget proposal that could balance the budget through spending cuts alone. They had strong support from white evangelicals and Christian Right groups, who argued that high taxes are harmful to the family because they force women into the workplace. Republicans in the senate were more attentive to the business community, who argued that Virginia's roads and highways need repair and expansion and that previous cuts had eroded the prestige of the state's colleges and universities. The Democratic governor proposed additional taxes, senate Republicans wanted a smaller and somewhat different tax hike, and the assembly wanted no new taxes.

Although economics dominated the legislative agenda, the legislature considered many other issues of interest to religious constituencies, although as elsewhere these groups sometimes lined up on opposite sides of issues. Overall, the scorecard for Virginia's Family Foundation (representing mainly white evangelicals and conservative Catholics) and the scorecard for the Virginia Interfaith Center for Public Policy (representing more liberal Christians and Jews) reflect the different priorities that have come to characterize these constituencies (Djupe and Gilbert 2003; Guth et al. 1997). The Family Foundation focused on measures on abortion, homosexuality, Internet pornography, and public displays of religious symbols, while the Interfaith Center made a priority of bills relating to food stamps, child support, the minimum wage, housing and homelessness, capital punishment, and religious freedom. Catholic lobbyists found themselves supporting and opposing items on both agendas.

Religious conservatives had victories and defeats. The legislature made it a double felony to kill a pregnant woman, and removed from a bill all language that would have instructed school personnel to mention the availability of emergency contraception to students who had been raped. It defeated measures that would have mandated that emergency contraception be covered in health plans but also defeated bills that would have required anesthetizing a fetus before an abortion, banned the dispensing of emergency contraception on college campuses, or required parental consent before dispensing emergency contraception to minors. The legislature also memorialized the U.S. Congress to pass a federal marriage amendment, passed a law nullifying any domestic partnership arrangement made in another state between same-sex partners, did not allow businesses to voluntarily extend health insurance to same-sex partners, refused to legalize homosexual relations despite a U.S. Supreme Court ruling invalidating the state law, and voted 97 to 1 in the assembly to recriminalize such relations in defiance of the Court.

Religious liberals also saw victories in minimum-wage legislation, food stamp outreach, and housing programs, but the legislature defeated efforts to abolish capital punishment, to impose a moratorium on capital punishment, to abolish the death penalty for minors, and to make it easier for convicted felons to prove their innocence.

Despite a plethora of bills of interest to religious constituencies, there were few religious lobbyists working the legislature's halls. Virginia's eight-week session, combined with a burgeoning workload, keeps legislators quite busy. Most religious groups that seek to influence state policy try to mobilize congregations and individuals to contact their representatives at the start of the session before the workload becomes overwhelming. Yet even grassroots lobbying is less common in Virginia than in many other states.

Religious conservatives have focused most of their efforts on electoral politics in recent years. Chuck Cunningham, formerly of the Christian Coalition, argues that "the best way to change policy in Virginia is to change politicians." Liberal groups do more direct lobbying, but these efforts are small compared to those in states with full-time legislatures.[1]

## THE RELIGIOUS AND POLITICAL CONTEXT

At first glance, Virginia might be expected to be home to significant religious lobbying. Clearly there is sufficient religious and cultural diversity to produce "culture wars" both between the political parties and within the GOP. Virginia's religious composition is more diverse than in most southern states. Surveys show that roughly half of voters are affiliated with an evangelical denomination and that 10 percent identify themselves as fundamentalists in surveys. Evangelicals are especially numerous in the southern and central parts of the state, where Southern Baptists (along with many other Baptist denominations) are strong (Rozell and Wilcox 1996).

A significant portion of these evangelicals are African American. Overall, one in five Virginians is African American, as is one in six of the electorate. The large black churches in Richmond and elsewhere are a key source of Democratic political mobilization, and nearly all Democratic candidates for statewide office make a tour of these churches in October. White evangelical churches in Virginia, like elsewhere, have moved strongly to the GOP camp and often feature mobilization efforts by Christian conservatives.

A quarter of Virginia's residents are mainline Protestants, and they are especially common in the northern Virginia suburbs and in the western part of the state. Particularly numerous are Methodist and Episcopal churches, which preach moderate mainline Christianity in the northern part of the state but a more evangelical doctrine in the south and west. The 2000 exit poll revealed that one in five of Virginia voters is Catholic. The Catholic Church is divided between the Arlington diocese, which is one of the most conservative in America, and the Richmond diocese, which is far more liberal.

Finally, the northern Virginia suburbs are home to growing numbers of non-Christians, including Jews, Muslims, Hindus, and many other faiths. Although they compose a small portion of the overall population, they constitute a significant number of citizens in these populous counties. Most non-Christian groups do not have lobbying strength in the state capital, but they are able to mount grassroots campaigns aimed at local governments.

Overall, the 2000 exit poll showed that 43 percent of the electorate claimed to attend church weekly or more often and that 39 percent attended a few times a year or less. Slightly fewer than one in five voters indicated that they considered themselves to be part of the "religious Right." Throughout most of the 1990s, however, an antifundamentalist coalition of moderate to liberal Christians and secular citizens mobilized against Christian Right–backed candidates (Rozell and Wilcox 1996).

## A CULTURE WAR IN VIRGINIA?

Virginia has traditionally been a culturally conservative state: Erikson, Wright, and McIver (1993) reported that Virginia voters and political elites were among the most conservative in the nation. Yet over time, exit polls have revealed a moderating trend in the electorate. In 1994, 40 percent of voters called themselves conservative and 15 percent liberal, but by 2000 these numbers had changed to 30 percent conservative and 20 percent liberal. It is not clear whether Virginia's electorate has become more liberal on concrete issues or whether the extremely conservative positions of some Republican elected officials has changed the yardstick by which individuals measure their relative ideology. What is clear is that there is also political diversity that might be expected to generate religious mobilization and lobbying.

The northern Virginia suburbs of Washington, D.C., have become the home to a booming high-tech industry that has attracted young, socially liberal voters. These populous and growing counties are among the best educated and most affluent in the nation. Many of the residents in the northern Virginia area have immigrated to Virginia from northeastern states with more liberal social policies and coexist somewhat uneasily with the more conservative native Virginians. Surveys show substantial support for abortion rights and gay and lesbian rights in northern Virginia, but voters there are also fiscally conservative and drawn to the Republican Party on economics.

Virginia is also in a sense the birthplace of the Christian Right in American politics. Lynchburg was home to the Moral Majority, the most prominent Christian Right group of the 1980s, and remains the home of Rev. Jerry Falwell's Liberty University and the huge Thomas Road Baptist Church. Chesapeake was home to the Christian Coalition, the premier Christian Right group of the 1990s, and remains home to Pat Robertson's Regent University and his large Christian Broadcasting Company.

The Christian Right has not always thrived in Virginia, however, and it has only recently come to exert significant policymaking power. Falwell and Robertson became involved in state Republican politics in the late 1970s, and for the next decade evangelical activists played a key role in the nomination of GOP candidates. Virginia's Republicans often choose their candidates in very large conventions with more than 10,000 delegates, making the party unusually permeable to social movements. In the 1980s, evangelicals attended these conventions in large numbers and helped nominate the most conservative candidate in the field. They then pressured these candidates to adopt relatively extreme positions on social issues, and this led to a string of Democratic governors during this period.

In 1988, Pat Robertson lost his home state badly in the GOP presidential primary, coming in last among five candidates still in the race. But delegates to the GOP national convention are selected through a series of local and district conventions and finally a state convention, and Robertson's supporters battled through each stage and ultimately won a majority of delegates. In the process, they took control of the state GOP committee, nominated the state's representatives to the Republic National Committee, and elected their own state Republican chair.

In the early 1990s, moderate Republicans and conservative Christians fought pitched battles within the GOP. In 1993, homeschool advocate and Christian Right activist Mike Farris ran for lieutenant governor, easily capturing the nomination by flooding the convention with supporters. Farris's backers were new to politics and were involved in shoving matches, throwing ice and debris, and other confrontational tactics. Moderate GOP Senator John Warner refused to back Farris, who had been the lead attorney for Concerned Women for America in the *Scopes II* trial in Tennessee (Bates 1993).

Democrats attacked Farris as too closely linked to Falwell and Robertson and ran ads linking him to censorship and extreme positions. Farris's combative writings over the years made him an easy target for charges of extremism. Ultimately, he lost the election despite strong victories by the GOP gubernatorial candidate and the attorney general. Farris's backers took over many local and county GOP committees across the state, however, and the new governor, George Allen, established many links to Christian Right groups (Rozell and Wilcox 1996).

In 1994, a slightly different set of Christian Right activists flooded the GOP convention to nominate Oliver North to challenge Democratic incumbent Chuck Robb for the U.S. Senate. North had spent many years cultivating Christian Right activists and speaking in churches, but he was also famous for his testimony in the Iran-Contra hearings, which made him unpopular with many Republicans. Warner again refused to back the Christian Right candidate and in fact recruited another candidate to run as an independent. Although Robb had been weakened by a sex scandal and there was a national Republican surge that swept in a new House and Senate majority, North lost the election.

By the end of 1994, the Republican Party was deeply divided, with Christian Right activists furious with Senator Warner for not endorsing "their" candidates and GOP moderates furious at these new Republican activists for taking over their party. A survey of party activists showed that moderates and Christian conservatives alike rated the rival faction more coolly than they rated the Democratic Party's candidates (Rozell and Wilcox 1996).

The intraparty culture clash dissipated during the late 1990s and into the new century, however. As in national politics, Republican policymakers moved to the right, as conservative activists worked hard in party primaries, caucuses, and conventions. In 1999, Republicans gained a narrow majority in the assembly and then performed a masterful job of partisan gerrymandering to increase their margin from 52–47 to 64–35 in 2001. Christian conservatives who had been biding their time in local party committees took full advantage of the newly created seats, and the resulting GOP majority was large and very conservative. The 2001 convention for the gubernatorial race again pitted a Christian conservative against a more secular conservative, but unlike previous years, there was this time little rancor and no real disagreement on issues such as abortion or gay rights. The eventual winner was a Christian Right candidate who lost to a wealthy Democratic businessman (Rozell and Wilcox 2000).

Thus, by 2002, religious alignments in Virginia resembled those in the nation at large. Conservative white evangelicals were a key partner in the GOP coalition, along with the most conservative Catholics and mainline Protestants. More moderate Protestants and Catholics, black Protestants, and Jews were aligned with the Democrats. But the Republican Party had firm control of one wing of the state legislature and a workable majority in the other, while the Democrats held the governorship (Rozell and Wilcox 2003).

## INSTITUTIONS MATTER: WHY RELIGIOUS LOBBYING IS UNCOMMON IN VIRGINIA

Although there are considerable religious and cultural differences in the Virginia electorate, and although the government considers a wide range of policies that interest religious elites and can be linked to religious values, there is relatively little religious lobbying in Virginia. The explanation seems to rest with political institutions.

Writing in 1949, V. O. Key Jr. noted that Virginia was a "political museum piece" and that compared to "all the American states, Virginia can lay claim to the most thorough control by an oligarchy" (Key 1949). The Byrd Democratic political machine was organized through county courthouses and maintained its control by restricting participation and by limiting the power of government officials. The poll tax, the literacy tests, and many other restrictions on voting are long gone, but Virginia remains one of only two states to elect its state officials in odd-numbered years, when there are no national elections to increase interest and draw citizens to the polls. Participation rates have increased dramatically from the 6 percent turnout in the Democratic primary of 1945 (then tantamount to general election victory), but they remain low in state elections.

More important, state legislative seats are extraordinarily safe. Republicans redistricted not only to dramatically increase their vote share but also to decrease the number of competitive districts. In 2003, fifty-three of the one hundred assembly races were uncontested, and another twenty were won with more than 61 percent of the vote. Virginia ranks as the third least competitive state legislative races in the country. These uncompetitive districts make grassroots lobbying less effective. When most incumbents do not fear electoral defeat, the mobilization of moderate numbers of religious constituents may not sway their legislative votes. Religious groups do mount grassroots campaigns—in the 1990s, the Christian Coalition and the Family Foundation had rapidly mobilized networks—but they are less visible and less effective than elsewhere.

The Virginia legislature is in session for only sixty days in even-numbered years and only forty-five days in odd-numbered years. Over the years, the legislative workload has increased so that the legislators are quite busy during their sessions. Former Christian Coalition political director Chuck Cunningham notes that "it is hard to contact legislators during the session because they are so busy, and hard to contact them out of session because they are back to their regular jobs." The short session is one of the main reasons why religious groups do not retain full-time lobbyists in the state capital. There is little denominational lobbying outside the Catholic Church; instead, there are broader religious coalitions that represent religious liberals and conservatives in the process. Even these coalitions do less lobbying in Virginia than in other states.

Governors have more time to develop policy proposals, but Virginia is the only remaining state in the union with a single gubernatorial term. As soon as they assume office, governors are immediately lame ducks, and by the time they have figured out how to be governor and begun to flesh out their agendas, they are looking forward to their next job, and candidates are already running to replace them. Governors do frequently incorporate members of religious coalitions into their administrations. Perhaps the most striking of these was the administration of George Allen (now a U.S. senator from Virginia). Allen's top advisers in education (including the state secretary of education) were Christian conservatives who opposed sex education and favored prayer in schools. His secretary of health and human services was Kay Coles James, a prominent pro-life activist who had worked in the first Bush administration and had blocked an AIDS pamphlet aimed at teens because it advocated the use of condoms. The head of Virginia's Family Foundation became the director of the governor's personnel and training operation (Rozell and Wilcox 1996). Yet after four years, the Allen administration had accomplished far less than Christian conservatives had hoped for because Virginia's political institutions are stacked against nonincremental policymaking.

## RELIGIOUS RIGHT LOBBYING

Virginia's white Protestant evangelicals were politically mobilized through individual churches before the formation of broader Christian Right groups, and many individual congregations remain active in politics (Wilcox 1999). In 1978, before he formed the Moral Majority, Baptist pastor Jerry Falwell successfully mobilized his huge church and other Bible Baptist Fellowship congregations to oppose a referendum that would have permitted pari-mutuel gambling. Church-based mobilization on moral issues continues to play a prominent role in Virginia. Members at Kempsville Presbyterian Church in Virginia Beach take some credit for bringing riverboat gambling legislation to a halt at the state capitol in 2004. "We took a busload of people for riverboat gambling," Majorie Powers said to *Citizen Magazine*, a publication of Focus on the Family.[2] "In the end, it was not voted on. But it would have been had we not been there." Powers and her husband, both in their late seventies, led a "Faith, Freedom and Citizenship" class at Kempsville Presbyterian that taught church members how to apply biblical teachings to public policy. The class and subsequent lobbying was organized through the help of the Family Foundation, the most visible and effective Christian conservative lobbying group in the state. More recently, the Family Foundation's latest endeavor is the Defending Faith, Family and Freedom Grassroots Workshop, which was held recently at Immanuel Bible Church in Springfield. The workshops are meant to inform Christians about public policy and equip participants with talking points when contacting their state legislators. Recent speakers include lobbyists from various conservative organizations as well as state legislators from the evangelical community, such as Delegates Dick Black and Ken Cuccinelli.

Because the state legislature is so rarely in session, conservative religious lobbying groups in Virginia have made efficient use of the calendar year by working to organize evangelical congregations between legislative sessions, encouraging members to become more active. Christian conservative groups work separately to organize churches, but they cooperate to lobby the state legislature. A coalition called the Capitol Group—composed primarily of Christian conservative and pro-life groups but also including anti-tax organizations—meets three to four times a year to compare notes and prepare for the legislative season. They also meet at least three times while the legislature is in session. The Family Foundation facilitates the group. "We believe that all our efforts will be enhanced by a connected network," says the Family Foundation's legislative director, Victoria Cobb.[3] "It's an informal relationship. We come together to check where our energies are at and how we can assist each other."

The Family Foundation claims to be Virginia's oldest and largest pro-family organization and claims to represent some 200,000 members with a budget of $500,000 per year. It is affiliated with both Focus on the Family in Colorado Springs, Colorado, and the Family Research Council in Washington, D.C. The members of the Family Foundation are primarily white evangelicals and conservative Catholics, although the group is ecumenical and its rhetoric generally secular and focused on "pro-family" policies. The Family Foundation's lobbyists visit and educate state legislators, testify at committee hearings, and seek to increase civic activism within the pro-family ranks through workshops at churches. They distribute report cards for each session, voter guides, and e-mail alerts regarding important legislation. The foundation employs four full-time staff and a few part-timers when the legislature is in season.

The Concerned Women for America (CWA) has a Virginia chapter and many local chapters as well and has long emphasized grassroots lobbying and electoral politics. The CWA of Virginia Citizen Action Guide is distributed in the organization's quarterly newsletter and explains how members can be involved in public policy. The group hosts an annual lobby day while the legislature is in session for members to gather and speak to their representatives in groups. The CWA of Virginia has regional Prayer/Action Chapters that meet monthly throughout the state. At a recent meeting in Arlington, the president of the Eagle Forum, Helen Blackwell, was the guest speaker. The CWA's rhetoric is more biblically centered than that of the Family Foundation, but the preferred policies are almost identical.

Virginia also has a state chapter of the Eagle Forum, which is more influential than in some other states because of the political ties and acumen of its director, Helen Blackwell. In 2004, in the midst of the state's budget debate, Blackwell and the Eagle Forum sponsored Bread Day to oppose a tax increase. Homemade bread was delivered to each legislator with the following quote from Thomas Jefferson attached: "Government shall not take from the mouth of labor the bread it has earned. This is the sum of good government." Both the CWA and the Family Foundation assisted in the effort, which was eventually unsuccessful. A tax increase was passed.

One denominational family has a full-time lobbyist in Richmond. The Virginia Assembly of Independent Baptists is directed by Jack Knapp, who is also its sole lobbyist. Representing 500 independent Baptist churches and supported by donations from the congregations, he talks with legislators and informs them of the churches' positions on various issues. This group holds positions similar to the groups mentioned earlier.

## THE CONSERVATIVE CHRISTIAN AGENDA

For Christian Right groups in Virginia, pro-life legislation is the top priority. In the 2004 session, the religious conservative groups successfully pushed the legislature to pass a prenatal protection law that makes the killing of a woman and her unborn child two distinct crimes. Numerous bills broadening the availability of emergency contraception were defeated. For example, a Family Life Education bill originally required that the Board of Education include a discussion of emergency contraception in its curriculum guidelines for sex education classes. After enormous work by the Family Foundation, the final version removed the reference to contraception and inserted in its place a discussion of "steps to take to avoid sexual assault" and "the importance of immediate medical attention and advice."

"We are still not pleased," says Cobb on behalf of the Family Foundation. "We'd prefer to have the entire thing killed. It still provides an opening for Planned Parenthood." Cobb's primary complaint was that supporters of emergency contraception were exploiting the rape issue to get contraception in schools. "To say a pill is the answer to rape is to overlook the whole person. . . . In some cases, using emergency contraception at the school may be an alternative to taking them to the hospital where they can be cared for and rape can be reported." Cobb said she spent time educating legislators about the abortive feature of the pill as they worked on the amendment. The Family Foundation even brought a child of a rape victim to speak in front of the committee to argue against mandating the teaching of emergency contraception in the schools. "It helps to put a face on the issue," explains Cobb.

Christian conservative groups also made gay-rights issues a top priority. The legislature banned civil unions and the state's recognition of any same-sex contracts that might provide marital benefits of any kind. The state also passed a Federal Marriage Amendment Resolution, which tells Congress that Virginia will support an amendment to the U.S. Constitution defining marriage as between one man and one woman. Christian Rights groups moved successfully to defeat hate-crime legislation and bills allowing benefits to same-sex partners and to overturn a Fairfax County ordinance that banned discrimination in Fairfax County government employment. The assembly also restated Virginia's criminalization of sodomy, although a recent Supreme Court decision makes that law unenforceable.

Education remains a top priority of the Christian Right in Virginia and an issue where they can at times find common ground with African American churches. A number of black churches in the capital city, Richmond, have started private inner-city schools. The Family Foundation has brought students at one such school, the Elijah House Academy, to testify before the legislature in regard to school choice. Currently, the students are privately funded, but the Christian Right (and other religious groups) seeks the use of public funds through vouchers. In addition, Christian Right groups successfully pushed to allow homeschool parents to choose their own curriculum. Previously, parents had to pass a standardized test or else adopt a curriculum recommended by the state.

Christian Right groups faced off against religious liberal groups on a bill that would have required clergy to report suspected child abuse. "This would have been an intrusion, an interference with a pastor's ability to counsel," said Knapp, who worked for the legislation's defeat on behalf of the Independent Baptists.[4] The bill was ultimately defeated despite support from Christian Left organizations. In addition, conservative groups responded to the display of the Ten Commandments monument in an Alabama courthouse (that caused national controversy over the display of religious symbols) by successfully persuading the House of Delegates to pass a resolution that urged Congress to grant the states the freedom to decide religious liberty issues for themselves. Delegate Robert Brink (D-Arlington) called the resolution "an embarrassment to the House, to the General Assembly and to the commonwealth" and accused Republicans of "throwing a little red meat to its political base."

At the end of the session, it was discovered that the legislature had mistakenly repealed a portion of an old law, creating in the process the right of nonmanagerial employees to refuse to work on one weekend day. Business groups quickly mobilized to call for a special session to reinstate the old law, which would have fined a business $500 and required triple-time pay for any employee required to work during his or her designated day of rest. Christian Right groups were noticeably silent on the issue despite the obvious implications of the bill for religious freedom and families. "Nobody on our side was prepared for it," says Walt Barbee, the founder of the Family Foundation.[5] "So I see it as another brick chipped out of the constitutional wall protecting religious freedom, under the category of right of religious persons."

## CAUGHT IN THE CENTER: CATHOLIC RELIGIOUS LOBBYING

Catholics in Virginia find themselves torn between the two large religious coalitions and between the two parties. Drawn to Christian conservative positions on sociomoral issues such as abortion and gay rights and to liberal religious positions on aid to the poor and disadvantaged, Catholics in Virginia are also divided by geography. There is no statewide Catholic Conference in Virginia. Instead, Virginia is home to two Catholic dioceses, the Diocese of Arlington and the Diocese of Richmond. The Arlington diocese is one of the most conservative in the nation, but the Richmond diocese is far more liberal.

The Richmond diocese is one of the oldest in the country. Pope Pius VII established the diocese in 1820, and at that time, it included all of Virginia and what is now West Virginia. Because it is headquartered in the state capital, it employs a full-time registered lobbyist, Steve Collecchi, who is at the capitol nearly every day the legislature is in session. In comparison, the Arlington diocese was started in 1974, and though similar in population size to today's Richmond diocese, it does not have a registered lobbyist. Instead, the director of family life of the diocese, Bob Laird, serves as an educator to the legislature. Laird visits the capitol roughly once a week while the legislature is in session.

In 2004, the two dioceses jointly adopted a 2004 legislative agenda but then focused on different parts of that agenda, reflecting perhaps the interests and priorities of each bishop. The jointly adopted agenda includes the following: the protection of human life, the protection of family life, the promotion of international solidarity, and the promotion of social justice. According to Laird, the Arlington diocese tends to focus on abortion and the traditional family structure, while the Richmond group focuses on issues relating to poverty and injustice. The different foci are reflected in job titles: Laird is the director of family life, while Collecchi is the director of the Office of Justice and Peace.

Each diocese appears to participate in different religious coalitions as well. Laird works closely with the Family Foundation on bills dealing with contraception and homosexuality. He attends meetings of the Capitol Group with other conservative lobbyists. Like those who run the Family Foundation's workshops, Laird spends time educating congregants about public policy. He leaves letters to legislators at the back of Catholic churches—on leaving Mass, congregants can sign their names to a particular letter urging their representative to vote a certain way. Laird got 23,000 signatures on a letter in defense of a bill dealing with parental notification for minors seeking an abortion. Although the Richmond diocese also promotes conservative positions on sociomoral issues, it does not emphasize them in its lobbying and does not work with the Family Foundation.

While both dioceses have official representation on the board of the Virginia Interfaith Center for Public Policy (VICPP), Richmond is more active within this coalition. Collecchi has worked with the VICPP to address poverty issues. Moreover, Collecchi started a branch of a national program called "Sowers of Justice" in the Richmond diocese. The group is founded primarily on the biblical principle to act justly and love mercy, as stated in Micah 6:8. Sowers of Justice is a network of Catholic groups that organize with groups from other faiths to work for social justice by attending local or national demonstrations or writing to legislators about policy issues. Collecchi also instituted a Parish Legislative Advocacy Network (PLAN) within the Richmond diocese to coordinate calls to legislators and trips to the capitol. Many Sowers are active in PLAN, and PLAN members are urged to become members of the VICPP.

## RELIGIOUS LEFT LOBBYING

Religious liberals work primarily through the VICPP. The Interfaith Center brings together mainline Protestant denominations such as United Methodist churches and Episcopal dioceses (as well as Catholic dioceses), African American churches, and Jewish and Muslim organizations. Member organizations of the Interfaith Center unite around an agenda that is concerned primarily with supporting those in need, including children, the poor, the homeless, and the accused, as well as those in opposition to the death penalty. The Interfaith Center does not address issues such as abortion or homosexuality, likely because there is not complete agreement on those issues among its members. Instead, the Interfaith Center focuses on issues where there is agreement. According to the Interfaith Center's executive director, Rev. C. Douglas Smith, "In most every faith there is a clear call to be involved on behalf of the poor and marginalized."[6] Smith explains that the Interfaith Center's agenda is "not liberal, but rather looks out for common people."[7]

The Interfaith Center is the primary advocacy arm for many of its members. The Interfaith Center has a $170,000 budget, two full-time staff, and two interns. Advocacy activities include meetings with elected officials, publication of a scorecard and weekly legislative action alerts, and grassroots lobbying through nine regional chapters.

Individual denominations generally advocate on a much more limited basis, and these smaller-scale efforts are typically led by part-time volunteers or are sometimes hired out to professional lobbyists paid to advocate for a specific cause for a limited time. For example, the United Methodist Church has an annual lobby day for its members as well as several volunteers who monitor select legislation and occasionally advocate. But overall, the Methodist's efforts at lobbying are limited, and they usually coordinate those efforts with the Interfaith Center.[8]

The Interfaith Center formed in 1982 largely out of the lobbying arm of the Virginia Council of Churches (VCC), an organization representing eighteen different denominations, including Catholic, Orthodox, and mainline Protestant churches—a membership that overlaps significantly with the Interfaith

Center. The VCC focuses on building Christian unity and ecumenical cooperation as well as supporting social outreach efforts. The VCC has difficulty achieving consensus among its members on a legislative agenda, except in opposition to the death penalty, according to General Minister John Barton.[9] Even before the Interfaith Center was created, politics was not a primary activity for the VCC, and now the VCC does only a very limited amount of advocacy itself.

In 2004, one of the Interfaith Center's primary emphases was to ensure that funding in the budget was "fair and adequate" for social services. Given the strong opposition by Christian conservatives to any tax increases to fund such programs, the final budget was considered a modest success. The organization also blocked efforts to limit local minimum-wage ordinances as well as successfully increased outreach for food stamp programs. However, the Interfaith Center made only very limited progress in its efforts against the death penalty. Efforts to impose a moratorium on capital punishment and to abolish the death penalty for minors failed. A small victory on the death penalty came when the Interfaith Center and its allies secured improvements in the ability of capital defendants to introduce new evidence after the existing twenty-one-day window has closed.

Non-Christian groups, including Jewish organizations and the Virginia Muslim Coalition, joined with the Interfaith Center to defeat legislation that would have amended the Virginia Fair Housing Law to allow the display of religious symbols, such as crosses. These groups argued that the change would have been discriminatory: the use of religious symbols creates a presumption even if the intent is not to discriminate. Preventing religious discrimination and ensuring the separation of church and state are the key issues for the Jewish community, according to Miriam Davidow, a lobbyist who has worked for years with several Jewish organizations in Virginia, including the Jewish Community Federation. Jewish organizations tend to play defense on these issues in Virginia, and the short legislative session helps this effort. "Our presence makes it hard to pass laws through a very busy legislature," Davidow notes.[10]

## THE BLACK CHURCH AND LOBBYING

While African American churches are still a regular stop on the election circuit for many politicians, in Virginia they are not as engaged in advocacy efforts as they once were. "Other than ten to twenty days before an election, most black churches now are not very politically involved," says the executive director of the Virginia state conference of the NAACP, King Saliam

Khalfani.[11] Leaders for two of the largest statewide organizations of black churches agree that advocacy is down from historic levels. According to the Reverend Cessar L. Scott, executive minister of the Baptist General Convention, "We are choosing to be less involved because politics doesn't produce that much for our needs, like increased economic opportunity, that are less obvious than segregation."[12] The Virginia Baptist State Convention president, Robert J. N. Jones Jr., argues that politics can still produce results for the black community but notes that "the vast majority of churches don't get involved between elections."[13]

Despite the reduction in advocacy from historic levels, the black church appears to still be involved in some advocacy efforts through their denomination or statewide affiliation. The Baptist General Convention, formed in 1899, represents 1,000 black churches in Virginia. The Baptist General Convention primarily lets the Virginia Interfaith Center for Public Policy take the lead on its advocacy efforts, according to Executive Minister Scott, though it does some limited work on its own on the issues of housing, jobs, and education and in opposition to the death penalty.

The Virginia Baptist State Convention represents 700 black churches throughout the state, many of which are also members of the Baptist General Convention. While the Virginia Baptist State Convention works with the Interfaith Center, it is also active on its own primarily through its Social Justice Commission. "We need to be involved because many times black issues are not the same as the issues for everyone else," notes Virginia Baptist State Convention President Jones.[14] The volunteer-led Social Justice Commission works on a range of issues and is involved with writing letters to government officials, meeting with elected officials, and occasionally organizing broader member support for legislation. In recent years, efforts have been focused primarily on the issues of racial profiling and unequal prison sentencing. Because of the State Convention's communications with Governor Warner, several of its members have been placed on police boards charged with addressing the issue of racial profiling.

## CONCLUSION

Although there is some lobbying by individual churches and by denominations, most religious lobbying in Virginia is done through large organizations that represent many denominations and churches. Religious lobbying groups on the Right and those on the Left have successfully carved out their niche in Virginia state politics. Each side has its range of issues it is most concerned about, and there is very little overlap. When asked if the Family Foundation worked with groups concerned with poverty, Cobb said, "The awareness is growing that we need to be concerned [with poverty]. . . . We haven't been as effective in that area because we have a different perspective on the government's role." Similarly, the Interfaith Center does not lobby on abortion. Catholics are caught between these two religious coalitions, with the Arlington diocese working with both coalitions and the Richmond diocese active primarily in the Interfaith Center.

Yet religious lobbying is not widespread in Virginia. Working with small staffs and limited funding, even the most sophisticated of these political-religious groups do only limited direct lobbying and hope that their training of grassroots activists will generate additional political clout. The Family Foundation holds civic workshops within local congregations to help bolster its grassroots capacities, and Collecchi at the Richmond diocese hopes that Sowers of Justice will evoke a concern for social welfare from its parishioners. Yet in a state with few contested elections and an overworked amateur legislature that does not attract quality challengers, there are real limits to grassroots pressure. Indeed, in recent years the Christian Right has focused as much on primary elections as on general elections, seeking to change the members who represent the many safe GOP districts. And one-term governors do not generally afford religious groups the opportunity to establish long-term relationships or to develop complex agendas.

Virginia is a case that reminds us that institutions matter. In a state with a culture divide sufficient to produce significant conflict around religiously motivated politics, the electoral and governing institutions combine to quiet that conflict and to provide only limited opportunities for religious groups to exercise their prophetic voice. In the brief and busy sessions of the Virginia assembly, the small number of religious lobbyists usually discuss different issues, hurrying past one another to meet with different members. Although the state legislature is solidly in the hands of the GOP and is controlled by religious conservatives, there is little time for them to plan long-term policies. Instead, they battle over the budget and focus on symbolic issues.

## NOTES

1. For a general discussion of religious lobbying, see Hertzke (1988) and Hofrenning (1995).
2. See Cushman (2002) in *Citizen Magazine*, a publication of Focus on the Family.
3. Phone interview, Virginia Cobb, June 9, 2004.
4. Phone interview, Jack Knapp, June 15, 2004.
5. Personal interview, Walt Barbee, April 20, 2004.
6. Phone interview, Douglas Smith, May 26, 2004.

7. Phone interview, Douglas Smith, May 26, 2004.
8. Phone interview, Gary Robins, July 23, 2004.
9. Phone interview, John Barton, June 11, 2004.
10. Phone interview, Miriam Davidow, May 26, 2004.
11. Phone interview, King Saliam Khalfani, August 18, 2004.
12. Phone interview, Cessar L. Scott, August 20, 2004.
13. Phone interview, Robert J. N. Jones Jr., August 20, 2004.
14. Phone interview, Robert J. N. Jones Jr., August 20, 2004.

## WORKS CITED

Bates, Stephen. 1993. *Battleground: One Mother's Crusade, the Christian Right, and the Struggle for Control over Our Classrooms.* New York: Simon & Schuster.

Cushman, Candi. 2002. "Patriot Pastors." *Citizen Magazine* (July), www.family.org/cforum/citizenmag/features/a0021232.cfm (accessed September 12, 2005).

Djupe, Paul A., and Christopher P. Gilbert. 2003. *The Prophetic Pulpit: Clergy, Churches, and Communities in American Politics.* Lanham, Md.: Rowman & Littlefield.

Erikson, Robert S., Gerald C. Wright, and John P. McIver. 1993. *Statehouse Democracy: Public Opinion and Policy in the American States.* New York: Cambridge University Press.

Guth, James L., John C. Green, Corwin E. Smidt, Lyman A. Kellstedt, and Margaret M. Poloma. 1997. *The Bully Pulpit: The Politics of Protestant Clergy.* Lawrence: University Press of Kansas.

Hertzke, Allen. 1988. *Representing God in Washington: The Role of Religious Lobbies in the American Polity.* Knoxville: University of Tennessee Press.

Hofrenning, Daniel. 1995. *In Washington but Not of It: The Prophetic Politics of Religious Lobbyists.* Philadelphia: Temple University Press.

Key, V. O., Jr. 1949. *Southern Politics in State and Nation.* Reprint. Knoxville: University of Tennessee Press, 1984.

Rozell, Mark J., and Clyde Wilcox. 1996. *Second Coming: The Christian Right in Virginia Politics.* Baltimore: Johns Hopkins University Press.

———. 2000. "Virginia: Prophet in Waiting?" In *Prayers in the Precincts: The Christian Right in the 1998 Elections*, edited by John C. Green, Mark J. Rozell, and Clyde Wilcox. Washington, D.C.: Georgetown University Press.

———. 2003. "Virginia: Birthplace of the Christian Right." In *The Christian Right in American Politics: Marching to the Millennium*, edited by John C. Green, Mark J. Rozell, and Clyde Wilcox. Washington, D.C.: Georgetown University Press.

Wilcox, Clyde. 1999. "The Christian Right in Virginia: A Mixed Blessing for Civil Society." Paper presented at the Conference on Civil Society and Good Governance in the United States, Center for the Study of Voluntary Organizations and Services, Georgetown University, Washington, D.C.

# 4

## The Influence of Christian Conservatives in the Empire State of the South

*Charles S. Bullock III*

Public policy is set in the churches in the South.

—Georgia State Representative Karla Drenner

Organized religion has always been important in the civic life of the South. Although divided into various denominations and sects and even some cults, most southerners are Protestants. Since the South participated only in a small way in the in-migration from eastern Europe a century ago, the region has relatively few Catholics or Jews outside of urban areas. In Georgia, like the other Deep South states, other than Louisiana, the Protestant denominations were led by a variety of Baptists. Among the churches found in most county seats would be a Methodist, a Presbyterian, and at least one representative of a conservative, smaller following, such as the Church of God, or perhaps a fundamentalist church unaffiliated with any domination. In cities, the range would be greater and include Episcopalians and Catholics and, in the largest cities, a Jewish synagogue.

While churches were numerous both in the city and in the countryside and public figures almost always belonged to a congregation, only recently have religious groups taken an active role in Georgia's politics. Traditionally, conservative Protestants strongly supported separation of church and state. Fundamentalist religious leaders usually avoided political involvement. In both the 1928 and the 1960 presidential campaigns, some southern preachers opposed the Democratic presidential nominees (Al Smith and John Kennedy) because of concerns that the election of a Catholic might breach the wall separating church and state.

In a dramatic shift for conservative Christians, first Jerry Falwell and later Pat Robertson used the pulpit and their television shows to encourage their followers to become politically involved. Robertson's Christian Coalition found fertile ground in Georgia. Many of these early activists won their spurs in his 1988 presidential campaign. After their favorite faded in the presidential sweepstakes, a number of the newly mobilized turned their attention to Republican county organizations.

This chapter focuses on the emergence of Christian conservatives as a force in Georgia politics. The mobilization of this component of the electorate played a critical role in the rise of the GOP, a dramatic rise over little more than a decade that has reduced the once dominant Democratic Party to underdog status. While religious conservatives cannot legitimately claim all of the credit for the transformation of the Peach State's partisan politics, they brought both numbers and vigor to the long-stagnant GOP. More recently, as the Georgia GOP's support has broadened, religious conservatives have seen their grip on the nomination process weakened as the party increasingly selects candidates who do not fully embrace the most conservative policy positions. Nonetheless, even the more moderate candidates who are now carrying the GOP standard in general elections are careful to genuflect in the direction of Christian conservatives.

Since conservative Christians became the GOP's core constituency, their agenda has been entangled in partisan underbrush. Republicans have pushed evangelicals' demands for pro-family policies. Through the 2004 session, Democrats controlled at least one chamber of the legislature, enabling them to thwart efforts to restrict access to abortions, but they could not keep an anti–gay marriage constitutional amendment off that year's ballot. The 2004 election delivered the statehouse to GOP control so that in 2005, for the first time, the Republicans served as governor, speaker of the house, and president pro tempore of the senate. With majorities in both chambers, conservative Christians anticipate that their agenda will be enacted. This chapter examines the influence of religious conservatives both in the Georgia electorate and in the state legislature.

## BACKGROUND

Ralph Reed, who grew up and was educated in Georgia, is often credited with being the political trainer who produced an electorally muscular Christian Coalition. The Emory history Ph.D. provided tactical skills that made Pat Robertson's concerns a potent political force that could elect some candidates and influence the stands taken by others. What the messages preached by

Robertson and other ministers mobilized Reed harnessed. In Georgia, when the Christian Coalition burst on the scene, it came with all the surprise of an enemy submarine that suddenly surfaces in a peaceful harbor.

The surprise was heightened by the political weakness previously displayed by religious leaders. Zell Miller won the governorship in 1990 by promising to institute a lottery to generate funds for education. He made this the centerpiece of his campaign despite warnings that a lottery would offend too many religious conservatives. Unlike in Alabama, where the religious community foiled Governor Don Siegelman's effort to implement a program based on what Miller proposed, Georgians overcame ministerial opposition and narrowly approved the Peach State lottery.

At the same time that religious leaders, along with various others who saw a lottery as bad public policy, were losing the prerequisite referendum, they were awakening to possibilities in electoral politics. In 1992, candidates with ties to religious conservatives competed in Republican congressional primaries; five won nominations, but only one went on to serve in the U.S. Congress. In contrast, Paul Coverdell, who was not the preferred candidate among Christian conservatives, managed not only to win the GOP nomination but also to upset Senator Wyche Fowler by 17,000 votes. The religious Right had moved into electoral politics but achieved only modest success. Part of the reason that religious conservatives did not enjoy success commensurate with that achieved by the GOP in 1992 and later was that while the religious vote typically lined up behind all Republican candidates, Republican voters who did not identify with the religious Right often eschewed nominees fully committed to the more extreme ideology (Smith 2001). This interpretation is in line with the results in table 4.1.

In 1994, the Christian Coalition turned its attention to the Georgia legislature. Its initial involvement coincided with the coming to fruition of GOP candidate development efforts. Republicans, frustrated by an inability to capitalize on the strong showings of Presidents Reagan in 1984 and Bush in 1988, launched a program, first to identify districts offering reasonable prospects for GOP legislative candidates and second to recruit and fund candidates to compete in the most promising districts (Bullock and Shafer 1997). The Christian Coalition worked aggressively to teach followers the steps to political involvement while also encouraging members to run for office themselves (Gartland 1994).

In addition to encouraging candidacies and training workers, the Christian Coalition launched two publications in 1994 designed to influence voters. *Legislative Scorecards* calculate the percentage of time that legislators voted for the Coalition position on a set of family issues. *Voter Guides* report responses to selected issues probed in surveys distributed by the organization to

**Table 4.1.   Share of White Georgians Identifying Themselves as Members of the Religious Right and Their Partisan Support (%)**

|  | | % of White Electorate | Support for GOP Candidate | | | |
|---|---|---|---|---|---|---|
| **1994** | | | | | | |
| | Religious Right | 26 | Governor | 77 | | |
| | Not religious Right | 74 | | 40 | | |
| **1996** | | | | | | |
| | Religious Right | 21 | President | 80 | Senate | 75 |
| | Not religious Right | 75 | | 37 | | 39 |
| **1998** | | | | | | |
| | Religious Right | 19 | Governor | 70 | Senate | 83 |
| | Not religious Right | 78 | | 38 | | 45 |
| **2000** | | | | | | |
| | Religious Right | 20 | President | 83 | Senate[a] | 63 |
| | Not religious Right | 78 | | 42 | | 33 |
| **2004** | | | | | | |
| | Evangelical/born-again | 35 | President | 84 | Senate | 85 |
| | Not evangelical | 65 | | 45 | | 44 |

Source: Voters News Service exit polls.
[a]Since the 2000 Senate election was to fill the vacancy created by the death of Paul Coverdell, it was non-partisan. While the ballot carried no partisan identification for the candidate, the interim appointee and winner of the election, Zell Miller, was closely identified as a Democrat as a result of his service as lieutenant governor (1975–1991) and governor (1991–1999). His leading opponent, Mack Mattingly, was Georgia's first popularly elected Republican senator (1981–1987), and the media regularly identified him as a Republican.

candidates for Congress and for statewide and legislative offices. These widely disseminated evaluations of legislators' records and of the stands taken by opposing candidates concentrate on what the Christian Coalition identifies as family values. The Coalition often taps attitudes about abortion and the role of homosexuals in society in its evaluations of candidate policy position; however, the scope of the questionnaire has expanded so that in 2004 its eighty-two questions covered much of the state's legislative agenda (Salzer 2004).

While the numbers of *Voter Guides* that Christian Coalition leaders report distributing has dropped from a peak of 1.5 to 2 million, the organization continues to send out half a million copies. Almost a quarter of a million copies go to households in the organization's database (Fields 2004). Additional copies are placed under the windshield wipers of cars in church parking lots on the Sunday before election. Others are passed out in Sunday schools or are available for the taking in church vestibules.

Democrats have criticized the assessment of candidates' positions on a few of what the Coalition called "family-friendly issues" as being little more than Republican propaganda. Democrats have also expressed displeasure with the choice of roll calls used to calculate the legislative scorecards prepared by the Christian Coalition. A liberal Democrat groused about the survey used for the *Voter Guides*: "It's designed to give high ratings to Republicans. That is the bottom line" (Salzer 2004). In 1994, fourteen of seventeen GOP senators got scores of 89 percent or higher, while no Democrat managed more than a 50 percent correct vote (Bullock and Grant 1996).

Coincident with the unprecedented Christian Coalition activity in 1994, Republicans made significant gains in the general assembly, winning more than a third of the seats for the first time in more than a century. In other contests, Republicans won seven congressional seats and three statewide constitutional offices. The dean of the state's political writers observed that many of these new officeholders owed their victories to Christian Right support (Shipp 1994; see also Bullock and Grant 1995).

In 1996, candidates favored by evangelicals won the GOP nomination for the two statewide offices to be filled—a U.S. Senate seat and the post of secretary of state (Bullock and Smith 1997). However, neither of these managed to win election. Many believed that had Johnny Isakson, like Coverdell, a moderate former state legislator, won the Senate nomination, he could have succeeded in November. But Isakson ran a television ad in which he embraced a more tolerant position on abortion than the free-spending runoff winner and that made him unacceptable to religious conservatives in the GOP.

The 1998 election cycle welcomed a new player to Georgia's GOP theater as Ralph Reed left the Christian Coalition to create an Atlanta campaign consulting firm. Some believed that hiring Reed's consulting firm, Century Strategies, to handle a campaign gave candidates instant credibility in the religious community. Reed-managed candidates won GOP nominations for three statewide positions. The gubernatorial nominee also had strong ties to evangelicals, helped in part by the widely announced fact that his wife hosted prayer meetings in their mansion. While candidates with close ties to the Christian Right won some legislative seats, none of the four statewide candidates most closely identified with religious conservativism succeeded in November.

Some GOP consultants with close ties to the religious Right attributed the 1998 GOP stumble to the failure of candidates at the top of the ticket to stake out positions sufficiently conservative to excite the Christian Right despite Reed's involvement (Bullock and Smith 2000). Although the Christian Coalition continued disseminating the *Voter Guides*, the newness that had sparked so much interest four years earlier had worn off. A Republican legislator who is also a minister cited "an overall general sense of disinterest" with the GOP ticket in the religious community (Walker 1999).

Over the course of four years, the relationship of Christian conservatives to the GOP had changed. In 1994, concentrations of religious conservatives added votes above what would be expected on the basis of past partisan voting. By 1998, Republicans did worse, after controlling for past partisan voting, in counties with large numbers of evangelicals. The change in slopes for Guy Millner, who sought support from religious conservatives and who beat Isakson in 1996, is instructive. When he ran for governor in 1994, he did significantly better in counties with higher percentages of fundamentalists (b = .127). Two years later, when he narrowly failed in a bid to become U.S. senator, the relationship between percentage of evangelicals and his vote share remained slightly positive but not statistically significant (b = .032). In his second bid for the governorship, Millner ran significantly worse in heavily evangelical counties (b = −.073) (Bullock and Smith 2000).

A GOP campaign consultant and lobbyist says of Christian conservatives, "They have become the Republican Party. They are the activists and the public officials. A number of them have become county Republican chairs." Sadie Fields (2004), executive director of the Georgia Christian Coalition, agrees: "Our community has assimilated into the process. A number of our people began by starting Christian Coalition chapters, and serving as their leaders and then ran for [public] office." She continued, describing the advice she gives her members concerning involvement with the GOP, "They need to be the people who put up the yard signs and lick the stamps. Go back and offer to serve. The heart of Christianity is to serve. People need to stay involved and do grassroots organizing. If you do that then you have a seat at the table."

## SIZE OF THE RELIGIOUS RIGHT

Each political party has a core constituency that displays extraordinarily high levels of party loyalty. These voters have an enhanced influence in the nomination process because they are especially likely to participate in party primaries. Georgia Democrats have an advantage in identifying members of their core constituency. African Americans, who vote for Democrats at rates often exceeding 90 percent (Bullock and Dunn 1999), can readily be identified because Georgia is one of five states that include race in the information collected on registration forms. The task for Republicans is more challenging. Their core constituency is composed of Christian conservatives, and a person's religious leanings are not recorded in the course of voter registration.

Republican candidates who believe that Christian conservatives faithfully turn out strive, at a minimum, to avoid incurring the ire of this group. This may necessitate walking a tightrope suspended between being conservative enough to keep off the religious conservatives' hit list and moderate enough to appeal to swing voters. A Republican legislator explained, "You can't be their nemesis. There is a lot of fear of what they'd to you if you crossed them. The key is getting them not to work against you" (Bullock and Grant 1995, 57). While some Republicans take a "let sleeping dogs lie" approach to religious conservatives, many candidates appeal for support, as will be described later. But before looking at how candidates solicit support from Christian conservatives, we examine the size of this electoral bloc.

## General Electorate

Exit poll responses provide one way to determine the size of the Christian conservative community. Beginning in 1994, exit polls conducted by the media asked white voters whether they considered themselves to be part of the religious Right. Table 4.1 provides recent Georgia data. Across four elections, conservative Christians had their greatest presence in 1994, when just over a quarter of the white electorate identified with that movement. In the next three elections, the share of the white electorate identifying with the religious Right hovered around 20 percent.

The distinctiveness in the voting behavior of those who identify with the religious Right is shown in the candidates preferred. Of the contests for which exit poll data exist, white voters who identify themselves as supporters of the religious Right are at least thirty percentage points more likely to vote Republican than are other white voters. For example, in the 1994 gubernatorial election, 77 percent of the religious Right voters supported Republican Guy Millner compared with only 40 percent of the whites who did not identify with the religious Right. The largest differences occur in presidential elections, where at least 80 percent of the Christian conservative voters supported the Republican nominee compared with only approximately 40 percent of the remaining white voters.

The smallest difference came in the 2000 senatorial election, and this contest did not provide the same partisan cues as did the other elections in table 4.1. The 2000 senatorial election filled the remaining four years of Paul Coverdell's (R) term. Governor Roy Barnes (D) named his predecessor as the interim senator. Special elections in Georgia do not carry partisan identification, so all candidates interested in the remainder of the term ran in a single contest with a majority vote needed for victory. The two leading candidates were interim senator Zell Miller, whose partisanship was well known after his quarter century as governor and lieutenant governor. His chief opponent, Mack Mattingly, had served one term as a Republican senator and since his defeat in 1986 has been something of an elder statesman of the GOP who frequently gets his name in the papers. Attentive voters would know of the partisanship of Miller and Mattingly, but some voters new to the state or who paid less attention to political news would be unaware of the partisan differences. Nonetheless, even without a party label on the ballot, a thirty-percentage-point difference exists with Mattingly getting 63 percent of the vote from religious conservatives contrasted with only 33 percent from other white voters.

In 2004, the exit polls asked whether whites were evangelicals or born-again rather than asking about identification with the religious Right. The difference in the wording may account for the much larger share of whites who responded favorably, as 35 percent of the whites told interviewers they were evangelicals or born-again.[1] The voting patterns are similar to other years with the share of believers who supported the GOP candidates being approximately 40 percent greater than the share of those who had not been born again. The pattern in the presidential election was almost identical with four years earlier. The voting in the Senate contest was very similar with that in 1998, the most recent year in which the ballot carried partisan identification of the Senate candidates.

## Primary Electorate

As table 4.2 shows, the number of voters participating in Georgia primary elections has remained relatively constant since 1990 with the exception of especially low participation in 1994. In other years, between 900,000 and 1.4 million voters have helped choose party nominees.

While the number of voters has been relatively constant, their partisan choices have changed dramatically. Since Georgia does not have partisan reg-

**Table 4.2. Participation in Georgia Primaries**

| Year | Total | Democrat | Democrat % Black | GOP | % GOP |
|------|-------|----------|------------------|-----|-------|
| 1990 | 1,171,131 | 1,053,013 | 24.6 | 118,118 | 10.1 |
| 1992 | 1,151,971 | 875,149 | 22.1 | 276,822 | 24.0 |
| 1994 | 761,371 | 463,049 | N.A.[a] | 298,322 | 39.2 |
| 1996 | 1,187,717 | 718,302 | 22.5 | 464,866 | 39.1 |
| 1998 | 950,871 | 519,412 | 36.4 | 426,679 | 44.9 |
| 2000 | 976,950 | 613,901 | 31.3 | 340,001 | 34.8 |
| 2002 | 1,110,058 | 567,728 | 45.2 | 533,982 | 48.1 |
| 2004 | 1,418,838 | 731,111 | 47.2 | 671,961 | 47.4 |

Sources: Turnout figures come from the Georgia secretary of state. Figures for the Democratic percentage from black voters are estimates for 1990–1996 and were estimated by the author; more recent figures are the secretary of state's calculations derived from voter sign-in sheets. My estimates for 1998 and 2000 are 38.0 and 29.8 percent, respectively. Figures for 2004 are the sum of the votes in each party's U.S. Senate primary and therefore do not include voters who registered no preference in this contest.
[a]N.A. = not available.

istration, voters can select a Democratic or a Republican ballot or opt for a ballot that includes only contests for nonpartisan offices, such as judgeships. In 1990, approximately 90 percent of the primary voters asked for a Democratic ballot. In the two most recent primaries, almost half the electorate picked the Republican ballot.

As the fourth column in table 4.2 shows, the racial makeup of the Democratic primary electorate has undergone a marked change. Until 1998, African Americans cast less than one-quarter of the Democratic ballots. In 2004, blacks accounted for 47 percent of the Democratic turnout. This change occurred as the size of the Democratic primary electorate fell by 300,000 voters. An obvious consequence demonstrated in table 4.2 is that the core Democratic constituency (African Americans) has doubled and assumed a greater role in the selection of its party's nominees.

At the same time, the Republican primary turnout increased by 550,000 between 1990 and 2004. If one assumes that the Republican core constituency turns out in primaries in higher percentages than other voters less committed to the GOP, then the core constituency may have cast a larger share of the vote in earlier Republican primaries, when fewer primary voters selected Republicans ballots. An estimate from 1996 was that Christian conservatives accounted for approximately 40 percent of the Republican primary (Foskett 1996). Christian conservatives' share of the Republican primary electorate will have decreased, unless their numbers have kept pace with growing GOP turnout. Republican activists interviewed for this chapter agreed that the numbers of religious conservatives participating in GOP primaries has failed to keep pace with growth in primary voters.

Returns for selected 2004 primary contests offer insight into the size of the Christian conservative vote in the most recent election. The Christian Coalition's Sadie Fields (2004) points to the 2004 Court of Appeals primary to demonstrate what the Christian Coalition can do for a candidate. Mike Sheffield was the only candidate for that office to respond to the Coalition's survey that asked whether candidates agreed with a set of U.S. Supreme Court decisions that the Coalition felt touched on family values, a fact emphasized in the half million *Voter Guides* distributed by the organization. Sheffield, who mounted an underfunded effort, polled 20 percent of the vote in this nonpartisan contest in which all primary voters could participate, which was, by a narrow margin, good enough for second place.[2] Some observers point to the Sheffield vote as an indicator of the turnout that the Christian Coalition can mobilize since he was reviewed so favorably in the organization's *Judicial Voter Guide* and lacked the funding needed for a vigorous campaign and had no television presence. If all of Sheffield's votes came from individuals who participated in the GOP primary, it would constitute just over 30 percent of the Republican primary participation. No doubt, however, Sheffield got some votes from participants in the Democratic primary, and some GOP voters who identify with the Christian Coalition preferred one of the five other candidates to Sheffield.

If conservative Christians have become a smaller factor in GOP primaries, then candidates associated with these beliefs will encounter increased resistance, and that has been the pattern over the past decade. As noted earlier, in the first half of the 1990s, strident abortion opponents often won GOP nominations only to meet rejection in November. As will be described later, now candidates favored by the Christian Coalition and Georgia Right to Life (GRTL) often come up short in their bids for nominations. A GOP campaign manager illustrated this point by recounting how he had lined up backing from the two religious groups and a number of ministers thinking that would secure the nomination to a countywide office for his candidate. The favorite of the religious Right struggled to get a third of the vote in a three-candidate contest. The discouraged activist saw the religious Right as ineffectual: "Candidates backed by the Christian Coalition and the conservative religious Right who did well were good candidates. Poor candidates with Christian Coalition and GRTL backing lost."

The declining success of the religious Right, highlighted by the inability of its favorites to win high-profile nominations in 2004, coincides with other indicators that the movement has lost steam over the past decade. A national survey conducted in 1994 assessed Christian conservatives' influence with Georgia's GOP as strong—one of eighteen states placed in that category (Persinos 1994). Eight years later, a follow-up survey concluded that religious conservative strength in the GOP has subsided into the moderate range (Conger and Green 2002). As further evidence, the Christian Coalition distributes far fewer copies of its *Voter Guides* today than a decade ago. It is also reported to be operating on a tighter budget, which could account for distributing fewer *Voter Guides*. In the 1990s the Christian Coalition concentrated on creating chapters in as many counties as possible (Bullock and Grant 1995). Now it has little interest in maintaining chapters and, instead, relies on a database of almost a quarter million (Fields 2004). Among those in the database are key activists tied to the Atlanta headquarters via the Internet who help with distributing materials.

## 2004 REPUBLICAN PRIMARIES

Religious conservatives, with GRTL in the lead, had as their chief objective in the 2004 Republican primaries derailing the Senate bid of Johnny Isakson.

Isakson, a longtime state legislator and three-term member of Congress, had earned a reputation as a moderate who could work effectively with Democrats. This alone sufficed to raise questions about his commitment to conservative principles among some on the far Right.

In 1996, Isakson confirmed religious conservatives' suspicions when he released a television ad that took a moderate stand on abortion. Isakson, who was locked in a desperate struggle to keep the Republican front-runner from wrapping up a majority and thus the nomination in the initial primary, explained that while he opposed abortions, he questioned the appropriateness of having government determine the conditions under which they should be granted. Flanked by his wife and teenage daughter, Isakson looked into the camera and said, "I trust my wife, my daughter and the women of Georgia to make the right choice" (Tharpe 2004a, D7). With that announcement, he conceded the support of the more conservative element of the Republican Party, even though most observers acknowledged that his moderate stand on abortion pulled him to within striking distance of the unreservedly pro-life front-runner.

In 2004, Isakson confronted two conservative challengers for the nomination to the Senate seat being vacated by Zell Miller. Initially, the stronger challenger was thought to be Mac Collins, a colleague in the Georgia congressional delegation. Joining Collins was political neophyte Herman Cain, the former chief executive officer of Godfather's Pizza. Cain had grown up in Georgia and had recently returned to his native state after living in Omaha for a number of years.

The television advertising done by the three candidates reveals the significance each attached to the religious Right's opposition to abortion. In separate ways, each contender appealed to pro-life forces.

The more conservative challengers emphasized the differences they had with Isakson. In a frequently run television ad, African American entrepreneur Cain caught viewers' attention with, "There's a big difference between me and Johnny Isakson. And it's not just the color of our eyes. I believe in life from conception. Johnny's voted pro-abortion 14 times." Collins began his televised attacks calling Isakson a "moderate." Collins boasted that he rated 100 percent on scorecards done by Right to Life and the Christian Coalition and a zero from Planned Parenthood. Early in 2004, just in time for the meeting of the Families in Freedom, a pro-family organization, Collins mailed a two-minute video to 20,000 conservatives. In it, he charged Isakson with having voted for abortion more than a dozen times. Rather than choosing between the two conservatives, GRTL gave a dual endorsement.

The moderate Isakson touted his pro-life credentials by emphasizing a 92 percent positive rating from the Christian Coalition and pointing out that he had presided over the U.S. House floor debate on the legislation banning partial birth abortions. He also noted that he had an 88 percent support score from Right to Life (Tharpe 2004a).

In response to charges that he voted for abortion, Isakson explained that while he personally opposes the procedure and would never countenance public funding for abortions, he supports allowing military women to obtain abortions in military hospitals overseas. His rationale is that it provides the same access to abortions that a woman could get in the United States (McMurray 2003). Roll calls to permit women posted with the armed forces abroad to pay to have abortions in military hospitals accounted for most of the fourteen roll calls criticized in Herman Cain's ad (Tharpe 2004a).

While pro-life groups opposed Isakson, unlike in his earlier bids, he managed to draw support from some individuals with strong credentials among religious conservatives. Isakson visited a number of the leaders among Christian conservatives to demonstrate his faith and to seek support. One of Isakson's television ads showed him teaching a Sunday school class. In response to Isakson's outreach, he had in his corner in 2004 the Republican whip in the statehouse, a former president of the Georgia Christian Coalition chapter. Jerry Keen downplayed the relative importance of taking the one-exception stand on abortion and emphasized the importance of having a Senate that will confirm conservatives nominated to the federal bench by President Bush (Baxter 2003). Keen sized up Isakson as more electable than his more conservative opponents. This fit neatly with Isakson's television ads in which he promised to be a strong supporter of Bush judicial candidates.

Sadie Fields (2004), the head of Georgia's Christian Coalition, sat out the Senate contest. Indicative of her organization's growing pragmatism, Fields explains that while she was disappointed that Isakson continues to support allowing women to obtain abortions in military hospitals abroad, he has enough good qualities and has been sufficiently supportive to compensate. A political operative summed up what he believes to be the new outlook of the Christian Coalition: "They are learning that someone who is your 90 percent friend should not be considered to be a 10 percent enemy." With Isakson having a substantial lead from the outset of his candidacy, the Christian Coalition may have calculated that it would be preferable not to take on the individual likely to be Georgia's next senator. An Isakson staffer volunteered that Coalition pragmatism may reflect the realization that a strong performance by Isakson in November could facilitate the election of religious true believers to down-ticket offices like the legislature.

Isakson's refusal to embrace the single-exception approach to abortion may have been less significant in 2004 than earlier. Republican campaign consultants observed that for many religious conservatives, gay marriage has supplanted abortion as the primary threat to family values. Expanded participation in the GOP primary helped Isakson win the Republican nomination without a runoff. With 650,000 voters marking ballots in the Republican Senate primary, the influence of religious conservatives was diluted. The number of people voting in the Republican primary had increased by 200,000 since Isakson lost the 1996 Senate nomination to a more conservative opponent.

Aside from the Senate nomination, religious conservatives had a mixed record of success at best. A key staff member of the Republican state headquarters reports that Christian conservative organizations played little if any role in the GOP primaries to fill two open seats in heavily Republican congressional districts. The state senator seen as the favorite of the religious Right in the Sixth Congressional District made it into the runoff but failed to overtake the front-runner. On the other hand, Nancy Schaefer, founder of Family Concerns, a conservative religious entity and a strong supporter of public displays of the Ten Commandments and opposed to domestic partnership benefits, won an open state senate seat. We turn next to the efforts of the Christian Coalition in two statewide judicial contests.

## JUDICIAL ELECTIONS

Georgia judicial elections are usually sterile affairs. Until 2004, the bar's canon of ethics prevented judicial candidates from commenting on the policy preferences of their opponents. It was thought to be inappropriate to challenge a sitting judge on the basis of decisions rendered by that jurist. The Supreme Court recently struck down as an unconstitutional limitation on freedom of speech the prohibition on raising policy questions in the course of a judicial campaign.

In the aftermath of the elimination of the ban on policy debates for judicial candidates, a challenge to a sitting member of the state supreme court ensued. The object of this challenge, Leah Sears, was the first African American woman to serve on that body. Some of her opinions infuriated conservatives. She also alienated Republican Governor Sonny Perdue when she sided with the majority and rejected his efforts to rein in Democratic State Attorney General Thurbert Baker in a battle over who determines Georgia's position on legal matters.

Georgia judicial elections are nonpartisan and in the past attracted few challengers and relatively little interest or information. In 2004, the Christian Coalition stepped into this void. It sent questionnaires to the two candidates running for the supreme court as well as to six candidates competing for an open seat on the court of appeals. The questionnaire, which was designed by a conservative attorney, asked the candidates whether they supported the opinion of the court or the dissent in five cases heard by the supreme court between 1992 and 2004. One opinion dealt with abortion rights, while a second involved a state antisodomy law.[3] Also included in the five opinions posed to the judicial candidates were a ban on sectarian prayers at public school graduations, the use of vouchers at parochial schools, and a ban on use of public funds for training ministers.[4]

A group headed by former American Bar Association President William Ide formed the Georgia Committee for Ethical Judicial Campaigns. Ide urged judicial candidates not to respond to the Christian Coalition questionnaire, warning that the responses might give the impression that a judge would be biased should a similar case come before the panel for a decision (Jacobs 2004). The president of the Georgia bar also came out against having judicial candidates respond to questions such as those posed by the Christian Coalition (Barwick 2004).

Of the eight candidates whose opinions were solicited by the Christian Coalition, only two responded. Grant Brantley, who challenged Sears for the supreme court slot, took the conservative view on each of the five cases posed. Justice Sears refused to respond, and the Christian Coalition's *Judicial Voter Guide* distributed to about half a million voters (Wyatt 2004) as well as posted on the organization's website noted her refusal to participate. The *Judicial Voter Guide* identified Sears as part of the majority that struck down Georgia's law against sodomy.

Brantley stressed "family values" by including in his four-page mailer a picture of his extended family along with an indication of his church membership. He castigated Justice Sears, charging that she supports gay and lesbian marriage and wants to weaken statutory rape laws.

The Sears campaign acknowledged the importance of the religious vote and made its own appeal. Her mailer described Sears as "a woman of faith, integrity [who has] respect for the sanctity of traditional marriage and family values." In defending herself against the suggestion that she is not sufficiently religious, Sears noted, "My daughter attends Southwest Atlanta Christian Academy, where they pray and praise every morning" (Rankin 2004, A9).

In the contest for justice of the court of appeals, the one respondent to the Christian Coalition survey, Mike Sheffield, embraced the conservative stand in each of the five cases. The *Judicial Voter Guide* noted Sheffield's position along with the lack of response from the other five candidates. A Sheffield mailer distinguished him from Howard Mead, the candidate against whom he vied for the second slot in the runoff. Mead, who has close ties to several high-ranking Democrats, was the only court of appeals candidate to advertise on Atlanta television. Sheffield compared himself with Mead on four dimensions. On one of these, "Community Involvement," Sheffield noted his membership in a Presbyterian congregation, while for Mead he reported "Involved in various Democratic *Campaigns* and ultra-liberal causes" (emphasis in the original). On a second dimension identified as "Georgia Values," Sheffield "Pledges to protect traditional marriage." For Mead, the Sheffield mailer charged, "Currently refuses to address this important issue. Georgia families at Risk!" As a further appeal to conservatives, the campaign literature stated that "Mike Sheffield is an unapologetic constitutionalist who is pro-life, pro-family and who believes in upholding Georgia's capital punishment laws for convicted murderers."

Neither candidate who completed the Christian Coalition questionnaire did well in the nonpartisan primary. Brantley was routed with only 38 percent of the vote. As noted earlier, Sheffield struggled to place second in the court of appeals primary with a 20 percent vote share.

## DISAGREEMENTS AMONG CONSERVATIVE RELIGIOUS ORGANIZATIONS

While some see religious conservatives as a single movement, others note a division with the Christian Coalition becoming more pragmatic while GRTL has taken the more extreme position on the ideological spectrum often embraced by the Coalition in the 1990s.[5] The two have moved to different positions on availability of abortion. Few if any serious Republican candidates would qualify as pro-choice. However, GRTL has upped the ante for getting its endorsement as a right-to-life candidate by requiring that a candidate tolerate abortion only to save the life of the mother. After backing him in the primary, GRTL withdrew support for Saxby Chambliss in the 2002 Senate race on discovering that he embraced the three-exceptions approach that permits abortions in the case of rape or incest as well as to save the mother's life. While Chambliss rejected the sole-exception position, his views on abortion came much closer to that of GRTL than the incumbent, Democrat Max Cleland. Since campaign polling identifies less than a third of *Republican primary voters* as single-issue, one-exception abortion supporters, taking the GRTL stand may not only make winning the nomination difficult but also risk pushing candidates to take such extreme positions that they become unelectable in November.

The Christian Coalition leadership has quietly come to accept candidates who take the three-exceptions stand. A longtime GOP activist sees in Ralph Reed's redefinition of himself a model for change in the Christian Coalition.[6]

According to this source, Reed came to Georgia with the goal of becoming head of the GOP. Once he achieved that objective, he insisted that when appearing on radio or television shows he be identified as the GOP executive director and not in his former role with Pat Robertson. He also downplayed the abortion issue in his meetings with the media. Abortion has also become less central to the Christian Coalition, as it has emphasized issues that find widespread support in the public, such as opposition to gay marriage and partial birth abortion.

## ORGANIZED RELIGION AND STATE POLICYMAKERS

So long as Democrats controlled state government, religious conservatives had little prospect for legislative success. Many of their top priorities, such as restricting the availability of abortions, never got out of Democratic-controlled legislative committees. Even conservative Democrats like Tom Murphy, who held the record for the longest tenure as a house speaker (1974–2002), opposed efforts to restrict access to abortion. Antiabortion bills went to the House Judiciary Committee, which was chaired by a succession of the speaker's loyal lieutenants. Judiciary chairs could be trusted to keep abortion bills off the floor, thereby deflecting cross pressures for a number of rural, conservative Democrats. With the election of a Republican governor and Republican ascendancy in the senate, religious conservatives hoped that their agenda would fare better (Galloway 2003).

Sadie Fields, the executive director of the Christian Coalition, assured her followers that "the governor-elect is very in tune with our values and wants to work with us on accomplishing our goals. We have a seat at the table and I am honored to have been asked by the [Perdue] team to be your voice and representative during this critical time" (Cook 2002, A1, A19). Beth Cope, the executive director of the Georgia Abortion and Reproductive Rights Action League, agreed that the context had changed and characterized the new administration as "the most hostile political environment we have ever faced" (Cook 2002, A19).

### Family Values under a Republican Governor

Governor Perdue came to office saddled with a growing budget gap. To plug this gap, he proposed a tax increase that shocked and outraged many of the Republicans who had been rejoicing in their party's first chief executive in 130 years. The economic crisis meant that the Christian conservative objectives would not dominate the governor's agenda. Indeed, religious conservatives' concerns were not even the top cultural divide that the governor confronted in 2003. Contributing to Perdue's upset victory was anger over Governor Roy Barnes's decision to remove the St. Andrew's cross associated with the Confederate flag from Georgia's flag.[7] Perdue had promised that if elected, he would hold a referendum on Georgia's flag. To honor that pledge, Perdue spent many hours on issues such as what flag options to put on the ballot and the voting rules that would be used to settle the issue.

While not at the top of his concerns, the governor did embrace efforts to restrict abortions. Abortion opponents believed for several years that if allowed to vote on the issue, they would be able to restrict access to abortions. The item selected for emphasis in 2003 was the Women's Right to Know bill. This proposal would impose a twenty-four-hour delay before a woman could obtain an abortion. Before getting an abortion, she would have to be told of alternatives and warned of possible complications from the procedure. In addition, she would be given a color brochure showing the fetus at various stages of development. The senate, where Republicans enjoyed a thirty to twenty-six advantage, passed this legislation with eighteen dissenting votes. That, however, was the last triumph for pro-life forces. Once the bill reached the house, it met the same fate as efforts to restrict access to abortions in previous years. The speaker assigned the legislation to the Judiciary Committee, which was chaired by one of the chamber's most liberal members. And there the bill stayed. Not only was the bill not considered in 2003, but the committee took no action on it during the next year.

A number of other ideas favored by the religious conservatives also failed to receive sufficient support for enactment. One proposal would set aside part of each day in public schools for students to talk about their religious beliefs. This failed to attract widespread Republican support. The proposal by a member of the house to have an attorney appointed to represent the fetus at a hearing that would be required before an abortion generated little enthusiasm.

Pro-choice supporters worried that the Republican governor might seek to eliminate money for family planning. Eric Johnson, the Republican leader of the senate, supported this effort and promised that "we will find and rule out any money going to groups like Planned Parenthood" (Cook 2003, A9).

## 2004 Session

Governor Perdue stressed two initiatives designed to please religious conservatives in his second year. One of these, the faith-based initiative, would allow the state to offer funds to religious entities that provide social services. This idea followed a similar proposal by President George W. Bush at the national level. Governor Perdue pointed out that Georgia placed more restrictions on the use of public funds than the federal government imposed on the usage of federal dollars. Georgia's prohibition goes back to the Blaine Amendment adopted in the nineteenth century by Georgia and a number of other states, although rejected at the national level. Before religious entities could get state dollars to help in serving the needy, it would be necessary to repeal this prohibition. This repeal, which would require approval of two-thirds of the membership of both chambers, suffered the same fate as the Woman's Right to Know bill in the previous year, dying in a house committee.

The major objective of religious conservatives in 2004 was a proposed constitutional amendment banning gay marriage. Georgia law already restricts marriage to a man and a woman, but the decision of the Massachusetts Supreme Court striking down similar limitations in the Bay State touched off concerns in Georgia and several other states. Advocates of the amendment argued that since the Massachusetts court had interpreted the law there to permit gay marriages, a court in Georgia might conceivably do the same thing if banning these types of unions were limited to statute, and thus, they argued, it became necessary to incorporate the prohibition into the state constitution.

The gay marriage ban became the chief cultural war waged in the halls of the capitol. "I had not seen an issue that had such grassroots appeal since abortion," observed Christian Coalition leader Sadie Fields (2004). Day after day, citizens on either side of the issue filled the hallways hoping to convert legislators to their positions. They waylaid legislators trying to get to their offices, committee hearings, or the floor. Lobbyists noted the lack of sophistication of some of these ardent supporters who were making their first visit to the capitol and grabbed everyone passing through the halls who looked like a possible legislator. One lobbyist reported that she and her colleagues began holding up their yellow name tags identifying themselves as lobbyists when they tried to run the gauntlet. Legislators who wanted to avoid the onslaught took off their distinctive badges when passing through the hallways. In addition to the presence of supporters and opponents of the amendment in the capitol, pressure for the amendment came from religious leaders who both mobilized their congregants and made personal appeals to legislators. Joining this effort were black ministers, including the leader of one of Atlanta's largest megachurches, who concentrated on getting black legislators to back the amendment. The overwhelming majority of the Black Caucus rejected these overtures, and in doing so they aligned themselves with ministers who saw gay marriage as a civil rights issue. Ultimately, the religious community that opposed homosexuality succeeded in bringing enough African Americans over to get the gay marriage ban through the house.

Supporters of the amendment cited scripture to bolster their claims that sex acts between members of the same sex violated the laws of God and nature.

Augmenting biblical appeals were threats to recruit and support challengers to legislators from conservative districts should they oppose the amendment. Opponents argued that failure to acknowledge love between members of the same sex not only violated Christian principles but also contravened the Equal Protection Clause of the U.S. Constitution.

As with many other aspects of the Christian conservative agenda, the senate had little trouble mustering the two-thirds vote needed for approval. The senate passed the proposal, 40 to 14. All Republicans voted "aye" and were joined by ten of the twenty-six Democrats. Amendment opponents included the ten members of the Legislative Black Caucus and the chamber's one Hispanic, who relied on strong support from the gay community to defeat an African American woman in a heavily black district (Galle 2004). Joining the eleven minority legislators were three white Democrats from DeKalb County, an older suburban area that as of the 2000 census had become majority black. Rural Democrats uniformly opposed this legislation, as did two white Democrats from metro Atlanta.

Achieving passage in the house proved far more difficult. The one openly gay member, Karla Drenner, a second-term legislator from DeKalb County, led the forces opposing the amendment. This effort included some religious leaders. Drenner (2004) explained, "We started with gay ministers and gay churches. We worked through the Episcopal Church and the Atlanta Presbytery. One day I was called off the floor and there were ten or twelve ministers. I didn't know what to expect. They said, 'We're here for you.'" However, Drenner acknowledges the disadvantageous position from which her supporters worked. "The legislators know that these groups have no *Voter Guides* and they do not have an organization with 265,000 members behind them," she said, making a comparison with the Christian Coalition.

On the initial vote, the amendment attracted support from a solid majority of 117 legislators but was three short of the two-thirds majority required. The key to the outcome was held by the thirty-nine members of the Legislative Black Caucus. Two of these had supported the amendment before the Rules Committee, the body through which legislation goes before being placed on the calendar and thus becoming eligible to come to the floor. But on the vote on the merits, one of these African Americans voted against it, while the other ducked the vote altogether. The legislator who failed to cast a ballot, Randal Mangham, had appeared to be a supporter when he explained in the course of the house debate that "this is not a civil rights act. It's not against your civil rights. Though God loves us all, and God protects even homosexuals, he hates the sin called homosexuality" (Baxter and Galloway 2004). Eight African American Democrats along with two white Democrats who represented predominantly black districts failed to vote on the proposal. Only one Republican, a DeKalb County suburbanite and former neighbor of Drenner, voted against the gay marriage ban.

The Democrats who cast ballots divided almost equally with forty-seven voting in favor of the amendment and forty-nine opposing it. Of the forty-nine opponents, thirty were African Americans, while another was the chamber's one Hispanic Democrat. White Democrats overwhelmingly joined with Republicans in favor of the limitation. Only seventeen white Democrats opposed the ban, while forty-six voted in favor. Eleven of the seventeen white Democrats voting against the amendment were women. Of the Democrats who voted for the amendment, five rural ones changed to the Republican Party later in the spring. Only six metro Atlanta Democrats backed the amendment.

The gay marriage amendment split the Democratic leadership. The speaker pro tempore, majority leader, and majority caucus vice chair (all rural males) voted in favor of the amendment. Joining the forces against the amendment were the majority whip (a white female), the caucus chair (a black male), and the caucus treasurer (a white female), all representing urban districts. The speaker, who by custom votes only to break a tie, did not participate in the roll call.

Supporters of the ban on gay marriage immediately pushed for reconsideration. An opponent of the amendment reports that a majority of the House Democratic Caucus took a secret vote that came out against reconsideration. Speaker Terry Coleman represents a rural, conservative, Republican-leaning district, and he faced pressure from his constituents, led by local ministers, to schedule a second vote. Ultimately, he indicated that if necessary he would cast the deciding vote to put the amendment on the November ballot. The chair of the Rules Committee, an urban African American, hesitated to bring the issue up for another vote but finally relented after Coleman made a personal appeal to the committee.

On reconsideration, the proposal achieved the two-thirds support necessary and won, 122 to 52. As on the earlier vote, all but one Republican voted to place the proposed amendment on the November ballot. Two Democrats who had voted for the proposal shifted into opposition. These two defections were more than offset, however, when seven new Democrats signed on in support. Key here was the conversion of four African Americans, one of whom is married to a minister. Three of these had not cast ballots in the earlier vote. These votes came despite a warning from the president of the Georgia Association of Black Elected Officials, who is also a senior member of the Legislative Black Caucus, that placing the proposal on the November ballot might well spur enough Republicans to the ballot box that Democrats would lose control of the house (Tharpe 2004b).

While many criticized the lobbying tactics, they likely had an impact. "We no longer scatter shoot," explained Fields (2004) of the Christian Coalition. "We target to people who vote and let them know what is happening and what they can do about it." Even the critics have acknowledged that the Christian Coalition efforts swayed the votes of a few legislators, and with the outcome being so narrowly decided, a few legislators proved critical. Representative Drenner (2004) recounts that several legislators told her privately that they opposed the anti–gay marriage amendment but feared that should they vote their conscience, their constituents might also be led by their consciences and retire the incumbents. Drenner estimates that the lobbying efforts of the Christian Right may have influenced as many as twenty votes.

The gay marriage amendment proved to be a classic wedge issue. While Republicans united in support, it split the Democratic Caucus in both chambers. Fields (2004) agrees: "The gay marriage issue polarized people; it cut across all kinds of cleavages. It cut across race, party, and income." Conservative, white, rural Democrats joined with their ideological confederates in the GOP. Some representatives acknowledged privately that fear of defeat motivated their votes to put the amendment on the November ballot. Non-Anglo Democrats stood united in the senate, and even on the final house vote suffered few defections. Joining the opponents of the proposed constitutional change were a disproportionate share of female Democrats and Democrats from central cities and inner suburbs, areas that tended to be more progressive in their outlooks and often had relatively large numbers of politically active gays and lesbians.

In seeking to ban gay marriage, religious conservatives had an issue that drew support from a broad swath of Georgians. In November 2004, 76 percent of the Georgians who voted favored adding this prohibition to the state constitution.

## The 2004 Election and Beyond

Like many states, turnout in Georgia rose dramatically in 2004, reaching almost 500,000 more than in 2000. The anti–gay marriage amendment contributed to the heightened political interest. "The pastors are amazingly engaged," observed GOP campaign consultant Joel McElhannon (2004). "The preachers are telling their congregations that it is very important to get out and vote this year. The motivation for this is gay marriage. The religious community sees gay marriage as part of a fundamental assault on moral values."

The top-of-the-ticket offering of the Democratic Party, a set of candidates that most Georgians found to be unattractive, also promoted turnout. With the three statewide Democratic candidates (presidential nominee John Kerry,

Senate nominee Denise Majette, and Public Service Commission nominee Mac Barber) struggling to attract 40 percent of the vote, Republicans had unprecedented success down ticket.

Republicans increased their senate majority from thirty to a secure thirty-four and added twenty-one house seats to achieve a majority of ninety-six seats that quickly swelled to ninety-nine when three rural, conservative Democrats changed parties. The convening of the 2005 session found Republicans positioned to enact their agenda regardless of Democratic objections.

In his State of the State Address, however, Governor Perdue ignored many Christian conservative policy preferences. He said nothing about the desirability of circumscribing access to abortions, nor did he reference proposals to promote the display of the Ten Commandments in courthouses. Only when he urged the legislature to enact his faith-based initiative did Perdue's priorities coincide with those of the conservative religious community. Even with the Republican gains in the 2004 election, revocation of the Blaine Amendment will require support from some conservative Democrats, which may remain elusive in the house.

Even though the governor did not recommend adoption of new preconditions for getting an abortion, GOP legislators are likely to offer multiple proposals. Instituting a twenty-four-hour waiting period that is favored by the Roman Catholic Archdiocese of Atlanta and the Christian Coalition is the idea most likely to secure a majority. Among other abortion bills that have been offered in recent years and are likely to reappear in 2005 are proposals to require parental notification when a minor seeks an abortion and a "Laci and Connor Peterson" bill that would make it a crime to injure a fetus at any time during a pregnancy.

## CONCLUSION

Religious conservatives continue to struggle to elect their preferences to top-of-the-ticket offices in Georgia. Indeed, the influence of the ideological purists in this component of the electorate seems to be slipping when it comes to highly visible offices. A decade ago, religious conservatives often won Republican nominations only to come up short in the general election. Today, candidates who are their favorites less often win the nominations for statewide and congressional offices. The 2004 primary season yielded little in high-profile contests for Christian conservatives to celebrate. While they are increasingly shut out of the top offices, religious groups on the Right can chalk up successes in electing state legislators. Several key legislative leaders are prepared to push the evangelical agenda.

The electioneering strategy of religious conservatives has ceased to be monolithic. The Christian Coalition that was seen in the 1990s as doctrinaire and extreme—at least that was the perception of many Democrats—has adopted a more pragmatic approach. Although Ralph Reed has yielded his leadership position within the Christian Coalition, the Georgia chapter is following the course he charted when still with the national organization. Reed, a shrewd tactician, recognized much earlier than many Christian conservatives that half a loaf is more satisfying than the few crumbs obtained from unbending commitment to positions unable to attract majority support. The clearest evidence of the pragmatic approach was the decision not to get behind either of the more conservative U.S. Senate hopefuls in 2004 even after Isakson, in the midst of the campaign, cast another vote that permitted abortion under limited circumstances.

While leaders in the Christian Coalition tolerated the Isakson approach—a position that polls indicate comes closer to where most Georgians are than did his rivals—GRTL held firm to its one-exception approach. Now that GRTL has staked out a position farther to the right on the abortion spectrum, it commands a position of electoral irrelevance. It could not stop Isakson's nomination just as in 2002 retracting its endorsement could not prevent Saxby Chambliss's election. GRTL provides an option that allows those who would countenance abortion only to save the mother's life to feel good, but it has little political potency. By positioning itself to the right of the Christian Coalition, GRTL helps make the former appear closer to the mainstream.

While religious conservatives control neither the GOP nominations nor general election outcomes, Republican candidates genuflect to them. In campaign materials, candidates trumpet their commitment to policy concerns of Christian conservatives. Like children eager to please authority figures, they seek the approbation of leaders of conservative religious groups. But while Republicans sense that support—or at least the absence of hostility from conservative religious organizations—is valuable, the winners now are reluctant to move too far to the right if that is the price demanded for support.

Religious conservatives experienced policy disappointment even as the GOP star rose. While supportive, the state's first Republican governor in more than a century did not throw his full weight behind the religious conservative agenda. Even if Governor Perdue had made their agenda his agenda, Democratic control of the statehouse would have proven an insurmountable obstacle. Access to abortion became no more difficult through 2004. However, with the GOP boasting a majority in the house in 2005, it will be surprising if restrictions to abortion are not added by the newly elected legislature.

Religious conservatives did attain one major goal in 2004—a goal that may have supplanted regulation of abortion as a top priority. After a prolonged

struggle, a constitutional amendment banning gay marriages passed the legislature and won overwhelming ratification in November. This success came as
the Christian Coalition played hardball politics, and their threats to mobilize
voters or recruit opponents deterred Republicans considering voting "no" and
brought along some Democrats, who at least privately told antiamendment
leaders that their personal preference was not to change the constitution.

So what is the present influence of religious conservatives in Georgia?
When they come into the mainstream, as in their tacit acceptance of Isakson's
candidacy or support for the gay marriage ban, they find themselves in the
winners' circle. When they take less popular stands, as in their efforts to influence the outcome of the two judicial contests in 2004, their efforts come
up short. In statewide and congressional contests, Christian conservatives
need allies for their preferred candidates to win, and that means that they cannot demand that the candidate fully embrace their policy agenda—an agenda
that remains too conservative for most Georgia voters. If conservative Christians back moderate to conservative Republicans, Democratic electoral
prospects are dim.

The situation, not surprisingly, changes when the focus shifts to smaller
constituencies. In some state senate and house districts, religious conservatives have much greater influence since their stands are compatible with the
policy preferences of the district's voters. A number of Republican legislators,
including some chamber leaders, now come from the conservative Christian
community, and others owe their elections to support from those voters. With
Republicans having consolidated their hold on the legislature in the 2004
election, it will be surprising if more of the Christian conservative policy
package is not enacted. Access to abortion and divorce will probably become
more difficult. The Blaine Amendment may be repealed. The state may even
offer financial assistance to counties that get sued after they post the Ten
Commandments in their courthouses.

As this is being written in early 2005, Republicans are relishing their first
opportunity to chart the direction of Georgia government in generations.
Their evangelical allies who worked to elect Republicans and were repeatedly
thwarted by powerful Democrats have high hopes for the new legislature.
Some feel that since their ranks provide the most consistent support for GOP
candidates, they are entitled to have their agenda enacted. That demand, if
fully acceded to by Republicans, could hold the key that opens the way to
Democratic resurrection. While Governor Perdue carefully avoided signing
on to all features of the conservative Christian agenda, if aspects of it that are
outside the mainstream are enacted, he will be saddled with defending it in
his 2006 reelection. Moderate white women who voted for Republicans in the

last two elections and narrowed the gender gap so that Republicans could win may bolt to the Democratic side if the legislature makes it impossible for their daughters to get an abortion.

## NOTES

1. In the postelection inquiry to discover why the early exit polls showed John Kerry winning key states, those responsible for the polls attributed their errors to a greater willingness of Kerry than Bush supporters to respond. If that pattern existed in Georgia, then the share of white voters who have been born again exceeds 35 percent.

2. The candidate who finished third secured an injunction that prevented holding the runoff scheduled for August 20 that would have picked the new judge.

3. The abortion case was *Planned Parenthood v. Casey*, 505 U.S. 833 (1992); the sodomy case was *Lawrence v. Texas*, 539 U.S. 558 (2003).

4. The graduation prayer opinion was *Lee v. Weisman*, 505 U.S. 577 (1992); the use of vouchers is *Zelman v. Simmons-Harris*, 536 U.S. 639, 122 S.Ct. 2460 (2002); and the training of theology majors decision is *Locke v. Davey*, 540 U.S. 712, 124 S.Ct. 1307 (2004).

5. The political action committee of GRTL is headed by Daniel Becker, who, when running for Congress in 1992, ran television ads that included pictures of aborted fetuses.

6. Some see Reed's continued evolution taking him on an increasingly secular course as he and his firm work with corporate clients (Stone 2004). For years there have been rumors that Reed will seek statewide office in Georgia. If true, this could explain why Reed would move toward positions designed to make him electable.

7. Barnes attributes his defeat exclusively to the backlash to the flag changes.

## REFERENCES

Barwick, William D. 2004. "Iffy Poll Questions Hurt Judicial Candidates." *Atlanta Journal-Constitution*, May 21, A15.

Baxter, Tom. 2003. "Right's View of Isakson Softens." *Atlanta Journal-Constitution*, August 9, E2.

Baxter, Tom, and Jim Galloway. 2004. "Black Lawmakers Held Key to Amendment's Defeat." *Atlanta Journal-Constitution*, February 27, D6.

Bullock, Charles S., III, and Richard E. Dunn. 1999. "The Demise of Racial Redistricting and the Future of Black Representation." *Emory Law Journal* 48: 1209–53.

Bullock, Charles S., III, and John Christopher Grant. 1995. "Georgia: The Christian Right and Grass Roots Power." In *God at the Grassroots: The Christian Right in* the 1994 Election, edited by Mark J. Rozell and Clyde Wilcox. Lanham, Md.: Rowman & Littlefield.

———. 1996. "Evangelical Christians and the 1994 Georgia Elections." Paper presented at the Citadel Symposium on Southern Politics, Charleston, South Carolina, March 7–8.

Bullock, Charles S., III, and David J. Shafer. 1997. "Party Targeting and Electoral Success." *Legislative Studies Quarterly* 22 (November): 573–84.

Bullock, Charles S., III, and Mark C. Smith. 1997. "Georgia: Purists, Pragmatists and Electoral Outcomes." In *God at the Grassroots, 1996: The Christian Right in the 1996 Elections,* edited by Mark J. Rozell and Clyde Wilcox. Lanham, Md.: Rowman & Littlefield.

———. 2000. "Georgia: The Christian Right Meets Its Match." In *Prayers in the Parishes: The Christian Right in the 1998 Elections,* edited by John C. Green, Mark J. Rozell, and Clyde Wilcox. Washington, D.C.: Georgetown University Press.

Conger, Kimberly H., and John C. Green. 2002. "Spreading Out and Digging In: Christian Conservatives and State Republican Parties." *Campaigns and Elections* 23 (February): 58–65.

Cook, Rhonda. 2002. "Georgia Abortion Fight Brews." *Atlanta Journal-Constitution,* December 26, A1, A19.

———. 2003. "Perdue, GOP Pledge to Curb Procedure." *Atlanta Journal-Constitution,* January 23, A9.

Drenner, Karla. 2004. Telephone interview, August 18.

Fields, Sadie. 2004. Telephone interview, August 23.

Foskett, Ken. 1996. "Religious Conservatives Figure Big in Tuesday's Vote." *Atlanta Journal,* July 8, B3.

Galle, Sara. 2004. "The Latino Legislative Anomaly." Unpublished honors thesis, University of Georgia.

Galloway, Jim. 2003. "Perdue Talks to Abortion Foes." *Atlanta Journal-Constitution,* January 26, C7.

Gartland, Pat. 1994. Telephone interview, February 9.

Jacobs, Sonji. 2004. "Group Presses Judicial Hopefuls." *Atlanta Journal-Constitution,* May 14, C1.

McElhannon, Joel. 2004. Telephone interview, June 12.

McMurray, Jeffrey. 2003. "Isakson Tries to Shed Stigma He's Not Conservative Enough." *Athens Banner Herald,* September 28, D4.

Persinos, John F. 1994. "Has the Christian Right Taken Over the Republican Party?" *Campaigns and Elections* 15 (September): 21–24.

Rankin, Bill. 2004. "State GOP Goes After Supreme Court Seat." *Atlanta Journal-Constitution,* July 3, A1, A9.

Salzer, James. 2004. "Christian Quiz Touches All Bases." *Atlanta Journal-Constitution,* September 2, D1, D5.

Shipp, Bill. 1994. "Big Winners: Bowers, Perdue." *Georgia Trend,* December 15.

Smith, Mark C. 2001. "With Friends Like These . . ." Ph.D. diss., University of Georgia.

Stone, Peter H. 2004. "Go-To Gay." *National Journal* 36 (July 17): 2234–38.

Tharpe, Jim. 2004a. "GOP Race Turns to Debate on Abortion." *Atlanta Journal-Constitution*, January 30, D7.

———. 2004b. "Same-Sex Marriage Ban Finds Support." *Atlanta Journal-Constitution*, March 3, B1, B5.

Walker, Lynn. 1999. Telephone interview conducted with Mark C. Smith, January 15.

Wyatt, Kristen. 2004. "Georgia Group Releases First Judicial Survey." *Athens Banner-Herald*, July 7, A8.

# 5

# Religious Advocacy in the Texas Legislature

*Brian R. Calfano, Elizabeth Anne Oldmixon,*
*and Peter VonDoepp*

A nation without God's guidance is a nation without order.
Happy are those who keep God's law!

—Proverbs 29:18

$S$tacey Emick works as the legislative director for Texas Right to Life. Among religiously inspired political advocates, she is not alone in characterizing her work as a "witnessing opportunity" (interview with Calfano, July 20, 2004). She and her colleagues, regardless of denominational family, are guided in politics by the sentiment of the Proverb: they seek to bring "God's guidance" to bear on public policy. Lobbying, then, takes on a larger significance than simply pursuing one's interests. Indeed, religiously inspired political advocates pursue what they perceive to be God's interests.

The state of Texas provides an interesting environment in which to pursue God's interests. In a socioeconomic and demographic sense, it is extraordinarily diverse. In a religious sense, it is dominated by Protestant religious traditionalism, though there is a substantial Catholic population. In an ideological sense, it has been a bastion of conservatism, regardless of partisanship. Finally, as any Texan will attest, it is a state unto itself, not quite South, not quite Southwest. Rather, it has the unique experience among states of having been its own republic, with its own founders and its own founding myth. There can be little doubt that this distinctive history has produced a level of individualism—and, to a certain extent, provincialism—that characterizes the culture of Texas even today.

Though not unfailing in its dominance, the Christian Right, as the standard-bearer of religious traditionalism, plays an influential role in Texas politics.

Christian Right groups have pursued enviable elector strategies, working diligently to stake a foothold in the Republican Party and elect fellow travelers to state office. Accordingly, they tend not to "wine and dine" legislators in the traditional manner. Having elected equally committed religious conservatives, the production of favorable public policy is a problem that solves itself. To the extent that they do engage in direct lobbying, many groups use volunteers that rotate through Austin since they do not need and are suspicious of professional "hired guns." That said, the sheer dominance of conservatives in the state provides an environment in which the pro-business and religiously oriented wings of the conservative movement come into conflict with one another. Religious conservatives, then, work diligently to educate constituents so that they apply pressure on legislators.

Religious conservatives face competition for influence in the public space, and the Catholic Church provides a distinctive alternative voice. By their own account, the Christian Right and the Catholic Church both pursue pro-family policies. However, the Catholic Church espouses a broader interpretation of that concept that leads it to support an expansive social welfare agenda. This puts it at odds with Christian Right groups. Ultimately, when the conservative wings of the Republican Party are united, public policy in Texas is marked by religious traditionalism, much to the satisfaction of Christian Right advocacy groups. Catholic, mainline Protestant, and liberal religious groups also advocate for their own vision of "God's law," and to the extent that their agendas overlap with the Christian Right agenda, they meet success. This is sometimes the case for the Catholic Church on moral issues but not on social welfare issues, where the major religious traditions of the state agree to disagree.

## THE RELIGIOUS AND POLITICAL CONTEXT

As table 5.1 illustrates, Texas is a highly religious state. Texans, in the 2000 American National Elections Study, reported that religion is personally salient and that they engage in frequent religious practices. For example, 89 percent of Texas respondents indicated that religion is important to them, and 83.5 percent indicated that religion provides them with either "quite a bit" or "a great deal" of guidance. Almost 65 percent of Texas respondents indicated that they pray either "several times a day" or "once a day," compared to 54.3 percent of national respondents. While the national sample appears to slightly outpace the Texas sample in terms of weekly church attendance, 20.6 percent of Texas respondents reported almost weekly attendance, compared to 16.5 percent of national respondents. Similarly, 28.4 percent of Texas respondents

Table 5.1.  Religiosity in Texas and in the United States

|  | % Texas Respondents | % All Respondents |
|---|---|---|
| Church attendance |  |  |
| Every week | 35.3 | 38.5 |
| Almost every week | 20.6 | 16.5 |
| Once or twice a month | 28.4 | 21.7 |
| A few times per year | 15.7 | 22.6 |
| Never | 0 | 0.6 |
| Frequency of prayer |  |  |
| Several times a day | 36.8 | 31.8 |
| Once a day | 27.9 | 22.5 |
| A few times a week | 21.3 | 17.5 |
| Once a week or less | 8.8 | 15.9 |
| Never | 5.1 | 10.8 |
| Guidance from religion |  |  |
| A great deal | 52.9 | 50.0 |
| Quite a bit | 30.6 | 28.7 |
| Some | 16.5 | 21.3 |
| Importance of religion |  |  |
| Important | 89.0 | 76.3 |
| Not important | 11.0 | 23.7 |

Note: Data are taken from the 2000 American National Elections Study.

reported "once or twice a month" attendance, compared to 21.7 percent of the national sample.

Precise and reliable data on the size and distribution of religious communities in Texas are difficult to obtain, but research conducted by the Glenmary Research Center (Jones et al. 2002) provides some insight. Their work assesses the size of respective denominations by obtaining data from specific religious bodies regarding the size of their membership. Given that only established religious bodies are contacted and that different organizations have different criteria for counting members (Baptist churches, for example, count only baptized adults as members), the data are somewhat problematic. That said, their research provides an initial perspective on the religious mélange in Texas.

Two denominations dominate the religious landscape in Texas (see table 5.2): the Southern Baptist Convention (SBC), which is decidedly conservative in theological and political orientation, and the Catholic Church, which is a bit more bifurcated in its outlook. The largest is the Roman Catholic Church, which registers 37.7 percent of Texas adherents and 21 percent of the population overall. The SBC, at 30.4 percent of adherents, is the second-largest denomination in the state. The United Methodist Church follows, with 8.8 percent of Texas adherents. Other denominations follow distantly, with

**Table 5.2.    Predominant Religious Denominations in Texas**

| Denomination | % Texas Population | % Texas Adherents | Cultural Family |
|---|---|---|---|
| Roman Catholic | 21.0 | 37.7 | Individualistic |
| Southern Baptist Convention | 16.9 | 30.4 | Traditionalistic |
| United Methodist Church | 4.9 | 8.8 | Individualistic |
| Church of Christ | 1.8 | 3.3 | Traditionalistic |
| Assemblies of God | 1.1 | 2.0 | Traditionalistic |
| Presbyterian Church U.S.A. | 0.9 | 1.6 | Moralist |
| Episcopal Church | 0.9 | 1.5 | Individualist |
| Independent Charismatic | 0.8 | 1.4 | — |
| Latter-day Saints | 0.7 | 1.3 | Moralistic |
| Jewish (estimate) | 0.6 | 1.1 | Moralistic |
| Muslim (estimate) | 0.6 | 1.0 | — |
| Other | 5.3 | 9.9 | — |
| Total | 55.5 | 100.0 | — |

Note: Data are taken from Jones et al. (2002). Classifications are consistent with Morgan and Watson's (1991) revision of Elazar.

the remainder of Texas adherents affiliated, for the most part, with Protestant denominations. There are also small Jewish and Muslim populations. Notably, other research offers slightly different figures. Lamare, Polinard, and Wrinkle (2000), for example, suggest that 25 percent—not 21 percent—of Texans are Roman Catholic, while fully one-third of Texans are affiliated with the SBC. Almost another third are said to identify with some other Protestant denomination. However, missing from both of these assessments is a measure of the relative size of unaffiliated evangelical and charismatic churches. Many of these represent the "megachurches" that dot the Texas landscape, drawing large numbers of worshippers each Sunday.

Despite the challenges in obtaining a precise portrayal of the patterns of religious affiliation in Texas, we can say that the Roman Catholic Church and the SBC are the largest denominations. Beyond that, there are many other smaller Protestant mainline, fundamentalist, and evangelical denominations. It also deserves mention that there is a pronounced geographic religious divide in Texas that is not reflected in these data. Predominantly Roman Catholic counties are concentrated in south Texas along the Mexico border, while predominantly Baptist counties are concentrated in central Texas, moving north and east along the borders of Louisiana, Arkansas, and Oklahoma.

In a socioeconomic sense, Texas looks much like the rest of the country. As table 5.3 indicates, Texas is at or within striking distance of the rest of the country by socioeconomic measures. However, Texas does experience a higher level of racial diversity than the rest of the country. Non-Hispanic whites constitute 52 percent of the Texas population, compared to 69 percent

**Table 5.3. Demographic Overview of Texas**

|  | Texas | United States |
| --- | --- | --- |
| 2004 presidential vote |  |  |
|   Bush—Republican | 61% | 51% |
|   Kerry—Democrat | 38 | 48 |
|   Other | 1 | 1 |
| Racial composition |  |  |
|   White | 52 | 69 |
|   Black | 11 | 12 |
|   Asian | 3 | 4 |
|   Hispanic | 32 | 13 |
| Socioeconomics |  |  |
|   Median income | $39,927 | $41,994 |
|   White collar | 61% | 60% |
|   Blue collar | 25 | 25 |
|   Service industry | 15 | 15 |
|   College educated | 23 | 24 |
|   Rural | 17 | 21 |

Note: Demographic data taken from the 2000 U.S. Census.

of the U.S. population. Texas and U.S. black and Asian populations are about equivalent. However, the Hispanic population in Texas is more than double that in the rest of the country. Thirty-two percent of Texas is classified as Hispanic, compared to 13 percent of the U.S. population.

Regardless of the socioeconomic similarities between Texas and the rest of the country, the prevalence of religious denominations that embrace religious traditionalism produces a strong conservative bent to the political culture. This values-based conservatism is complemented by the profound hostility to government that dates back to the 1869 constitution. This fifth and penultimate constitution was ratified during Reconstruction and included certain provisions that were unpopular in Texas but required as a condition to reenter the Union. For example, it provided for universal male suffrage and created a strong central government. The governor under the 1869 constitution, Edmund Davis, was extraordinarily powerful. He was well paid, controlled the state police and voter registration, and had expansive appointment powers. Many viewed Davis, a Republican and former Union officer, as corrupt. He instituted compulsory education, appointed many friends to positions in government, and presided over an array of tax increases.

In the wake of Davis's tenure and as a reaction to the perceived corruption, Texans ratified their sixth and current 1876 constitution, which severely limited the powers of the political institutions. The governor's term of office under the new constitution was two years (this was later changed to four years by constitutional amendment), and the appointment powers of the office were limited. As a result, Texas has a plural executive. In an effort to limit cronyism and make the executive branch more responsive, many executive officers, such as the attorney general, the lieutenant governor, the comptroller, and the fifteen-member Board of Education, are independently elected. State judges, once appointed exclusively by the governor, are also elected in partisan elections under the current constitution.

The 1876 constitution also restricted the powers of the legislature. Arguably the most limiting aspect of the current constitution is that it takes power out of the hands of the legislature by requiring many substantive policy decisions to be made by constitutional amendment rather than statute. Since voters must ultimately approve proposed amendments, public input is ensured. The current Texas constitution has been amended more than 300 times. As is apparent from table 5.4, the bicameral Texas legislature is weakened in other significant ways. It can meet in regular session for only 140 days once every two years, and legislators earn $7,200 per year—this is a decidedly part-time, low-paying gig. However, the legislature does have full-time professional staff. As of 2000, there were 2,153 full-time equivalent staffers working for the legislature. In the house, 754 work in member offices and on committees, 554 work on the senate side in offices and committees, and the rest work for legislative support agencies (O'Connor et al. 2004). Finally, in an effort to curb spending, the constitution requires that the legislature pass balanced budgets. Thus, spending is limited by the revenue estimates of the independently elected comptroller. Yet even though the legislature is hamstrung to a certain extent by the constitution, it still appropriates billions of dollars. For the 2004–2005 bi-

**Table 5.4.  Characteristics of the Texas Legislature, Seventy-Eighth Session (2003–2004)**

|  | *House* | *Senate* |
|---|---|---|
| Constitutional characteristics |  |  |
| Chamber size | 150 members | 31 members |
| Pay | $7,200 per year | $7,200 per year |
| Term of office | 2 years, no term limits | 4 years, no term limits |
| Partisan breakdown |  |  |
| Republicans | 88 | 19 |
| Democrats | 62 | 12 |
| Racial demographics |  |  |
| White | 105 | 22 |
| Hispanic | 30 | 7 |
| Asian | 1 | 0 |
| Black | 14 | 2 |
| Gender breakdown |  |  |
| Men | 118 | 27 |
| Women | 32 | 4 |

ennium, the Legislative Budget Board (2003) recommended baseline appropriations of $126.6 billion.

Given the conservative tenor of Texas' political culture, it comes as no surprise that Texas is strongly Republican. It went for former Texas Governor George W. Bush with 59 percent of the vote in 2000 and 61 percent of the vote in 2004. What is surprising is that Texas has a long tradition of Democratic dominance, albeit *conservative* (or "Blue Dog") Democratic dominance. Bush was only the second Republican governor, and he was the first Republican governor to be reelected to a second term since Reconstruction. In the seventy-eighth session (2003–2004) of the Texas legislature, Republicans controlled both chambers. But until Republicans captured the senate in 1996, they had not secured a majority in either chamber since 1870. Republicans have kept the senate in subsequent elections, and in 2002 they took the house, giving the party unified control of the legislature and governorship.

Given the political and social landscape of the state, a moralistic political culture, as identified by Elazar (1966), never took root in Texas. Elazar identified three distinct political cultures in the United States: traditionalistic, individualistic, and moralistic. The moralistic culture, rooted in Puritanism, views society in an organic fashion and embraces government as a force for achieving the common good. Elazar identified Texas as largely traditionalistic. The traditionalistic culture supports an active government but in support of an established political order. Thus, power tends to be concentrated in the hands of a few elites. This culture originally took root in the South, as European settlers sought to re-create the feudal system. The individualistic culture is more entrepreneurial in spirit. It embraces limited government and individual achievement through competition in the marketplace. As the new middle class fled Europe to escape the feudal limits on upward mobility and merit-based achievement, many settled in the mid-Atlantic and established communities consistent with this ethic.

Subsequent analysis classifies religious denominations using Elazar's tripartite model and measures culture as a function of denominational presence. Using that technique, Johnson (1976) reclassifies Texas as individualistic. Morgan and Watson (1991) show a decidedly mixed pattern in Texas, with 54 percent of the population classified individualistic, 42 percent traditionalistic, and only 5 percent moralistic. With westward migration, both traditionalists and individualists took root in Texas, and the influence of both cultural groups is still apparent. Texans support small government and free-market individualism and are hostile to taxation and environmental regulation. At the same time, Texas politics has historically been heavily influenced by a handful of elite families and industries. Moreover, many Texans seem to embrace the idea that government can be appropriately used to legitimate and spread traditional religious values.

There is another cultural dynamic that plays out within the largely Catholic Tejano community, predominant in south Texas. These Texans support a conservative moral agenda, as do their brethren in the SBC and other conservative churches, but they also support a progressive social welfare agenda. This joining of a moralistic social welfare agenda and a traditionalistic moral agenda reflects the changes that took place in the Catholic Church in the mid-twentieth century. For many years, the Catholic Church in the United States provided a consistently conservative voice to the political landscape. But the Second Vatican Council (1962–1965), called by Pope John XXIII, called for Catholics to "apply their Christian values to the problems of the world" (Wald 2003, 252). In the years to come, that would include poverty, nuclear proliferation, the status of the Third World, social justice, and civil rights. Gradually, the Catholic voice took an active role championing an array of progressive causes.

## GOD'S ADVOCATES

While they may shy away from the "wine and dine" approach to lobbying, the major religious communities in the state are all associated with important organized political interest groups that play active roles in the political life of the state. As the seventy-eighth session of the legislature got under way in 2003, religious advocates were preparing "to address issues ranging from health care to criminal justice reform" (Flynn 2003, B1). The Catholic Church, mainline Protestant denominations, liberal religious groups, and Christian Right organizations all participate in this effort. And while Catholic Church and mainline Protestant organizations are quite visible in Texas politics, Christian Right groups eclipse their impact and activities.

### The Christian Right

A number of Christian Right organizations stand out as the most high profile and influential in Texas. Texas Right to Life is one of an array of single-issue interest groups that lobby the state legislature on abortion-related issues. The organization is affiliated with the National Right to Life Committee, which was founded in 1973 in the wake of the *Roe v. Wade* decision. While National Right to Life characterizes itself as a nonsectarian group that exists to secure legal rights for the unborn, it is clearly guided by religious principles. Texas Eagle Forum is an affiliate of Eagle Forum, a national organization founded by Phyllis Schlafly in 1972. Eagle Forum was an early and effective opponent of the Equal Rights Amendment and currently advocates at all levels of government for a "pro-family" agenda. Among the various conservative Christian groups in Texas, the Eagle Forum is one of the most conservative. Their leaders are highly active and influential in GOP politics.

The American Family Association of Texas is an affiliate of the American Family Association, which was founded in 1977 by United Methodist Minister Don Wildmon. According to its mission statement, "The American Family Association exists to motivate and equip citizens to change the culture to reflect Biblical truth." By its own description, the American Family Association promotes a "pro-family" agenda and is particularly concerned about the effect of the media on society. Texas Christian Coalition is an affiliate of Christian Coalition of America, founded by Pat Robertson in 1989 to promote a "pro-family" agenda and facilitate political participation and influence on the part of Christians who embrace traditional values. Richard Ford founded Heritage Alliance in 1985 to empower those who embrace Judeo-Christian values. The Christian Life Commission is an organ of the Baptist General Convention of Texas that advocates on an array of issues and facilitates activism among Baptists.

As discussed at various points in this chapter, the power and visibility of Christian Right groups derive less from their status as powerful interests who can easily bend the ear of legislators than from their effective capturing of key positions of power in important Texas political institutions. In the early 1990s, by exerting influence on local-level party meetings and organizations, conservative Christians were able to dominate the state Republican Convention and claim most of the high-ranking positions in the party. This has given them some leverage over the party and its elected representatives. Beyond this, conservative Christians have effectively organized, recruited, and funded candidates for state (and local) elected offices and provided support by mobilizing grassroots supporters and distributing voter guides. The frequent target of these efforts has been moderate Republicans. With successes in these contests, the Christian Right agenda obtains important voices and promoters within the corridors of power.

## Catholics, Mainlines, and Jews

Other religious groups compete for influence in the public space. The Texas Catholic Conference was founded in 1963 to facilitate communication and coordination between the fifteen Roman Catholic dioceses of the state of Texas. It lobbies the legislature on issues that concern the Church. While the Conference echoes the concern of the Texas bishops on abortion, it does not have a singular focus. Poverty, health care, and the death penalty, the latter of which is uniquely significant in Texas, are also important components of the Conference's advocacy agenda. Importantly, its focus on social welfare issues and life issues places the Texas Catholic Conference in a position of simultaneous cooperation and conflict with the Christian Right.

A group of religious leaders founded Texas Impact in 1973 in the wake of a state political scandal. Currently, the group derives its support mainly from mainline and liberal Protestant and Jewish organizations. Its main area of advocacy is directed toward progressive social welfare policies. According to its mission statement, the organization works to "provide a presence of religious social concern to the Texas Legislature . . . on behalf of the poor, the disadvantaged, and victims of discrimination" (www.texasimpact.org). Cecile Richards, daughter of former Texas Governor Ann Richards, founded the Texas Freedom Network in 1995 as a counterweight to the influence of the Christian Right and advocates for "commonsense, mainstream values." The Jewish Federation of Greater Houston is a chapter of the Jewish Federation system. The Houston chapter is the largest in Texas and was founded in 1936 to facilitate philanthropic activities and promote social welfare in the Jewish community. It lobbies the state legislature on issues ranging from education to elder care.

## The Impetus to Witness

The advocates interviewed for this chapter indicate that lobbying is a form of religious mission. They do it out of sense of religious obligation and persevere in the face of defeat (or incremental progress) "because of a higher calling" (Flynn 2003, B1). Suzii Paynter of the Christian Life Commission characterizes her lobby work as her "calling." She seeks "God's will in her personal life" (interview with Calfano, August 6, 2004). Cathie Adams of Texas Eagle Forum states that she "felt a sense of mission" to become involved in her current efforts (interview with Calfano, July 29, 2004). Her mission began during a presentation by a local crisis pregnancy center in Sunday school class. Adams joined their organization and eventually became director. It was in that capacity that she met Phyllis Schlafly, who invited Adams to head Eagle's Texas chapter, a position she has held for eleven years.

Mike Hannesschlager of the Texas Christian Coalition makes a similar connection between personal faith and religious advocacy. He became a "born-again" Christian in 1996 and went to work in Tom DeLay's district office later that year. Hannesschlager wanted a career in politics even "before God saved" him. The difference between now and his pre-Christian days is his sense of political mission: "God is giving me a real overriding concern for our culture and seeing it match up with His values. I have a zeal for right-eousness." Hannesschlager makes a direct connection between the work of the Texas Christian Coalition and the Bible. In conversation, he repeatedly refers to the "biblical principles of government" and offers, "I love when you open up the Bible and see truth. God has ordained three important institu-tions: church, family, and civil government. But the bigger the government gets, the worse it becomes" (interview with Calfano, July 28, 2004).

Lee Wunsch of the Jewish Federation found that his sense of mission was animated by politics when he became concerned about the status of Israel. He became "emotionally connected" to what he calls the "state issue." Personally, the status of Israel is his priority, though the provision of social services for the larger Jewish community—in Israel and among the Diaspora—is profoundly important to the Federation. Wunsch argues that a lobbyist could not engage in religiously animated advocacy effectively without being "connected to faith and the emotion of the issues." Thus, he does not favor so-called hired guns, professional lobbyists who are nonbelievers, because he does not think they would be effective (interview with Calfano, August 7, 2004).

Many echo this skepticism of hired guns. Adams points out that her work is based completely on her faith. When asked if one could work in her posi-tion if one's faith were in a different religion or nonexistent, she responds that she would be "suspicious" of such people. For Adams, a personal, Christian faith instills a sense of "selflessness" in the advocate. Such selflessness is necessary to further one's agenda in the political realm: "Good candidates need help." Hannesschlager believes that if the advocacy is not done by be-lievers, "God's not going to bless it." Part of his reasoning is based on the as-sertion that non-Christians put government in the place of God as the "Savior of mankind" (interviews with Calfano, July 28–29, 2004).

Emick agrees that her faith is central to her work: "God is our source; we are working on his terms." Ford of Heritage Alliance concedes that nonbe-lievers *could* be lobbyists but that he would never use them because lobbyists "have to live what they advocate." However, taking a more pragmatic ap-proach to religious advocacy, Brother Richard Daly of the Texas Catholic Conference concedes that hired guns could be used for specific purposes if they have a particular expertise required in a specific lobbying situation (in-terviews with Calfano, July 20, August 6, and August 20, 2004).

## THE AGENDA

All these religious advocates lobby the legislature on an array of issues. Abor-tion and gay issues appear central to the religious advocacy agenda of the conservative Right. However, there are many other issues that do not get the same level of sensational coverage but obtain considerable attention from both conservative and liberal religious advocacy groups.

## Abortion and Life Issues

Abortion has been the focus of a number of conservative Christian groups with broad agendas (Texas Christian Coalition, Texas Eagle Forum, and American Family Association) as well as those mobilized around that specific issue (Texans United for Life, Texas Right to Life, and the Austin-based Texas Alliance for Life). In 1992, the prospects for significant changes in state-level abortion policies increased with the U.S. Supreme Court's decision in *Planned Parenthood v. Casey*, which more clearly defined the restrictions that states could place on abortion. With the inauguration of a Republican governor (albeit a moderate one) in 1994, hopes increased among these groups that state policy would come to reflect their pro-life agenda.

The seventy-fourth legislative session (1995–1996) witnessed the reintroduction of a parental notification bill (a similar measure had died in committee during the seventy-third session in 1993). The measure represented the first effort to restrict access to abortion in the state since the 1973 *Roe v. Wade* decision. Texans United for Life, headed by Pastor Bill Price, and other groups offered vocal support for the measure. Yet the bill ultimately died in the senate, falling short of the three votes needed to halt the efforts of several Democratic senators seeking to block its passage. Although Christian conservatives controlled the Republican Party and counted many state legislators among their ranks, both the Texas senate and house of representatives remained in the hands of Democrats, and this stymied their efforts. In the wake of the defeat, Price and others redoubled their efforts to bring abortion to the forefront of the Texas public policy agenda. A highly visible campaign in 1996, for instance, sought to force Texas delegates to the Republican National Convention (including Senator Kay Bailey Hutchinson and Governor George W. Bush) to sign an antiabortion pledge.

As control of the Texas senate went to the GOP in 1996, the stage was set for significant pro-life legislative victories. Yet the seventy-fifth session (1997–1998) yielded mixed results for pro-life groups. On the one hand, Christian conservatives won passage of three key pieces of legislation: (1) a bill requiring parental notification before a minor could receive birth control pills or treatment for sexually transmitted diseases, (2) a conscience clause in larger bill giving HMOs with religious affiliations the option of refusing to provide reproductive services that conflict with their religious beliefs, and (3) restrictions on the flow of state-apportioned family planning funds to family planning organizations that offer abortions. On the other hand, despite their vocal support for the measure, the parental notification bill (by far the most important for these groups) again failed to pass in the wake of technical maneuvering by the bill's opponents. While the former measures were seen as victories by abortion foes, in the words of one activist, they did not "make up for the disappointment over the loss of the notification bill" (Lenhart 1997).

The seventy-sixth session (1999–2000) saw the reintroduction of the bill (once again), generating significant public efforts by antiabortion groups. These included major public rallies by abortion foes, including the Texas Christian Coalition and Texans United for Life. When passage of the bill seemed questionable, activists indicated that they would demand a special session from Governor Bush to ensure its success. The eventual passage of the bill represented the first major success for antiabortion groups, and more would follow with the increasing shift in power in the state to more conservative political forces.

A major watershed in this process was the 2002 election that gave Republicans control of the house, placing the legislature firmly in their command. As one Austin reporter put it in the wake of these elections, "Groups that oppose abortion right now have friends in very high places in the legislative process and think that 2003 might be their year at the Texas Capitol" (Herman 2002, A1).

Abortion opponents introduced and won passage for two significant bills during the seventy-eighth session (2003–2004), both of which had failed in legislative wrangles two years earlier. The first of these was the Prenatal Protection Act, which defined an embryo or fetus as an "individual" and allowed for the prosecution of a person who harms or kills it. While not specifically directed toward the abortion issue, the new law carried obvious symbolic significance in the abortion debate. The second was the Woman's Right to Know Act, which required that women seeking an abortion wait twenty-four hours and receive, among other things, printed material and photographs about fetal development, information about child care services in the state of Texas, and information about potential health risks associated with abortion procedures. One liberal interest group, Texas Freedom Network, describes Representative Frank Corte (R), the bill's sponsor, as one of the most hard-line religious Right representatives in the legislature (www.tfn.org). The American Family Association of Texas, the Texas Eagle Forum, Texas Right to Life, and the Texas Christian Coalition have all honored him.

Not to be overlooked in the antiabortion lobbying effort is the Texas Catholic Conference. As Brother Daly relates, abortion is arguably the most important political concern facing the Church (interview with Calfano, August 20, 2004). While Catholic efforts on abortion and reproductive policy comport with the efforts of conservative Protestant groups, their activism on this issue appears to be overshadowed by these groups. As said, what sets the Catholic Conference apart from its "pro-family" compatriots is its focus on a wider array of social policy and social justice issues, all of which fall under the "pro-family" rubric, as far as the Catholic Church is concerned. These issues are in conflict with the limited-government preferences articulated by Ford, Hannesschalger, and Adams. Interestingly, Texas is a contemporary battleground among social conservatives regarding the scope of the "pro-life," "pro-family" agenda. It is an internecine conflict that prompted former Christian Coalition maestro Ralph Reed (1994) to opine, "If the . . . pro-family movement forwards a limited agenda that only addresses one or two issues, we will not succeed" (232). Whether and how social conservatives in Texas can find consensus on the direction and breadth of their issue menu remains to be seen.

Perhaps as a sign of more cracks in the conservative alliance, the conservative Christian agenda with respect to abortion has brought some groups into conflict with other political conservatives working for tort reform in the state. In the current context, tort reform refers to capping the damages that are awarded in civil verdicts. Conservatives generally support tort reform because high jury awards are thought to encourage frivolous lawsuits, increase the cost of medical care, and drive some doctors away from certain practice areas, such as obstetrics. Social conservatives have tended to stand with the business community on this issue. However, some abortion opponents strongly oppose tort reform. The argument is that "physicians who don't perform abortions now because of malpractice liability might consider the procedure profitable if the damages were limited" (Williams 2003).

A tort reform campaign has been brewing in Texas for years. In 2003, the Texas house passed a tort reform bill, H.B. 4, that capped medical malpractice awards. David Welch, former director of the Christian Coalition, conceded that while the bill was good for the business community, it does not "fit with God's law" and it is not "pro-family." Cathie Adams agreed, stating, "People should have the right to go after those doctors that do a bad job" (interview with Calfano, July 29, 2004). Some social conservatives suggested that the legislation discriminated against stay-at-home mothers because under the bill, "mothers who work outside the home and prevail in malpractice suits could get awards" for lost wages that would be unavailable to homemakers (Williams 2003). After the house passed H.B. 4, the chamber proposed a constitutional amendment in order that the law would not be subject to judicial scrutiny. The proposed amendment passed by a very narrow margin in September 2003 over the considerable opposition of groups such as Texas Eagle Forum (Guerra 2003).

## Gay Issues

In addition to abortion, several groups with close connections to the Texas GOP, most notably the Texas Eagle Forum, the American Family Association, and the Christian Coalition, have taken very visible and assertive stances on issues related to gay and lesbian rights and protections. Efforts to promote such rights and protections have been a primary catalyst for such groups to engage the political process and mobilize followers to political activism. In 1994, for example, after the City of Austin initiated a policy offering domestic partner benefits to city employees, conservative Christian groups (including the Christian Coalition) initiated and successfully passed a proposition in city elections to repeal those benefits.

Since that time, efforts in the Texas legislature to address gay rights have elicited similar responses. Hate-crime legislation that included language regarding sexual orientation was considered by the legislature in both the 1995 and the 1999 session and actually passed several legislative hurdles (including a house vote in 1999) before dying in committee. Members of the Texas Eagle Forum and the American Family Association provided some of the loudest voices opposing the measure in public testimony on the bills. "This law would make name-calling a crime," claimed Loralei Gilliam, who spoke on behalf of the American Family Association (Griest 1999, B10). When a similar bill came before the legislature in 2001, these groups again rallied in opposition. "The hate crimes law," argued Adams of the Eagle Forum, "polarizes and divides our citizens and places our most precious liberties—the freedom to think and believe as we will—at risk" (Robison 2001, A30). When the bill passed the legislature and went to Governor Rick Perry's desk for signature, both the Eagle Forum and the Christian Coalition mounted a major effort to mobilize their followers to contact the governor to encourage him to veto it. Despite being flooded with calls and e-mails and despite his open opposition to the clauses including protections for homosexuals, the governor ultimately appended his signature. Conservative groups predicted that this would dampen enthusiasm for Perry in the next election. Nevertheless, Governor Perry was elected to a full term in 2002 with 58 percent of the vote.

## Education

Education has also been a focal point of Christian conservative activism. But in addition to efforts to influence the legislature, conservative groups have targeted other arenas, such as the Texas Board of Education. The board, consisting of fifteen elected members, shares responsibility over public education with the Texas Education Agency, headed by an executive appointee. Along with other conservative groups, the Eagle Forum has been very active in supporting Christian conservatives to run against moderate Republicans for the board. The strategy of targeting the board makes absolute sense given its central role in deciding key issues such as textbooks and the content of health and sex education programs. More fundamentally, elections to the board offer a viable means of placing Christian conservatives in positions of authority. As part of this electioneering strategy, moderate Republicans who have backed the "wrong" textbooks have been targeted for removal, as conservative groups have vetted and recruited candidates for the board and helped them locate sources of funding from powerful conservative political action committees and individuals in the state (Brooks 1996).

Beyond this, the Texas Eagle Forum has engaged in open advocacy to advance its educational agenda. For example, the Forum led efforts to open up proposed curriculum changes to greater public scrutiny and commentary. These kinds of efforts allowed the Forum to influence debates on education and the actual content of textbooks. Reflecting this, in 2002, publishers of textbooks revised book contents to meet the concerns of conservative groups and Board of Education members who claimed that the books contained factual errors. Liberals critiqued the changes claiming that the revisions "promote Christianity, attack Islam and distort the teaching of science and slavery." Defending the changes, board member David Bradley, part of the social conservative bloc on the board, proffered, "Promoting Christianity? That's a crime?" and "America was founded on Christian principles" (Hood 2002, 5B).

Liberal groups claim that textbook publishers now exercise a form of self-censorship as they develop books for review by the Texas Board of Education. The board held hearings to consider new high school health textbooks in 2004, for example. Of the four books submitted by publishers for consideration, only one mentioned condoms. This is part and parcel of "abstinence-only" sex education, of which Christian conservatives have been primary advocates (Elliott 2004). But the mainline and liberal groups do speak out on this issue. Samantha Smoot of Texas Freedom Network strongly opposed the abstinence-only health texts: "I happen to believe that the single most important piece of information a teenager should take from their health class is that if they are going to be sexually active, at any age, they should use a condom every time" (Castro 2004).

Their efforts and agenda with respect to education in the 1990s sometimes put conservative groups in opposition to moderate Republicans and even other conservative activists. For example, during the 1990s, then-Governor George W. Bush sought to reform the Texas education system, implementing changes that are today at the center of national education debates. These included testing and higher standards for students and experimentation with voucher programs. While many conservatives supported the voucher proposals and the push for standards, Bush's proposals brought the ire of the Eagle

Forum. In their view, standards remained too low, and the voucher program represented an intrusion on the integrity of private schools (Brooks 1998, A1; Gamino 1997, B5). According to Adams, voucher programs constitute "a backdoor approach to control every private school in Texas. Vouchers are coupons for control" (Stitz 1998, quoted in Lamare et al. 2000, 53).

Beyond this, some took issue with Bush's adoption of some of then-President Clinton's Goals 2000 education program and accused him of expanding the state education bureaucracy by promoting summer reading programs (Ratcliffe 1999). Other efforts promoted by Texas Republicans in the senate to expand the range of subjects for testing were also criticized. The key issue for the Eagle Forum was that these kinds of steps appeared to expand the control of the executive and bureaucratic agencies over education at the expense of the elected Board of Education and local elected officials. Unlike the issue of abortion, however, the Forum was less successful in mobilizing citizens for public pressure on the legislature and the executive. Indeed, a public march planned in 1997 in opposition to Bush's education initiatives fizzled because of a lack of public participation (Brooks 1997a).

Liberal and mainline groups such as Texas Freedom Network have offered vocal opposition to the Christian Right in the area of education policy. In addition to health education, Freedom Network opposed the Christian Right effort to remove or water down language related to evolution in textbooks. In a 2003 vote, the Board of Education voted 11 to 4 to adopt eleven new biology textbooks that present the theory of evolution. Religious conservatives were disappointed, but so too was Texas Freedom Network because the language in the textbooks had been changed to appease religious conservatives. Smoot notes, "There was a disturbing pattern of changes. . . . In a few of the books there were semantic changes here and there that created a pattern of questioning the theory of evolution." Publishers are forced to make these changes because Texas is such a large consumer market. In 2003, for example, "publishers responded to criticism of history books by changing references to the Ice Age and other events occurring 'millions of years ago' to read 'in the distant past'" in order that scientific time lines would not seem to contradict biblical time lines (Elliott 2003).

Freedom Network also opposes voucher programs, and this is an area where Freedom Network and the Catholic Conference part ways. In 1999, the Conference was highly supportive of a voucher pilot program. Brother Daly likened voucher spending to the GI Bill of two generations ago (Staff 1999). Governor Perry called a special session of the legislature in April 2004 to consider education funding and expressed his hope that a voucher/school choice bill would emerge for his signature. This was a measure that Freedom Network strongly opposed, and ultimately the legislature did not approve such a program (Shannon 2004). The legislature has flirted with voucher programs many times over the past decade, and these programs are consistent with the agendas of groups, like Heritage Alliance, that embrace the ethic of smaller government. At each stage, Freedom Network opposed such programs as it did in 2004.

## Gambling

Religious groups have also fought gambling in Texas. Proposals for casino and riverboat gambling, for instance, raised considerable opposition in the mid-1990s, generating a nearly united front among religious advocacy groups. As Weston Ware of Christian Life Commission noted at the time, "Many denominations will join together in a strong coalition to prevent passage of any constitutional amendment in the House or Senate" (Vara 1994, 1). Yet while opposition to gambling united many denominations, their reasons for opposing gambling are markedly different. Many Christian conservatives view gambling as immoral prima facie because it "sets up Lady Luck as your god" and encourages covetous impulses (Vara 1994, 1).

According to Brother Daly, the Catholic Church does not "view gambling as immoral per se" but opposes gambling to the extent that it produces destructive outcomes for families and individuals (Vara 1994, 1). Presumably, if one is not gambling with the milk money, the Church has no problem with the activity. That said, the Texas Catholic bishops issued a statement in 1995 opposing casino gambling because of the problems it creates for families that struggle to meet financial responsibilities. Moreover, the bishops suggested that the effort to bring gambling to Texas was an unjust and inequitable way to raise state revenues (Staff 1995, 3). Mainline and liberal organizations echo this sentiment and oppose gambling because they view it as a regressive tax on the poor. Sue Thornton of Texas Impact notes that her organization is far more likely to oppose gambling on "social and economic grounds" than moral grounds (Vara 1994, 1).

While religious groups have been successful in pushing back efforts to bring casino and riverboat gambling to Texas, more recently the state has grappled with the issue of slot machine gambling. While Governor Perry stated his opposition to casino gambling, he has promoted slots as a way to fund education and make up for budget shortfalls. Both Adams of the Eagle Forum and Hannesschlager of the Christian Coalition list the defeat of slot machine gambling legislation as one of their organizations' primary goals. Hannesschlager encouraged the Coalition's grassroots to contact their legislators to express opposition and added, "God willing, we will head this thing off." Christian Life Commission opposes the new measure and argues that while gambling is always tied to something good—such as education—it generally hurts the poor. What is more, the Christian Life Commission expresses concern that it could one day open the door to casino gambling (Parker 2004, 5B).

The governor's plan to expand gambling in Texas has again been a source for unity among liberal and conservative religious activists. Texas Eagle Forum, Texas Catholic Conference, Texas Impact, and the Christian Life Commission all express opposition to the governor's plan. Their hostility finds many fellow travelers in the legislature. In order to get the required constitutional amendment on the ballot for voter consideration, the governor would first have to get it through the house and senate. At this point, he does not appear to have the votes (Garcia 2004). Thus, while voters have traditionally approved of gambling, as they did when Texas instituted a lottery, an expansion in gambling may not make it through the institutional hoops, much to the pleasure of religious advocacy groups.

## Capital Punishment

The Catholic Church has been by far the most vocal opponent of the death penalty in Texas, and, indeed, Brother Daly of the Texas Catholic Conference identifies capital punishment among the key issues for the organization. Many of the Church's efforts regarding the issue have involved issuing public statements that raise questions about the practice. In 1997, the Texas Catholic bishops issued a statement opposing capital punishment, making the argument that it had been ineffective as a crime-fighting technique, that innocent people were occasionally convicted of capital crimes, and that it does not comfort victims' families. What is more, the bishops intimated that there is a racially informed pattern to capital convictions (Parker 1997, 8A). More recently, in the wake of former Illinois Governor George Ryan's institution of a death penalty moratorium, the bishops asked then-Governor Bush to halt executions in Texas and review the criminal justice system (Perkes 2000, B9).

The Church has also channeled its energies toward the legislature. In 2001, the legislature considered—and the Catholic Conference and Texas Impact vocally supported—a bill that would have placed a moratorium on the death penalty. In 2003, the Catholic Conference also supported legislation that would have prohibited the death penalty for minors and another bill that would have allowed juries in Texas the option of a "life without parole" sentence for defendants convicted of capital murder. Currently in Texas, the life sentence comes with the possibility of parole. Some believe this makes juries less willing to give that sentence. In all these instances, perhaps reflecting the extent of public support for capital punishment in the state, efforts to curb the death penalty failed.

## Health and Human Welfare

While some religious advocates are skeptical of government efforts to secure social welfare, groups such as Texas Impact and the Catholic Conference embrace an agenda that includes government activism in this area. Brother Daly indicates that this is among the priorities of the Catholic Conference, and Impact has worked for decades to convince legislators to open the state's purse strings for child health care, welfare, and education. In particular, Impact has been critical of the legislature's willingness to spend on prisons while giving children short shrift (McNeely 1995, A15). In 2003, Impact criticized the legislature for cutting social welfare programs, such as Medicaid benefits for children and the elderly, in an effort to cope with a budget crisis. Says Ben Moorhead, Impact's executive director, "It's the very first time the Republican Party has been in full control of Texas government, and their very first act is to decimate programs that reflect decades of bipartisan negotiation" (Selby 2003, 10A).

Conservative groups have also staked positions on social welfare issues, albeit from a different angle than their Catholic and mainline counterparts. Opposition to health coverage for uninsured Texas children has been a priority for many conservative religious advocacy groups in Texas, such as the Eagle Forum, Christian Coalition, and Heritage Alliance. Their position reflects a more general conservative opposition to "big government." Perhaps as a consequence, they tend not to characterize their opposition in theological terms. Hannesschlager, for example, comments, "I don't think that the government should be the source of social welfare." Similarly, Ford of the Heritage Alliance (a driving force behind the successful opposition to a state income tax in the mid-1980s) simply states, "The government has to watch what it spends on social programs" (interviews with Calfano, July 28 and August 3, 2004). However, the Christian Life Commission, the public policy and lobbying arm of the Baptist General Convention of Texas and a religiously conservative group, is strongly committed to health care accessibility.

## STRATEGIES AND SUBJECTIVE SUCCESSES

In their efforts to influence public policy in Texas, conservative Protestant groups have been very skilled at working within the Republican Party, as we have said. By attending precinct meetings, they have been able to select delegates to the state's party convention, write the platform, and structure the direction of the party. They have also been able to get like-minded candidates elected to office in the legislative and executive branches. Eventually, this made direct lobbying efforts quite simple. For example, Christian conservative groups such as the American Family Association consider their ability to get the Board of Education to divest stock in the Walt Disney Company—after the company extended benefits to the same-sex partners of employees—one of their biggest direct lobbying victories in the 1990s (Lamare et al. 2000, 50).

However, many of the religious advocates we interviewed indicated that educating constituents and legislators is at the heart of their strategy. The goal of Suzii Paynter's (Christian Life Commission) educational activism is to get Baptists and other Christians to consider issues such as gay marriage, abortion, education, and criminal justice "with a theological filter." To the extent that they do work directly with legislators, Paynter explains that "a part of our ministry . . . is to be the salt and light to our legislators." If they have educated people, they have done their job. But practically speaking, Paynter soberly acknowledges that success is also measured by "getting the right language in a bill" (interview with Calfano, August 6, 2004).

Adams also emphasizes an educational mission but notes that Texas Eagle Forum, like the national organization, exists more as a think tank rather than a mobilization group aimed at grassroots activity. They may not organize grassroots activism, but they do educate the grassroots. The Forum publishes legislative scorecards that cover between fifteen and thirty policy items. Recent scorecards have emphasized issues ranging from tax policy to immigration to the standard "pro-life, pro-family" issues. Eagle Forum also works directly with legislators, but it does not have lobbyists on payroll and does not have a budget to support "wining and dining." Instead, it uses volunteers who rent an apartment in Austin and rotate responsibilities. Notably, Texas Eagle Forum may not have the resources to support traditional lobbying activities given that a significant portion of its operational costs are subsidized by Adams's husband, according to Adams herself.

Adams tries to build advocacy coalitions and indicates that the organization works very hard to find Democrats to help with legislation. Indeed, she tries to position the Eagle Forum in both a collaborative and an educative posture relative to other conservative groups. The Forum works regularly with the Heritage Alliance, the American Family Association, Concerned Women for America, and the Texas Christian Coalition. The organization often takes a secondary, supportive role to lobbying efforts by these organizations. As do a number of her counterparts, Adams characterizes organizational success as turning on whether the Forum is "able to engage people and make them really think through the issues" (interview with Calfano, July 29, 2004).

Like Texas Eagle Forum, Heritage Alliance functions much like an educational think tank, according to Ford. They do not lobby in the traditional "wine and dine" sense and instead try to "inform, educate, and engage the constituents." That last point is particularly important. Ford focuses on constituents, not legislators, in an effort to bring constituent pressure to bear on legislators. Part of his strategy, then, is to provide financial support to the campaigns of fellow travelers and defeat opponents that "get out of line." As such, he currently targets many swing districts.

Emick of Texas Right to Life characterizes their educative mission as an effort to "teach people, to empower them to activate their passion" on life issues. They send out regular e-mails to members, hold seminars, use direct mail, identify important legislation, and issue voter guides and legislator scorecards. Unlike Heritage Alliance and Texas Eagle Forum, Texas Right to Life places a great deal of emphasis on mobilizing the grassroots, or what Emick terms "the ground troops." In her estimation, these "troops" are mainly single-issue voters and ripe for mobilization. Emick and Texas Right to Life are practical in their approach to political witnessing and engage in direct lobby to complement their grassroots efforts. Their primary strategy is to create, build, and maintain quality working relationships with legislators on both sides of the aisle, to look for an "in" at every opportunity, and to move their agenda forward. Stagnation would produce personal devastation. Notes Emick, "I would die if there wasn't progress on the abortion issue." While her advocacy sometimes produces incremental results, by her own estimation, she does not get discouraged. Her organization's ultimate goal is "to end abortion," but her personal philosophy is that "if you're not happy with the way things are, then change it." This motivates her to carry on, even in the face of legislative setbacks. Thus, if her organization can foster relationships with legislators—relationships that might one day bear legislative fruit—she considers that progress (interview with Calfano, July 20, 2004).

The Jewish Federation sees itself as an educational conduit for the Jewish community. It promotes grassroots lobbying on the part of its members and galvanizes supporters with e-mail. In addition, volunteers occasionally travel to Austin to lobby legislators directly and at receptions. In addition to these efforts, the Federation tries to build lasting relations with Texas legislators by sponsoring trips to Israel. One might not necessarily think that Israel would be an important issue in Austin, but Wunsch notes that the Texas and Israeli economies are interrelated, especially in the high-tech sector (interviews with Calfano, August 3 and 7, 2004). In its effort to secure policy favorable toward Israel in the legislature, the Federation has developed "very strong relationships with several Christian Right groups." Indeed, one of the Federation's biggest financial contributors is a Christian Right group, though Wunsch declines to mention it by name. These groups support Israel in part because of their dispensational eschatology, a subject on which Wunsch has had to educate himself. On the Federation's larger social agenda, it simply "agree[s] to disagree" with its Christian Right supporters. Ultimately, Wunsch defines organizational success by its efforts to create new alliances, encourage Jewish grassroots activity, and produce favorable legislative outcomes. He notes that "in order to be successful, you have to be vigilant in your long-term outlook" (interview with Calfano, August 7, 2004).

Of all the broad-based, multi-issue, conservative organizations in Texas, the Christian Coalition is perhaps the most effective at using its grassroots membership to pressure legislators. Getting the word out to the roughly 200,000 members is achieved through several strategies, including e-mail, direct mail, and, perhaps unique to Hannesschlager and his professional relationships, the opportunity to use free airtime on Texas Christian radio stations to make direct appeals to sympathetic audiences. He feels these new media approaches are necessary as a way to get around the "liberal media." The Coalition is best known for its *Voter Guides*, which are distributed to churches and civic groups. Hannesschlager expected the distribution of one million guides for the 2004 elections. These efforts are supported by an annual operating budget that fluctuates between $100,000 and $300,000. And unlike the national Christian Coalition, whose tax exemption was revoked by the IRS, the Texas chapter is a 501(c)3 nonprofit.

However, Texas Christian Coalition also engages in direct lobbying efforts. In a departure from his compatriots, Hannesschlager offers names on the Coalition's "go to" list for legislation, including Senators Ken Armbrister (D), Jane Nelson (R), and Tommy Williams (R). That one of these senators is a Democrat speaks to the Coalition's desire to reach out to both parties. With its use of direct and grassroots lobbying and electioneering, Hannesschlager sees the Coalition and its allied groups as having "unprecedented clout" in the state and suggests that success for the Coalition is defined as serving according to God's calling. However, he concedes that he wants to also "see progress in a temporal sense" on issues such as taxes, gambling, education, abortion, and gay marriage (interview with Calfano, July 28, 2004).

According to Brother Daly, 40 to 50 percent of the Catholic Conference's work is focused on lobbying for favorable policy outcomes. The rest is devoted to educational work, social services, and ministerial programs. Daly is a registered lobbyist, but he does not attend or sponsor receptions, fundraisers, and dinners. While he attempts to build relationships with legislators and staff, their preferred lobbying tactic is to provide support to other organizations that share the goals of the Catholic Conference. Thus, the Conference works hard to coordinate with many other advocacy groups. Daly notes that he is "the only person who would meet with the civil liberties people in the morning and the pro-life people in the afternoon." Indeed,

Daly would work with anyone to further the Conference's goals, including Planned Parenthood, with whom he has worked on welfare issues.

Since the bishops set the goals of the Conference, Daly does not place a great deal of emphasis on grassroots-style lobbying. He suggests that this would be difficult given the sheer number of Catholics in the state. What is more, this reflects the institutionalized and hierarchical nature of Church organization, and it provides a point of departure from conservative and mainline Protestant groups. The Catholic effort is a top-down, inside-game approach, while these other groups engage in grassroots and electoral strategies. That said, the Conference does try to educate Catholics, especially parish leaders and program coordinators. It disseminates information by holding conferences, giving presentations, writing columns for Catholic newspapers, crafting legislative memos, and maintaining a Conference website.

Daly measures conference success in a pietistic manner: success is achieved "if we are articulating in the public square the salvific message of Jesus Christ, and if we are faithful to the teachings of the Messiah and the leadership of the Church" (interview with Calfano, August 20, 2004). Practically speaking, the successes and failures of the Catholic Conference vary by issue and depend on whether its preferred policy outcome comports with conservative Protestant preferences. In a very real sense, the successes and failures of conservative Protestant groups on abortion and gay issues are its successes and failures, too. However, given the conservative tenor of the state, the remainder of the Catholic Conference's pro-family/pro-life agenda has fallen on the rocks. It joins mainline Protestant groups in opposition to the death penalty and in support of government resources directed toward social spending, but its progress on these issues is limited. The preliminary success of the Catholic Conference and mainline advocacy groups on slot machine gambling is noteworthy, but arguably it would have been unattainable if conservative Protestant groups had not concurred.

## CONCLUSION

Religious interest groups play a very visible and certainly important role in the state of Texas. Yet it deserves reiteration that the most powerful and active of these groups are those that represent conservative Christians. While a precise measure of their influence is not possible, it is clear that they have realized success in a number of respects. They have promoted and aided the passage of major legislation restricting abortion rights. They have headed off efforts to bring gambling to the state. And they have realized success in shaping the content of educational material used in Texas public schools. To be sure, they have not won every contest in which they have engaged. Most notably, despite dramatic efforts, they failed to halt the passage and signing of hate-crimes legislation that included specific language regarding sexual orientation. On balance, however, they have done quite well in the state of Texas. With continued Republican domination of the state, they will likely continue to shape the content of public policy.

As we have detailed throughout this chapter, Christian Right groups employ a diverse array of tactics—working through the parties, campaigning for fellow travelers, direct lobbying, educating and mobilizing the grassroots, and coordinating with one another when possible—to advance their goals. The institutional and cultural context in which they operate has encouraged the embrace of these wide-ranging tactics and enabled their success. Christian Right educational messages often juxtapose their political views to liberal, secular, and counterculture agendas seeping into Texas from without. Such messages resonate quite strongly in a society where family and traditional institutions are celebrated and where a legacy of autonomy from national trends and politics remains in the collective consciousness. Moreover, as Todd (1999) argues, interest groups in general operate in a fairly favorable institutional climate in the state of Texas. Restrictions on their activities have historically been minimal. And the structure of Texas government offers groups such as Christian Right organizations a variety of channels to pursue their interests. A divided executive and the existence of numerous elected offices for positions in powerful institutions, such as the Board of Education and the judiciary, create a favorable political opportunity structure for such groups. It is no surprise that these groups have taken full advantage of this structure.

In the present context, both political trends and the state's institutional context portend the continued importance of such groups for Texas. Yet their successes may be less frequent in the future. While these groups have won a number of important victories, there may be limits to how much farther they can go in advancing their agenda. To date, key aspects of their agenda have resonated quite clearly with popular sentiments. Yet as they climb the ladder of ambition, they will no doubt chase more far-reaching and sometimes uncompromising goals. Whether these will run afoul of such sentiments remains an open question. And, as the fight over tort reform suggests, these goals might bring them into conflict with the pro-business wing of the conservative movement.

Finally, on abortion, federal case law constrains the effectiveness of Catholic and conservative Protestant advocates in the legislative arena. In the decades since the *Roe v. Wade* decision, the Supreme Court has permitted some state-level abortion restrictions (see *Webster v. Reproductive Health Services* [1989] and *Planned Parenthood v. Casey* [1992]) but struck down others (see *Stenberg v. Carhart* [2000]). Moreover, the ultimate goal of eliminating abortion seems unattainable in the current context, requiring ratification of a constitutional amendment or a Supreme Court reversal of *Roe.* On this and other issues, the efforts of religious advocates in Texas and elsewhere will either be constrained or facilitated by the federal bench.

## REFERENCES

Brooks, A. 1996. "Question of Who's True to the Cause Divides GOP." *Austin American-Statesman*, January 8, B1.

———. 1997a. "Education Board OKs New Curriculum." *Austin American-Statesman*, April 11, B8.

———. 1997b. "Lawmakers Want to Out TAAS to the Test." *Austin American-Statesman*, June 12, B1.

———. 1998. "Vouchers Worry Private Schools." *Austin American-Statesman*, December 29, A1.

Castro, April. 2004. "SBOE Takes Public Testimony on Adoption of Health Books." *Associated Press State & Local Wire*, July 14.

Elazar, Daniel J. 1966. *American Federalism: A View from the States.* New York: Cromwell.

Elliott, Janet. 2003. "Biology Book Battle Abates; Debate over Evolution Calms as 11 Texts Get Go-Ahead." *Houston Chronicle*, November 7, 29A.

———. 2004. "Critics Say Texts Ignore Information on Contraception." *Houston Chronicle*, June 29, 20.

Flynn, Eileen E. 2003. "For Some Religious Groups, Obligation Includes Lobbying." *Austin-American Statesman*, February 3, B1.

Gamino, Denise. 1997. "Curriculum Overhaul Battle Lines Solidifying." *Austin-American Statesman*, February 20, 1997, B5.

Garcia, Guillermo X. 2004. "Texas Governor's Electronic-Gaming Plans Fail to Gain Popular Support." *San Antonio Express-News*, April 23.

Griest, Stephanie Elizondo. 1999. "Hate Crimes Act Named for Byrd Heads for House." *Austin American-Statesman*, March 12, B10.

Guerra, Carlos. 2003. "The Voters Have Spoken, and There Were More Than Expected." *San Antonio Express-News,* September 14, 1B.

Herman, Ken. 2002. "Bill Sets Stage for Abortion Disputes." *Austin American-Statesman*, November 27, A1.

Hood, Lucy. 2002. "Issues in Education." *San Antonio Express-News*, November 14, 5B.

Johnson, Charles A. 1976. "Political Cultures in the American States: Elazar's Formulation Examined." *American Journal of Political Science* 20: 491–509.

Jones, D. E., S. Doty, C. Grammich, J. E. Horsch, R. Houseal, M. Lynn, J. P. Marcum, K. M. Sanchargrin, and R. H. Taylor. 2002. *Religious Congregations and Membership in the United States 2000.* Atlanta: Glenmary Research Center.

Lamare, J., J. L. Polinard, and R. D. Wrinkle. 2000. "The Christian Right in God's Country: Texas Politics." In *Prayers in the Precincts: The Christian Right in the 1998 Elections*, edited by J. C. Green, M. J. Rozell, and C. Wilcox. Washington, D.C.: Georgetown University Press.

Legislative Budget Board. 2003. Summary of Legislative Budget Estimates for the 2004–2005 Biennium Submitted to the 78th Legislature.

Lenhart, J. 1997. "Abortion Foes Lose One, Win 3 Others in Austin." *Houston Chronicle*, June 15, 29.

McNeely, Dave. 1995. "Children Suffer Neglect of Lawmakers." *Associated Press State & Local Wire*, March 9, A15.

Morgan, David R., and Shiela S. Watson. 1991. "Political Culture, Political System Characteristics, and Public Policies among the American States." *Publius* 21: 31–48.

O'Connor, Karen, Larry J. Sabato, Stefan D. Haag, and Gary A. Keith. 2004. *American Government: Continuity and Change, 2004 Texas Edition*. New York: Pearson Longman.

Parker, J. Michael. 1997. "Bishops Condemn Executions in a Statement." *San Antonio Express-News*, October 21, 8A.

———. 2004. "Anti-Gambling Effort Comes to S.A.; Illinois Lobbyist Brings His Message to Area Baptist Leaders." *San Antonio Express-News*, May 1, 5B.

Perkes, Kim Sue Lia. 2000. "Texas Bishops Implore Bush to Reassess Capital Punishment." *Austin American-Statesman*, February 18.

Ratcliffe, R. G. 1999. "Conservatives Look for Bush to Fulfill Promise of Agenda." *Houston Chronicle*, February 7, A1.

Reed, Ralph. 1994. *Politically Incorrect: The Emerging Faith Factor in American Politics*. Dallas: Word Publishing.

Robison, C. 2001. "Opposition Blasts New Hate Crime Bill." *Houston Chronicle*, February 14, A30.

Selby, W. Gardner. 2003. "House Budget Strikes Blow to Bigger Government." *San Antonio Express-News*, April 20, 10A.

Shannon, Kelley. 2004. "Perry: All Families Deserve School Choice." *Associated Press State & Local Wire*, June 4.

Staff. 1995. "Texas Catholic Bishops Oppose Gambling." *Houston Chronicle*, January 21, 3.

———. 1999. "Marchers Back Bill for Cesar Chavez Holiday." *Austin American-Statesman*, April 1, B2.

Stitz, Terrence. 1998. "School Voucher Issues Divide Conservatives." *Dallas Morning News*, December 20, 1A, 8A.

Todd, John. 1999. *Texas Politics: The Challenge of Change*. Boston: Houghton Mifflin.

Vara, R. 1994. "Churches and Gambling; All Bets Are Off." *Houston Chronicle*, September 10, 1.

Wald, Kenneth D. 2003. *Religion and Politics in the United States*. 4th ed. Lanham, Md.: Rowman & Littlefield.

Williams, John. 2003. "Anti-Abortion Activists Fight Medical-Malpractice Lawsuit Caps." *Houston Chronicle*, February 26, 21A.

# 6

## Religious Group Advocacy in Michigan Politics

*Kevin R. den Dulk*

In 2004, the state of Michigan experienced two pitched battles in the so-called culture wars. A gubernatorial veto of a legislative ban on a late-term abortion procedure triggered one of the battles; the national debate over legalizing same-sex marriage precipitated another. After intense mobilization, citizen groups forced action on both issues. Right to Life of Michigan and other groups put the abortion ban before the legislature a second time by filing nearly a half million citizen signatures with the government, meeting a somewhat obscure petition requirement under the state constitution that prevented the governor, Democrat Jennifer Granholm, from vetoing repassage of the ban. On June 9, 2004, the Republican-controlled state house and senate voted to reinstate the prohibition on the procedure. Groups also garnered enough signatures and weathered a legal challenge to put on the November ballot a proposed constitutional amendment defining marriage as a union between one man and one woman. The initiative passed with nearly 60 percent of the vote in the 2004 election.

The policy implications of late-term abortions and same-sex marriage are fresh examples of the high-stakes moral questions that have often caught the attention of religious groups in Michigan. This chapter explores why, how, and to what effect these groups have mobilized their intellectual and tangible resources in addressing public policy issues over the past two decades. Religious groups in Michigan, like any other advocacy group in the state, take part in a rich political history with a host of ongoing political disputes, geographic and economic divisions, and strong public personalities. Michigan also has an amorphous and less understood political culture that combines streaks of moral conservatism, state-centered progressivism, and deeply rooted individualism. It is in this milieu that Michigan's religious groups advocate their goals.

The main contention in this chapter is that religion has not only provided a motive for Michigan's religious groups to mobilize but also shaped the strategies and tactics those groups use to pursue their goals. This contention draws from a variety of theoretical innovations and empirical analyses that seek to explain the emergence of political movements and organized political participation, particularly those approaches that consider how a group's resources, political environment, and cultural norms and values combine to explain mobilization (Hart 1996, 2001; McAdam, McCarthy, and Zald 1996). In the context of religious group advocacy, this theoretical synthesis suggests that worldview—distinctively religious ways of explaining and evaluating the social and political world—can shape a group's strategic decision making. Indeed, at least two studies argue that religious advocacy groups perceive their resources and political environment differently than their secular counterparts (Hertzke 1988; Hofrenning 1995).

The chapter focuses on three questions. I begin with the question of motives: What role does religion play, if any, in translating interests into the mobilization of religious groups in Michigan? In response, I present both a broad profile of religious traditions in Michigan and a detailed description of the groups that give political expression to these broader traditions. The chapter then moves to the contexts of religious group advocacy: Do the religious motivations of Michigan's advocacy groups affect the way they garner resources and respond to their political environment? Finally, the chapter explores the question of effectiveness: What influence do religious advocacy groups have? Addressing this final question requires a discussion of the standards for effectiveness, taking into account that religious groups often differ with scholars and politicians about the best criteria for judging their own success.

## A PROFILE OF MICHIGAN'S RELIGIOUS TRADITIONS

Michigan's religious traditions are as diverse as its politics. Both denominational studies and mass surveys suggest that Roman Catholics are the most numerous religionists in the state, with a quarter of the state's population, roughly parallel to the national proportion. The large Catholic population also reflects a familiar national pattern of Polish, Irish, and other immigrant dispersion across the United States in the nineteenth and early twentieth centuries as well as more recent Latino immigration into the state (Gaustad and Barlow 2001). The Religious Congregations and Membership Study 2000, conducted by the Glenmary Research Center, reports that denominations within the "evangelical" family are the second-largest religious grouping, followed closely by mainline denominations (Jones et al. 2002). In terms of individual Protestant denominations, the Lutheran Church—Missouri Synod and Christian Reformed Church, both legacies of German and Dutch immigration, respectively, are the largest denominations identified as "evangelical," while the Presbyterian USA, United Methodist, and Evangelical Lutheran Church of America are the largest mainline denominations. Michigan also ranks eleventh among all the states in its number of Jewish residents, with high concentrations in Detroit and surrounding areas in the southeastern part of the state.

According to the Glenmary study, the total levels of religious affiliation across Michigan place the state thirty-seventh on a religiosity ranking of all the states and the District of Columbia. But this ranking does not fully capture the affiliation rates in the states. The study relied on denominational membership estimates, but none of the traditionally African American Protestant churches provided estimates for the study. Hence, the study leaves out a sizable proportion of Michigan's citizens, especially in the Detroit area, and skews the ranking toward disproportionately white states (Utah, North Dakota, South Dakota, Massachusetts, and Rhode Island are the top five). National mass surveys tend to report a higher proportion of self-identified Baptists in Michigan (at least 15 percent) than the Religious Congregations and Membership Study, reinforcing the argument that the denominational study underreports Michigan's relative levels of black Protestant religious affiliation. Moreover, the population of Muslims in Dearborn and other areas of the state is large compared to most other states, adding to the religious diversity and levels of affiliation.

This profile of religious traditions and religiosity in Michigan is instructive in at least two ways. First, it points to the need for an accounting of the effects of Michigan's religious diversity on political culture in the state. Michigan has been the subject of several studies of the politics of organized groups, but they have focused largely on Christian Right electioneering (Penning and Smidt 2000; Smidt and Penning 1995). These studies are a point of departure for a broader survey of religious advocacy in the state in terms of both the range of religious traditions surveyed and the tactics those traditions employ.

Second, Michigan's religious profile suggests a high likelihood of religious political engagement in the state. Michigan includes many of the traditions or denominational "families" that political scientists and historians have identified as teaching their members that political engagement is not merely appropriate but in some sense obligatory (see generally Fowler et al. 2004; Reichley 2002; Wald 2003). Numerous studies of political behavior have revealed that a key indicator of worldview—and particularly of the role of worldview in political mobilization—is the religious tradition to which an individual belongs (see, for example, Green et al. 1996). Catholics, of course, have a long history of church–state accommodation and interaction, and various religious groups in Michigan—white evangelicals associated with Lutheran- and Calvinist-Reformed traditions, mainline Protestants, black evangelicals, and Jews—are committed to political engagement and advocacy to varying degrees.

## RELIGIOUS MOTIVATIONS AND GROUP ADVOCACY

Several Michigan-based groups illustrate the link between religious traditions and political mobilization. The Michigan Catholic Conference (MCC), founded in 1963 as the chief liaison of the state bishops to the Michigan state government, is clearly motivated by a distinctly Catholic imperative to active political engagement. Paul Long, the current vice president of public policy at the MCC, suggests the organization's response to any policy issue is driven by three questions: "Does [the policy] affect the institutional Church? Does it impact a specific Church teaching? And is it good for the people as a whole?"[1] These questions reflect the Church's historical teachings on political engagement, which have focused both inwardly on the protection of institutional autonomy and outwardly on the fostering of a vision of the "common good" (see, for example, U.S. Conference of Catholic Bishops 2003).

Yet there is scarcely a policy issue that does not threaten the Church's institutional autonomy, bear on a specific Church teaching, or impact the common good. For practical reasons—resources are not infinite—the MCC has had to make choices about its specific policy priorities. But those priorities themselves result from a unique religious commitment by the institutional Church. The "first and foremost" concern, as Long puts it, is human life, a point reinforced in the MCC's stated legislative priorities for 2003–2004 (Michigan Catholic Conference 2003a) and its voter education materials for the 2004 election (Michigan Catholic Conference 2004). Taking its cues from the bishops and recent papal pronouncements (John Paul II 1995), the MCC understands the pro-life cause as a broad and "consistent ethic" that includes not simply opposition to abortion rights but also a rejection of capital punishment, euthanasia, and government-sponsored embryonic stem cell research.

In addition to the pro-life cause, the MCC has committed itself to educational choice policies, which includes support of charter schooling and a lifting of obstacles to state aid for private schools. Again following the lead of the bishops' statements on the issue (Michigan Bishops 2000), the MCC frames these efforts primarily in terms of the "basic right" of parents to shape the education of their children and, consequently, the government has a responsibility to enable these parental rights through support for a range of educational options, including Catholic parochial schools. Put another way, the MCC combines an argument for the "common good" (parental rights to guide children's education) with a desire to foster a specific form of religious education (public support for Catholic schools).

The third prominent issue for the MCC is a cluster of policies that bear on poverty in the state, including health care policy, financial assistance to at-risk children, and a variety of other budgetary matters. Indeed, the MCC has explicitly treated the state budget as a "moral statement" whose strength lies in how well it addresses poverty, thereby "fulfilling [government's] responsibility to promote the common good" (Michigan Catholic Conference 2003b). Like pro-life and education issues, the bishops have given relatively clear guidance on these issues (U.S. Conference of Catholic Bishops 2003). In each of these policy areas, among others, the distinctively religious themes of government's God-given role in fostering the common good and the special status of Church institutions as partners with government come through with considerable force.

The MCC has perhaps the single strongest religious voice in Lansing, but it is certainly not alone. Another group with explicitly Christian—and, in this case, more specifically evangelical Protestant—underpinnings is Citizens for Traditional Values (CTV), a membership organization that is heavily involved in electioneering and civic education. The story of CTV's founder, James Muffett, is deeply intertwined with the organization's history such that it is impossible to disentangle his own motivations from the group's.

Muffett, a former pastor who came late to politics, "immediately became a pro-life activist" in the mid-1980s after viewing the antiabortion film *The Silent Scream*.[2] He cut his political teeth by organizing street protests against hospitals performing abortions (this was, importantly, before the emergence of national groups like Operation Rescue) but admits that he and other evangelicals at the time were politically naive and unsophisticated. Nevertheless, he was recruited as an operative for the Michigan Committee for Freedom, which coordinated Pat Robertson's presidential campaign in 1988—a campaign he describes as an "all-out war" within the Republican Party in which Robertson served as the conservative evangelical counterbalance to the Bush and Kemp campaigns. After Robertson pulled out of the race, Muffett was offered a job as the head of the Michigan Committee for Freedom, which had become little more than an organizational shell with a $200,000 debt. He quickly reduced the debt of the organization, changed its name to CTV in 1989, and started producing voter guides and engaging in other electioneering activities. In 1991, CTV formed a political action committee (PAC) and began developing the Foundation for Traditional Values, the latter an effort to engage in various forms of civic education (I discuss these subsidiary organizations later).

What is important for my purposes here is Muffett's "epiphany" after the experience with Robertson's campaign. Neither Muffett nor the organization he resurrected wavered from a commitment to a moral conservatism rooted in traditionalist Protestant Christianity. But Muffett was saddened by the self-righteous tenor of the campaign—"there was a lot of un-Christlike behavior by Christians," he recalls—and he spent some time in what he describes as a "statewide sackcloth and ashes tour" to restore relationships damaged by the campaign. Moreover, he learned a lesson in terms of political *strategy* that was based in his belief that Christians in that campaign had not heeded the biblical admonition from Luke 16:10: "Whoever can be trusted with very little can also be trusted with much."[3] The campaign, Muffett realized in retrospect, had tried to achieve the height of power before Robertson and his supporters had proven themselves faithful with power at a smaller scale. Consequently, Muffett redirected the focus of the post-Robertson organization to support socially conservative candidates in just ten to twenty state legislative races every election cycle.

Later, he added an educational dimension to CTV's work by establishing the Foundation for Traditional Values, which, among other things, sponsors an institute for high school students who wish to study state government in a hands-on way. The impetus for the foundation was again distinctively religious. Muffett became frustrated by a lack of "historical rooting" in Christians' understanding of American politics, and he convinced his board of directors that the solution lay in the "biblical teaching on generations," by which he means the biblical call that a religious worldview that is both spiritually and socially conscious ought to be transmitted from generation to generation.

Many other groups in the state are less conspicuous and/or organized than MCC and CTV but are just as explicit about religious motivations. An example is the American Family Association (AFA) of Michigan, an affiliate of a national umbrella organization that is associated with conservative Evangelicalism and is known for opposing what it perceives as threats to "family values" in entertainment media. Unlike CTV, AFA of Michigan is not organized to conduct serious electioneering or lobbying—it has no PAC and it is headquartered in Midland, nearly a hundred miles from the state capital in Lansing—but it does engage in civic education with the broad goal of "aggressively and effectively promoting and defending the traditional Judeo-Christian values of family, faith, and freedom."[4] Christian Coalition of Michigan also fits into this category, though it should be noted that leadership and other problems in the late 1990s rendered the organization effectively defunct (Smidt and Penning 2003).

Catholic and evangelical groups are the most prominent religious voices in Lansing, but Jewish and mainline organizations also have a presence. The Michigan Jewish Conference (MJC), for example, maintains a Lansing office that focuses on poverty, health care, and education as well as the traditional Jewish concern for the separation of religion and the state. Yet the MJC is less organized, possesses fewer resources, and is generally less conspicuous than various Jewish groups that are headquartered in the Detroit area, where Michigan's Jewish population is concentrated. The Jewish Community Council and Jewish Federation of Metro Detroit have spearheaded many projects over the past few years, including the Detroit Jewish Initiative, a community development effort. They have also partnered on various other issues with local Jewish groups, such as the Southeast Michigan Coalition on the Environment and Jewish Life and a local chapter of the National Council of Jewish Women. The contrast of the MJC and these Detroit-based groups suggests that there is greater Jewish attention to local or regional politics than statewide issues in Michigan.

Mainline denominations, which are organized for advocacy in Washington, D.C., through the National Council of Churches, have no equivalent center of gravity at the state level in Michigan. As I discuss in the next section, this lack of coordination can put mainline groups at a political disadvantage. Yet a few of Michigan's mainline denominations do have very specific purposes that have resulted in a presence in Lansing. The best illustration is Lutheran Social Services of Michigan (LSSM), an agency of the Evangelical Lutheran Church in America that coordinates a variety of social programs for the denomination. LSSM operates an Office of Public Policy and Advocacy, which focuses on legislation ranging from mental health services to foster care. LSSM's work reflects recent scholarly research that suggests that the mainline tradition's social and political influence, though less conspicuous and wide-ranging than in the past, nevertheless continues to be important (Wuthnow 2002).

Many other religious groups are small, clergy-led concerns, often ad hoc but sometimes organized for the long term. The Council of Baptist Pastors in Detroit, an organization composed largely of African American clergy, uses the bully pulpit to address a range of issues from affirmative action to educational vouchers, while the Ecumenical Ministers Association, a small PAC also headquartered in Detroit, enjoys the support of a hundred pastors who believe, as the name implies, that it is important for clergy to unify from various traditions to support financially state legislative candidates. Both the Concerned Clergy of West Michigan and the Religious Coalition for a Fair

Michigan (the latter part of the secular Coalition for a Fair Michigan[5]) have emerged as largely mainline clergy groups committed to gay rights and, most recently, the defeat of the state constitutional amendment to ban same-sex marriage. Another group, Citizens for the Protection of Marriage, spear-headed the effort to put the marriage amendment on the ballot, partly with the support of evangelical and (to a lesser extent) Catholic churches and organizations (Jarema 2004).[6]

Other groups, some of them well organized and influential, are not as overtly religious but may still be reasonably labeled "religious." The Michigan Family Forum (MFF), which is often associated with the same conservative evangelical roots as CTV and Michigan affiliates of the AFA and the Christian Coalition, is religiously motivated but not explicitly so. As Brad Snavely, the current executive director of MFF, describes the goals of the group, "We don't have an evangelical mission. We have a public policy mission."[7] Indeed, the group, which focuses on policy related to marriage, abstinence, and other family issues, has published numerous well-produced pamphlets, booklets, and reports that assiduously avoid explicitly religious language, choosing instead to frame their work in terms of available social scientific data (Michigan Family Forum 1998, 2003). Still, the group emerged in the late 1980s as an effort to bring a "credible professional voice" on traditional family issues to the state level—in effect, to do for Michigan what Focus on the Family had been developing nationally. Like Focus on the Family, MFF began its mission primarily with the support of evangelical Christians, and this support continues to this day. Accordingly, while Snavely notes that there is no religious "litmus test" that supporters of MFF must pass, he readily admits—indeed, embraces—the fact that it is typically evangelicals who have been drawn to the organization.

Other groups are neither overtly religious nor indirectly associated with any one religious tradition, though they may have disproportionately large religious memberships. Right to Life of Michigan, for example, serves a sizable Protestant and Catholic membership and provides resources to churches in both traditions; it defines itself as "nonsectarian" and, as a membership group, is open to supporters from other religious and nonreligious traditions.[8] Other groups are not as clearly religious but engage in political advocacy that bears on religious group agendas. The group in favor of a failed ballot initiative for state-funded private school vouchers in 2000, Kids First! Yes!, was non–church based and formally unrelated to any particular religious faith. Another group focused on the school funding is the Great Lakes Education Project (GLEP), a PAC that supports the cause of school choice in the form of charter schooling. While GLEP is not connected to any religious tradition or perspective, its founders and chief benefactors—the DeVos family, cofounders of the Amway corporation—are well known for their support of religious organizations across the state and for their eventual aim of introducing vouchers into state education policy.

## AGENDA BUILDING, RESOURCE MOBILIZATION, AND POLITICAL ENVIRONMENT

Taken together, these groups, among many others, paint a picture of active religious involvement in Michigan politics. Yet mobilizing for religious reasons is not the same thing as using religion to guide how a group will mobilize. Examining the ways groups build agendas at the grassroots, structure themselves, garner resources, and respond to their political environment provides some insight into how religion impacts group strategies.

### Organizational Structure and Leadership

The structure of organizations—that is, the rules and informal norms that differentiate decision-making roles within the organization—is among the most important resources for group mobilization. The primary reason structure matters is that it facilitates the use of *other* resources. Without certain kinds of organizational arrangements, the ability of a group to define goals, utilize expertise, raise money effectively and use it efficiently, and coordinate with other groups is severely circumscribed.

The hierarchical structure of the Catholic Church in the United States, for example, includes some 300 region-based dioceses, thirty-five state Catholic conferences, and a national organization (the U.S. Conference of Catholic Bishops) that serves as the apex of decision-making authority. This structure parallels American federalism, with suborganizations representing local, state, and national interests of the Church. The Michigan Catholic Conference draws substantial resources from the Church's structural arrangements, particularly through the support of Michigan's seven dioceses and over 800 local parishes.

The dioceses not only provide financial support to MCC but also present opportunities for the MCC to promote the Church's policy goals. The fact that, unlike other religious groups, the MCC carries the banner in state government for the Catholic Church as an institution—a Church that is larger than any other in the state—gives the MCC an advantage over other religious groups in the state. Its role as Church representative provides ready-made interest among state legislators and many opportunities to be the classic insider lobbyist. Paul Long and his staff regularly review legislation, contact legislators, testify at legislative hearings, and help draft legislation either at the invitation of elected officials or by their own initiative. In many ways, the MCC bucks the pattern of other religious groups, remaining somewhat aloof from the nitty-gritty of the policymaking process (see Hertzke 1988; Hofrenning 1995).

But the MCC's insider advocacy is not its only tactical focus. While shaping policy is a chief goal, the MCC also seeks to contribute to agenda building among ordinary Catholics through grassroots or "outsider" lobbying. The MCC's efforts in this regard are consistent with other values-driven groups, which often have as much or more concern for cultural attitudes as they do specific policy proposals (Berry 1997). Just as with insider lobbying, the MCC's grassroots lobbying benefits from the group's intimate connection to the institutional Church. The MCC connects to ordinary Catholics in at least two ways. First, the MCC publishes a newsletter, *Focus*, which is distributed to parishes throughout the state. *Focus* articulates the Conference's perspective on the Church's political teachings, timely policy debates, and upcoming elections. The MCC is understandably protective of the Church's tax-exempt status and therefore cautiously avoids even a whiff of candidate endorsement in the newsletter; the latest discussion of the elections avoids naming a single contender for elective office (Michigan Catholic Conference 2004). The MCC's goal is more broadly understood as setting out the priorities and teachings of the Church rather than its partisan preferences.

A second way the MCC connects with ordinary parishioners is the Catholic Legislative Action Network, a largely Internet-based mobilization effort. Members of the network sign up with the MCC for electronic mail alerts when relevant legislation is up for a vote or other governmental actions are pending, and they are encouraged to take various forms of action, from calling elected officials to writing newspaper editorials. But MCC takes the additional step of providing members a repository of information on elected officials, media outlets across the state, and governmental agencies, among numerous other things.[9] Hence, the call to action is joined with readily available information that enables action.

Other religious denominations have their own public justice divisions, but they rarely approach the breadth of regional and local coverage that the Catholic Church can muster. While most of the mainline and larger evangelical denominations have central organizations that focus on politics and political advocacy, they generally do not have resources or organizational arrangements for state-level political offices (Lutheran Social Services of Michigan notwithstanding), and they tend therefore to concentrate most of their attention on national (or even international) policy concerns. Even those denominations with national or international headquarters in Michigan itself pay relatively little attention to state-level politics. For example, the Christian

Reformed Church's Office of Social Justice and Hunger Action, a public policy arm headquartered in Grand Rapids, lists no issue of particular interest to Michigan state lawmaking on its official website.[10]

Instead, to the extent they focus on state-level politics, Protestant denominations in Michigan, and especially those associated with Evangelicalism, tend to rely on nonaffiliated membership organizations for political advocacy. As already noted, several organizations identified as part of the "Christian Right" movement have a presence in Michigan, including the MFF, CTV, AFA of Michigan, and Christian Coalition of Michigan. To be sure, both AFA of Michigan and Christian Coalition of Michigan have ties to a parent organization that provides some resources to the groups; MFF also has ties to the resources of the Family Research Council, though it is not formally affiliated. Right to Life of Michigan and its various local affiliates also benefit from the support of a national organization, the National Right to Life Committee. Nevertheless, the memberships of these groups—and therefore most of their resources of time, energy, and money—originate in Michigan.

Developing and maintaining a membership highlights a key element of organizational structure for these groups: leadership. As Daniel Hofrenning (1995) suggests in his study of national religious lobbies, leaders in groups must balance "an intriguing mix of democracy and oligarchy" (11). For the MCC, control over agenda formation is top-down, with leadership flowing from the bishops as representatives of the Church. But leaders of groups that rely more heavily on support from the grassroots must be more attentive to what Theda Skocpol (2002) has recently argued is the professionalization of today's advocacy organizations, with fewer ordinary members positioned to make decisions about organizational goals than just a few decades ago. This alienation from leadership can diminish a member's sense of efficacy—the perception that one's participation matters—and hence the best leaders will try to balance the need for management from the top with sensitivity to the grassroots.

Interestingly, Skocpol suggests that many conservative evangelical religious groups are particularly adept at striking this leadership balance. Advocacy groups associated with Evangelicalism in Michigan tend to have an individualist leadership model, with a strong personality at the center of the group. James Muffett, whose imprint on CTV is unmistakable, is an excellent illustration. But Muffett and leaders in similar groups also realize that they cannot overwhelm the organization with their own personalities—indeed, the near demise of the Michigan Christian Coalition is partly attributable to just this problem (Smidt and Penning 2003). Partly through a committed board of directors and partly through innumerable forms of direct contact with donors and members, leaders of successful groups must shape the goals of the organization while reaching out to the grassroots. It is partly for this reason that Muffett has placed a great deal of emphasis on training opportunities such as the Student Statemenship Institute, which educates members (and future members) about organizational goals. Brad Snavely at MFF, whose organization has engaged in similar forms of student and adult educational activities, echoes the point when he notes the profound importance of "having the community behind" the group's initiatives.[11]

## Money and Mass Expertise

These matters of organizational structure can also shape the prospects of groups in garnering resources such as money. The Catholic Conference operates on a patronage model, receiving its budget largely from the state bishops. But mass membership groups must raise funds independently. In some instances, these groups find patrons themselves; the DeVos family, for example, has given considerable funds to education and right-to-life causes in the state. But the fact that MFF and CTV, not to mention subsidiaries to parent organizations like the AFA and Christian Coalition of Michigan, remain small relative to other interests in the state is partly the result of the difficulties in developing and, perhaps more important, maintaining a sufficiently large membership base to fund organization activities.

Fund-raising can be a chore for any group, but it poses special problems for leaders of religious membership organizations. There are fund-raising tactics, for example, that can be highly effective but are perceived as contrary to religious witness. The imperatives of fund-raising and organizational maintenance have especially cross-pressured evangelical-associated groups like CTV and MFF, neither of which favor the conventional threat letters and "sky-is-falling" approach of similar groups. Part of the reason for their avoidance of reactionary solicitations is both groups' long-term visions. When addressing family-oriented policy in Michigan, for example, MFF is much more likely to engage in education and small-scale collaboration than direct political conflict. The collaborative approach, which has included activities ranging from preparing groups to take government Temporary Aid to Needy Families money to involvement in a program for incarcerated fathers, is particularly appealing to Snavely of MFF, who insists that incrementalism is more effective in the long run. Muffett's intergenerational perspective, reflected in his organization's work through the Student Statesmanship Institute on civic education for high schoolers, also illustrates the belief in the slow, deliberate, and somewhat behind-the-scenes approach as the most effective way of shaping political attitudes and behavior. This attention to a long-term vision can butt against the desire of supporters to tackle the hot issues of the day. As Snavely puts the problem, "We need a long-term view . . . but sometimes in groups there is a pull toward getting involved in more issues because this or that group of activists and donors are really into it."[12]

Moreover, both Snavely and Muffett are quick to point out that their approaches to advocacy are as much about tone and cultural witness as effectiveness. To "witness to Christ in the political process," as Muffett explains, means that in a group's work it must avoid "inflammatory" language in presenting a message to the group's constituents and to the public as a whole, even if that language would bring a short-term spike in revenue. In practical terms, this has translated into groups like MFF and Right to Life of Michigan avoiding religious language in their publications, focusing instead on available social scientific data and other forms of information that appeal to a broader audience than the groups' religious bases. Muffett at CTV, in his teaching on the role of religion in American history, has shifted from a "Christian nation" emphasis, which assumed a favored divine status for the United States, to what he calls a more "nuanced" view of the historical record.[13] In some respects, these groups represent at the state level what Matthew Moen (1992, 1997) identified in similar groups at the national level in the 1990s—a transformation from a particularist religious orientation to a broader, perhaps more pluralist presentation of themselves to the public.

The effort to change attitudes incrementally and widely points again to the importance of building broad-based expertise and employing outside lobbying. The MCC has developed this resource by drawing some professional staff from within the Church vocations and by educating lay Catholics about the legislative process through the Catholic Legislative Action Network and *Focus*. Following the lead of other state conferences, the MCC also sponsors an annual "Legislative Day" and "Student Legislative Day." Laypeople from across the state come to Lansing for legislative briefings with Conference staff and elected officials. The MFF sponsors a similar educational event called the "Peer Education Summit," though the meeting is less explicitly focused on legislative matters.

With the exception of CTV PAC, nearly every facet of CTV's organizational structure is built around the development of mass expertise. Activists and candidates can take part in CTV's Political Leadership Academy, which teaches the basic features of fund-raising and campaign communications techniques. Ordinary adults may sign up on an e-mail distribution list (called "Minute Man Alerts," suggesting the speed with which members will respond if mobilized on an issue), or they may get involved in CTV's innovative "From Pews to the Polls" project, a church-based get-out-the-vote effort in which church members coordinate distribution of voter guides and encourage members to vote through direct contact just prior to an election.[14] And high schoolers may take part in the hands-on experience of the Student States-manship Institute.

## Political Environment

While resources internal to groups are crucially important, they are useless without a political environment that is open to mobilization. In Michigan, that political environment has often been defined along geographic lines. Residents in Detroit and other eastern urban areas, along with the vast stretch of land north of the Straits of Mackinac called the Upper Peninsula, are often at odds with the western side of the state, where Grand Rapids, the second-largest city in Michigan, and many other midsize cities are located. To a great extent, these geographic distinctions reflect economic realities among the more than ten million residents of the state. The automobile industry, still the state's top-ranked manufacturer, has anchored the economy of Detroit and nearby areas, while tourism, health care, furniture manufacturing, and agriculture have had relatively greater influence in other regions. This combination of geography and economics can shape religious mobilization, from the conservatism of groups in western Michigan, where many evangelicals are located, to the economic progressivism of groups in the east that identify with labor and similar issues.

Yet Michigan politics is not simply the convergence of geography and economics. The state's political culture includes an ever-shifting set of competing attitudes and political orientations that combine moral conservatism, state-centered progressivism, and economic individualism. Elazar's (1972) characterization of the state as "moralistic," which he describes as an openness to use government to achieve disparate understandings of the public interest, helps explain why religious groups have been relatively active in the state over time. The recent efforts regarding abortion and same-sex marriage, which required intense participation on a mass level, exemplify the willingness of religionists across the state to use the power of government to pursue a vision of the common good.

Moreover, the relationship between groups and government is not unidirectional; groups themselves are subject to a host of influences, including the salience of particular policy issues in Michigan government itself. Beth Leech and her colleagues (2002) suggest that there is a "demand side" to group mobilization in which organized interests do not simply push their agendas on a legislature but mobilize in response to legislative invitation. The relationship between groups and government is perhaps best described as codependency—or, as Baumgartner et al. (2003) put it, "coevolutionary." The policy agendas of religious groups illustrate this coevolution. The MCC issued responses to a remarkable range of proposals emanating from the state legislature from 1999 to the present, including "conscience clauses" for health services, opposition to late-term abortion procedures and parental consent for abortion, the death penalty, the marriage amendment, and a host of education-related items.[15] Other groups, including many Christian Right organizations, share these policy concerns but tend to amplify some issues more than others, from opposition to casino gambling to support for term limits (see Smidt and Penning 2003).

The "demand" for lobbying is especially strong in Michigan because its legislature is highly professionalized, with above-average time commitments from elected officials, the third most highly paid legislators among all state governments, and relatively large staffs.[16] The state is also characterized by a high degree of party competition; consequently, parties have a keen interest in gaining any edge over their competitors. For groups, this means more political opportunities, with many points of access in Lansing and greater needs for the information lobbyists can provide. Moreover, the state initiated term limits in 1992, heightening the importance of interest groups in the recruitment and election of public officials and increasing the reliance of groups on the grassroots. The MCC's Paul Long suggests that term limits "prohibit us from developing long-term relationships," which led the organization to redouble its efforts with programs like the Catholic Legislative Action Network that can help the MCC make connections with up-and-coming public officials.[17]

## RELIGIOUS GROUP EFFECTIVENESS

Although Michigan's religious interest groups have obstacles to successful mobilization, taken together they are highly motivated and possess significant (though varying) stores of resources and political opportunities. But how effective have they been?

If one interprets the question in terms of candidates elected or policy agendas drafted into law, the answer is mixed for religious groups in general, just as Smidt and Penning (2003) found with Michigan's Christian Right more specifically. It is, of course, very difficult to disentangle the influence of advocacy groups from the host of other factors that can shape electoral or legislative success. We might look to two pieces of evidence, however, to sort out how broadly religious groups might affect Michigan politics relative to other groups in the state: PAC donations in the context of electioneering and the perceptions of political elites and peers in the context of lobbying over policy.

The 2002 election cycle, which included a gubernatorial race and nearly three-quarters of the senate seats left open because of term limits, gives us a snapshot of the role of religious groups in electoral politics. Among the top 150 fund-raising PACs, ranging from over $2 million (the House Republican Campaign Committee) to just under $300,000 (Michigan Laborers), there were only three groups with some discernible connection to religion—the Great Lakes Education Project (fifth on the ranking), Right to Life of Michigan (twenty-first), and CTV PAC (144th). Other interests dominate the list, including party PACs, labor (particularly the Michigan Education Association and United Auto Workers), health care, energy, housing development, and alcohol wholesalers (table 6.1). If we assume that PAC contributions can increase access and influence, religious groups are clearly at a comparative disadvantage.

Yet despite the dominance of other interest groups in election-related fund-raising and expenditures, religious groups still have other opportunities for electoral influence, sometimes in quite subtle and sophisticated ways. Many religious organizations disseminate some information about candidates for office, most often in the form of a voter guide that may be distributed in churches or directly to group members. Candidate education is also a way of influencing elections. James Muffett reports that the current state legislature includes fourteen members who completed CTV's Political Leadership Academy.[18] This attention to electoral and legislative education and advocacy—education that has become increasingly important to groups such as MFF and MCC as well—points to a measure of political influence and sophistication among religious groups. In addition, for groups like CTV or Right to Life of

**Table 6.1. Top Michigan Political Action Committees (PACs) and Lobbying Organizations**

| Ranking | Top Michigan PACs, 2002 Election Cycle | Top Single-Interest Lobbying Organizations, 2001 |
|---|---|---|
| 1 | House Republican Campaign Committee | Michigan Chamber of Commerce |
| 2 | Senate Republican Campaign Committee | Right to Life of Michigan[a] |
| 3 | Michigan Education Association PAC | Michigan Education Association |
| 4 | Citizens for Responsible Leadership | Michigan State Medical Society |
| 5 | Great Lakes Education Project[a] | Michigan Insurance Federation |
| 6 | The Leadership Fund | Michigan Association of Realtors |
| 7 | House Democratic Fund | Michigan Retailers Association |
| 8 | United Auto Workers/Voluntary PAC | Michigan Farm Bureau |
| 9 | Michigan Trial Lawyers/Justice PAC | Michigan Manufacturers Association |
| 10 | Senate Democratic Fund | Small Business Association of Michigan |

Sources: Ballenger (2001) and Moorhouse and Robinson (2003).
[a]Religious or religion-affiliated group.

Michigan that have established PACs, it is somewhat misleading to suggest that they are "ineffective" simply because they lack the funds to contribute to a wide range of campaigns. CTV PAC, for example, is focused quite deliberately on a relatively few races statewide, positioning the group to make a political difference in a targeted way. They may not have clout in every corner of the state, but they do in certain places.

Campaigning is not the same activity as governing, and some organizations are more focused on the latter than the former. But here, too, we see mixed results. In 2001, the Lansing-based political magazine *Inside Michigan Politics* surveyed lobbyists and political officials in the state about their perceptions of the most influential lobbies in Lansing. As table 6.1 shows, only one group associated with religion—Right to Life of Michigan—is included among the top Lansing lobbies, with the usual suspects—business and labor—occupying most of the top positions. One explanation is that, at least among Christian Right groups, there has been a tendency to tackle a very broad range of policy issues since the 1990s that leaves the groups spread too thin (Smidt and Penning 2003). Groups with fewer financial resources but targeted priorities are able to do more in concentrated areas than other groups that cast too wide a policy net. Still, there are certainly religious advocacy groups in Michigan that have matched their policy focus to their capacities; even primarily evangelical groups such as the MFF have refocused their attention in the past few years on issues pertaining to marriage and sex education in schools, leaving other issues to other groups. Indeed, that kind of division of labor is an important tactic when groups must compete for finite resources from a shared membership base.

Moreover, the lobbying survey itself focuses entirely on insider lobbying, while many of the groups in this study have an emphasis on "outsider" or grassroots tactics, that is, changing mass attitudes and mobilizing the population. One need only look at the citizens initiatives of 2004 to recognize some success among religious groups in grassroots mobilization: the so-called People's Override of Governor Granholm's veto of the abortion ban, the state constitutional proposal on the November ballot to prohibit same-sex marriage, and the state constitutional proposal, also on the November ballot, to limit the expansion of gambling in the state. In each instance, groups with religious memberships took the lead in gathering signatures to put the issues on the public agenda.

## CONCLUSION

Religious advocacy in Michigan, though diverse in levels of sophistication and organization, continues to thrive. The political culture of the state, coupled with a rich array of political interests and grievances, has provided a seedbed for religious mobilization. Some groups, chief among them the MCC, have adapted themselves to the classic tactics of insider lobbying; others have focused more fully on grassroots mobilization, using mass opinion on issues ranging from same-sex marriage to gambling to advance their political agendas in the state legislature and through the blunt instrument of the ballot initiative. While these groups have met significant obstacles to their efforts, they have had measurable success. Perhaps more important, they have also deepened their understanding of the political process itself, and this undoubtedly will have long-term effects.

Perhaps one legacy of increasing sophistication among religious advocacy groups will be higher levels of coordination and intergroup support among those groups in the future. In terms of lobbying and other forms of advocacy, groups might hold joint strategy sessions and exchange information, divide the labor of contacting legislators and media, and even supply staff or financial support to other groups. There is some evidence of such coordination among Michigan's religious advocacy groups already—the recent signature drives pulled together many groups, including some strange bedfellows—but coordination remains largely ad hoc and intermittent.

Coalition building is, of course, a key tactic of smaller groups, as most of Michigan's religious advocacy groups are compared to their chief competitors. Without such coalitions, groups are especially susceptible to countermobilization. Religious groups in Michigan have formidable opponents (depending on ideological commitments and goals), from state teachers' unions to abortion rights groups, as well as a host of national organizations that take an interest in Michigan politics on occasion. In the past, these opponents' own coalitions have scuttled religious group efforts on everything from vouchers to health care to funding for faith-based social services. Perhaps we should expect interaction across religious traditions to be somewhat low given the often-invoked "culture wars" thesis, which holds that American culture is riven by deep divisions (Hunter 1991). Soldiers in these wars often march under religious banners. But traditional religious lines are also frequently blurred, as we have seen recently and repeatedly at the national level. Polarization exists between groups and can even be acute, but it can also be—and often is—overcome for the sake of common goals.

## NOTES

1. Author interview with Paul Long, August 3, 2004.
2. Interview with James Muffett, August 16, 2004.

3. Luke 16:10 (New International Version).

4. www.afamichigan.org.

5. www.coalitionforafairmichigan.org/Coalition.htm.

6. See www.protectmarriageyes.org. The assessment of Catholic involvement is based on an author interview with Paul Long, August 3, 2004.

7. Author interview with Brad Snavely, August 3, 2004.

8. www.rtl.org.

9. http://capwiz.com/micatholicconference/state/main/?state=MI.

10. www.crcjustice.org.

11. Author interview with Brad Snavely, August 3, 2004.

12. Author interview with Brad Snavely, August 3, 2004.

13. Interview with James Muffett, August 16, 2004.

14. Note that CTV does not seek church membership lists. As a former pastor, CTV's President Muffett calls such tactics a "reprehensible" intrusion into church life. Interview with James Muffett, August 16, 2004.

15. Based on news releases from 1999 to the present, archived at www.micatholic conference.org/public_policy/news_releases.html.

16. www.ncsl.org.

17. Author interview with Paul Long, August 3, 2004.

18. Interview with James Muffett, August 16, 2004.

## WORKS CITED

Ballenger, Bill. 2001. "Cawthorne Tops Lobbyist Survey; State Chamber Repeats as Top Firm." *Inside Michigan Politics*, February 12, 6–7.

Baumgartner, Frank R., Beth L. Leech, and Christine Mahoney. 2003. "The Co-Evolution of Groups and Government." Paper presented at the meeting of the American Political Science Association, Philadelphia, August 28–31.

Berry, Jeffrey M. 1997. *The Interest Group Society.* 3rd ed. New York: Longman.

Elazar, Daniel J. 1972. *American Federalism: A View from the States.* 3rd ed. New York: Crowell.

Fowler, Robert Booth, Allen D. Hertzke, Laura R. Olson, and Kevin R. den Dulk. 2004. *Religion and Politics in America: Faith, Culture, and Strategic Choices.* 3rd ed. Boulder, Colo.: Westview Press.

Gaustad, Edwin S., and Philip L. Barlow. 2001. *New Historical Atlas of Religion in America.* New York: Oxford University Press.

Green, John, James Guth, Corwin Smidt, and Lyman Kellstedt. 1996. *Religion and the Culture Wars: Dispatches from the Front.* Lanham, Md.: Rowman & Little-field.

Hart, Stephen. 1996. The Cultural Dimension of Social Movements. *Sociology of Religion* 57: 82–99.

———. 2001. *Cultural Dimensions of Progressive Politics: Styles of Engagement among Grassroots Activists.* Chicago: University of Chicago Press.

Hertzke, Allen. 1988. *Representing God in Washington*. Knoxville: University of Tennessee Press.

Hofrenning, Daniel. 1995. *In Washington but Not of It: The Prophetic Politics of Religious Lobbyists*. Philadelphia: Temple University Press.

Hunter, James Davidson. 1991. *Culture Wars: The Struggle to Define America*. New York: Basic Books.

Jarema, Morgan. 2004. "Clerics Oppose Push to Define Marriage." *Grand Rapids Press*, June 22.

John Paul II. 1995. Evangelium Vitae: *The Gospel of Life*. Washington, D.C.: U.S. Conference of Catholic Bishops.

Jones, Dale E., Sherri Doty, Clifford Grammich, James E. Horsch, Richard Houseal, Mac Lynn, John P. Marcum, Kenneth M. Sanchagrin, and Richard H. Taylor. 2002. *Religious Congregations and Membership in the United States 2000*. Nashville: Glenmary Research Center.

Leech, Beth, Frank R. Baumgartner, Timothy La Pira, and Nicholas A. Semanko. 2002. "The Demand Side of Lobbying: Government Attention and the Mobilization of Organized Interests." Paper presented at the meeting of Midwest Political Science Association, Chicago, April 25–28.

McAdam, Douglas, John McCarthy, and Mayer Zald. 1996. "Opportunities, Mobilizing Structures, and Framing Process: Toward a Synthetic, Comparative Perspective on Social Movements." In *Comparative Perspectives on Social Movements*, edited by D. McAdam, J. McCarthy, and M. Zald. Cambridge: Cambridge University Press.

Michigan Bishops. 2000. *A Just Beginning for All*. Lansing: Michigan Catholic Conference.

Michigan Catholic Conference. 2003a. "Michigan Catholic Conference 2003–2004 Legislative Priorities." *Focus* 31, no. 1 (March).

———. 2003b. "The 2004 State Budget: A Moral Statement." *Focus* 31, no. 4 (December).

———. 2004. "The Issues, the Candidates, and Your Vote 2004." *Focus* 32, no. 2 (July).

Michigan Family Forum. 1998. *From This Day Forward: The 1998 Michigan Marriage Report*. Lansing: Michigan Family Forum.

———. 2003. *Family Health Indicators: A Survey of Michigan Counties*. Lansing: Michigan Family Forum.

Moen, Matthew. 1992. *The Transformation of the Christian Right*. Tuscaloosa: University of Alabama Press.

———. 1997. "The Changing Nature of Christian Right Activism, 1970s–1990s." In *Sojourners in the Wilderness: The Christian Right in Comparative Perspective*, edited by C. Smidt and J. Penning. Lanham, Md.: Rowman & Littlefield.

Moorhouse, Barbara R., and Richard L. Robinson. 2003. *A Citizen's Guide to Michigan Campaign Finance 2002*. Lansing: Michigan Campaign Finance Network.

Penning, James, and Corwin E. Smidt. 2000. "Michigan 1998: The 'Right Stuff.'" In *Prayers in the Precincts: The Christian Right in the 1998 Elections*, edited by J. C. Green, M. J. Rozell, and C. Wilcox. Washington, D.C.: Georgetown University Press.

Reichley, A. James. 2002. *Faith in Politics*. Washington, D.C.: Brookings Institution Press.

Skocpol, Theda. 2002. *Diminished Democracy: From Membership to Management in American Civic Life*. Norman: University of Oklahoma Press.

Smidt, Corwin E., and James Penning. 1995. "Michigan: Veering to the Right." In *God at the Grass Roots: The Christian Right in the 1994 Elections*, edited M. J. Rozell and C. Wilcox. Lanham, Md.: Rowman & Littlefield.

———. 2003. "The Christian Right's Mixed Success in Michigan." In *The Christian Right in American Politics: Marching to the Millennium*, edited by J. C. Green, M. J. Rozell, and C. Wilcox. Washington, D.C.: Georgetown University Press.

U.S. Conference of Catholic Bishops. 2003. *Faithful Citizenship: A Catholic Call for Political Responsibility*. Washington, D.C.: U.S. Conference of Catholic Bishops.

Wald, Kenneth D. 2003. *Religion and Politics in the United States*. 4th ed. Lanham, Md.: Rowman & Littlefield.

Wuthnow, Robert. 2002. *The Quiet Hand of God: Faith-Based Activism and the Public Role of Mainline Protestantism*. Berkeley: University of California Press.

# 7

## Religious Advocacy in the Wisconsin Statehouse

*David Yamane*

John Huebscher's day begins early at his eleventh floor office on Wilson Street, three blocks from the state capitol building in Madison, Wisconsin. Like many of his fellow legislative advocates—typically called, whether descriptively or derisively, "lobbyists"—he first checks for important faxes and e-mail ("action alerts") that may have come in overnight from Washington, D.C. or Milwaukee. Finding nothing pressing, he scans the *New York Times*, pausing to enjoy a few escapist minutes with the crossword puzzle. He confers with his administrative assistant and two associates and then, on this particular morning, walks—efficiently and orderly, as befits his Swiss heritage—to his monthly breakfast meeting with four other advocates who share some of his legislative concerns. They generously share ideas, information, and strategies over coffee and bagels at one of Madison's many coffee shops. As the most experienced member of the group, Huebscher has more than his share of opportunities to offer commentary on the current legislative situation and prospects for the initiatives they favor. His colleagues listen intently as he makes predictions about the outcome of three of four bills currently pending—predictions that are born out more often than not. They also discuss the advisability of issuing a joint statement on a bill that would adversely affect the organizations they represent.

When he returns to his office, Huebscher spends an increasing amount of time at his computer. For better or worse, the key written materials he relies on are now offered electronically. The *Wheeler Report*—a digest of the activities of the Wisconsin legislature that has been published since 1972—is available as an e-newsletter, which Huebscher reads. The many documents produced for the legislature each day that were once printed and distributed through a document room are now posted on the legislature's website. Huebscher mouses and scrolls his way through a score of newly introduced bills, committee hearing and floor session schedules, and the like. Although he has seen many of the bills before—some of them inevitably return, like bell-bottom pants—the cost of missing an important piece of legislation is high. So he carefully scans the seemingly endless stream of words on his computer monitor to see what kind of trouble the legislature is getting into. In any given legislative session, Huebscher and his staff will flag one hundred or so bills for monitoring. Of those, they will take a public position on a third and give serious consideration to ten. A large part of the morning staff meeting is dedicated to vetting the bills, assessing their likely future, and planning a strategy for engagement.

That strategy almost always entails explaining their position to the legislative or executive branch via letters and public testimony. So, later in the day, Huebscher and his associate, Kathy Markeland, head to the north wing of the capitol building. In an ornate hearing room, Huebscher appears before the Assembly Committee on Labor to offer testimony on a bill that would permit an employer "to refuse to employ, or to bar or terminate from employment, an individual who has been convicted of a felony." It is at this moment that we begin to see how he differs from the other lobbyists whose days in the capitol otherwise resemble his quite closely. Huebscher begins his testimony by declaring, "On behalf of the Wisconsin Catholic Conference, I am offering this testimony in opposition to Assembly Bill 353." He then outlines the basis for his opposition:

> Our stance on criminal justice issues is guided by the social teaching of the Catholic Church and insights gained from long experience ministering to prisoners, ex-offenders, crime victims, and their families. This experience guided development of the WCC's 1999 statement, *Public Safety, the Common Good, and the Church: A Statement on Crime and Punishment in Wisconsin.*
>
> The statement identifies several principles for evaluating public policies in the criminal justice area. Three of these principles that speak directly to issues raised in AB 353 are (1) that criminal justice policies serve the common good, (2) that they foster restoring victims and offenders to the community, and (3) that they exercise an option for the poor and marginalized. On this latter point, policies must be assessed in light of their impact on racial minorities.

Of course, Huebscher was not the only lobbyist to appear before the assembly committee in opposition to this "felon bias" bill. But he was unique in grounding his opposition in a *religious* authority, principally "the social teaching of the Catholic Church" manifested in a statement issued by Wisconsin's Roman Catholic bishops.

Huebscher—like his breakfast companions—is a *religious lobbyist*. Indeed, he is considered by many to be the dean of religious lobbyists in Madison. Huebscher has worked for the Wisconsin Catholic Conference since 1987 and served as its executive director since 1992. The Catholic Conference was founded in 1968 by the Roman Catholic bishops of the state's five dioceses to fulfill the mandate of the Second Vatican Council that the Church be more involved in the world. As its literature states, "With the message of the Gospel and the social teachings of the Church as its foundation, the WCC offers a specifically Catholic contribution to state and federal public policy debates."

Although it is, by all accounts, the leading religious advocacy organization in Wisconsin, the Catholic Conference is also typical of religious advocates in the state in its organization, motivation, practices, and understanding of success. After a brief consideration of Wisconsin as a context, this chapter will look at faith-based political advocacy in terms of these four issues.

## CONTEXT

A brief consideration of the history, culture, and political organization of the state of Wisconsin is necessary to understand the context within which religious advocates work. As we will see, a number of these factors make Wisconsin a relatively conducive environment for religious advocacy.

Wisconsin was originally settled by seventeenth-century French explorers, Jesuits, and fur traders. When the American colonies won the War of Independence from Britain in 1783, they took formal control over all the land east of the Mississippi River, including what is now Wisconsin. At that time, Wisconsin was part of the Northwest Territory and later the Indiana Territory (beginning in 1800), though the British still effectively controlled the area until after the War of 1812, when the U.S. government took active control of the Great Lakes region from Britain. Wisconsin was then part of the Illinois Territory and later the Michigan Territory (in 1818) before Congress created the Wisconsin Territory in 1836. Wisconsin was admitted to the Union as the thirtieth state on May 29, 1848, with Madison as the capital city.[1]

Wisconsin's self-characterization as "The Dairy State" suggests one of the state's major economic emphases. Although the number of people working in agriculture continues to decline, as it has nationally, the proportion of the population working on farms continues to exceed the national average (3.0 to 1.9 percent). At the same time, a higher-than-average percentage of workers in Wisconsin work in manufacturing (22 vs. 14 percent). This combination is reflective of the fact that "the state's economy is that of a borderland between the more industrial East and the more agricultural prairie West."[2] Among industrial workers, Wisconsin has a strong history of labor union activity. As historian Robert Nesbit has observed, "In 1939, Wisconsin ranked third among the states in the extent of union organization of its non-farm workers; Milwaukee at one time was probably the most completely unionized major city in the United States." Nesbit attributes this to inheriting "a European tradition of labor organizations, particularly from the skilled German and British workmen in the metal fabricating, machinery, and brewing industries."[3] Wisconsin's economy, like others in the northern industrial rust belt, has struggled at times. Still, the median household income in Wisconsin ($43,791) is higher than the national average ($41,994), while the rates of poverty (8.7 percent) and unemployment (5.5 percent) trail the national averages (12.4 and 5.8 percent, respectively).[4]

The 2000 U.S. Census count of 5,363,675 makes Wisconsin the eighteenth most populous state. This figure represents a 9.6 percent increase over 1990. Still, Wisconsin's share of the U.S. population shrank to 1.9 percent, continuing a decline first seen in the 1910 Census, when the state's share dropped from 2.7 to 2.5 percent. In 2000, Wisconsin was one of ten primarily rust belt states to lose a congressional seat to the faster-growing states of the sun belt.

Although there are pockets of diversity, Wisconsin is still largely a racially homogeneous midwestern state, with 87 percent of the population identifying themselves as non-Hispanic whites in the 2000 Census. Indeed, people of German ancestry alone constitute almost 43 percent of the population. Irish, Poles, and Norwegians together make up another 29 percent. These four ethnic groups, therefore, make up nearly three-quarters of Wisconsin's population. The balance of the population breaks down as follows: 5.6 percent African American, 3.6 percent Latino, 1.7 percent Asian, 0.8 percent Native American, and 1.2 percent other (including multiracial).

Sociologist Stephen Tordella's observation a quarter century ago remains true today: "The religious and ethnic composition of modern Wisconsin is almost a direct reflection of that composition at the turn of the century."[5] As is to be expected in a state dominated ethnically by Germans, Irish, Poles, and Scandinavians, Catholics and Lutherans are overrepresented in Wisconsin's population. Nearly half the population (48.6 percent) is claimed by the Roman Catholic Church, Evangelical Lutheran Church in America, Lutheran Church—Missouri Synod, and Wisconsin Evangelical Lutheran Church. At the same time, membership in some mainline denominations (United Methodist Church, United Church of Christ, Presbyterian Church USA) as well as evangelical Protestant churches is lower than that seen nationally.[6]

The prominence of German and Norwegian Lutherans and German, Irish, and Polish Catholics in Wisconsin has resulted in a state culture with strains of both moral conservatism and progressivism. In Elazar's typology of political cultures, Wisconsin is classified as *moralistic*, and Schroedel has recently found Wisconsin to be strongly pro-life in terms of the restrictiveness of its abortion laws. At the same time, it ranks sixth out of fifty states in terms of policy liberalism, according to Erickson and his colleagues.[7] This configuration provides ample opportunities for a broad spectrum of religious group involvement, as these groups focus the bulk of their attention on "conservative" life and family issues and "liberal" social justice issues.

Although the residents of Jackson, Michigan, would surely dispute the title, Ripon, Wisconsin, claims to be the birthplace of the antislavery Republican Party in 1854. Thus, it is not surprising that for its first century, Republicans dominated Wisconsin politics. This included a period of ascendancy of a sect calling itself the "Progressive Republicans," led by Robert M. ("Fighting Bob") LaFollette, who served as governor from 1900 to 1906 and U.S. senator from 1906 to 1925. (LaFollette also won 17 percent of the vote running as a Progressive in the 1924 presidential election.) Under the influence of the Progressive movement, Wisconsin lived up to its motto ("Forward") in passing pioneering laws on workers' compensation, child labor, unemployment compensation, and women's rights. From the 1960s forward, party competition in Wisconsin has been more robust, with party control of both houses of the legislature and the governor's mansion alternating with some frequency. In 2002, Democrat Jim Doyle was elected governor, but Republicans widened their majority in the assembly (58 to 41) and regained control of the senate (18 to 15). Unlike in California, for example, where one party dominates state government, the political situation in Wisconsin creates opportunities for religious groups across the theological spectrum to make inroads in the political process.

Finally, the Wisconsin legislature is highly professionalized, ranking twelfth out of fifty states in level of professionalization, as measured by member's salary, staff, and time spent in session. This professionalism has a long history in Wisconsin. The state's Legislative Reference Bureau was created in 1901 to provide a nonpartisan source of policy research and expertise, and a Legislative Council was created in 1947 to study issues, make recommendations, and provide continuity between legislative sessions. Also, in their comprehensive analysis of the overall impact of interest groups on public policy in the American states, Thomas and Hrebenar classified interest groups in Wisconsin as "complementary" (as opposed to dominant or subordinate). Wisconsin is one of eighteen states that fall in this middle category. That organized interests do not dominate is due in part to Wisconsin's very restrictive lobbying regulations. Opheim ranks Wisconsin (along with New Jersey and Washington) as having the nation's strictest regulations. Finally, in Gray and Lowery's population ecology of interest representation in the states, no state is more "average" than Wisconsin in terms of the "density" (the number of interest organizations) and the "diversity" of the lobbying community (the percentage of not-for-profit interests in the overall population).[8] All this creates a fairly level playing field for religious advocacy organizations in Wisconsin compared to other states.

## ORGANIZATION

Religious advocacy organizations have been growing in number, both nationally (as Hertzke demonstrated in his landmark study *Representing God in Washington*) and in the states. When the Wisconsin Catholic Conference was founded in 1968, it joined the Christian Science Committee on Publication for Wisconsin and the Wisconsin Council of Churches as one of the three religious advocacy organizations in the state. By the time I undertook my dissertation research in the mid-1990s, I was able to identify no fewer than sixteen organizations. A decade later, the number of religious advocacy organizations has truncated some, to about a dozen. This decrease is attributable to the disappearance of the state affiliates of such conservative organizations as Morality in Media and the Christian Coalition and to reorganization in the Catholic Church that eliminated the lobbyists for the Archdiocese of Milwaukee and the Catholic Health Association of Wisconsin. Presently, religious groups from across the denominational landscape are represented in Wisconsin. This includes, of course, numerically predominant groups like Catholics and Lutherans but also religious minorities such as Christian Scientists and Jews. There are also three paradenominational groups that are issue oriented: the Family Research Institute, Pro-Life Wisconsin, and Wisconsin Capitol Watch.

As table 7.1 indicates, these religious advocacy organizations are modest in size, averaging just two full-time equivalent staff members. This is particularly true in comparison to their secular peers. As interest groups, religious advocates are part of the same organizational environment as teachers' unions, chambers of commerce, bankers' associations, manufacturers' associations, organized labor, utility companies and associations, state bar and trial lawyers' associations, municipal leagues and counties' associations, and state farm bureaus. Studies of interest groups consistently rank these organized interests as the most effective in lobbying state government.[9] Examining the most effective advocacy organizations reveals certain characteristics that are simply beyond the reach of religious advocates.

First of all, the most effective lobbying organizations spend far more time and money lobbying than other interest groups. Consider the data from the Wisconsin legislature given in table 7.2. In the first year of the 2003–2004 biennium,

**Table 7.1.  Overview of Religious Lobbying Organizations in Wisconsin (2004)**

| Organization | Year Founded | Staff Full-Time Employees | % Public Affairs | Who Is Represented? |
|---|---|---|---|---|
| Christian Science Committee on Publication for Wisconsin | 1900 | 1.5 | 100 | Christian Science churches and practitioners in Wisconsin |
| Milwaukee Jewish Council for Community Relations | 1938 | 3.5 | 5 | Twenty-eight member organizations, agencies, and synagogues in the greater Milwaukee metro area |
| Wisconsin Council of Churches | 1946 | 3.0 | 25 | Twenty-two judicatory units of twelve mainline Protestant denominations in Wisconsin |
| Wisconsin Catholic Conference | 1968 | 4.0 | 100 | Roman Catholic bishops of the five dioceses of Wisconsin |
| Interfaith Conference of Greater Milwaukee | 1970 | 3.5 | 30 | Catholic, Protestant, Jewish, and Islamic judicatories |
| Lutheran Office for Public Policy in Wisconsin | 1983 | 1.0 | 100 | Six Evangelical Lutheran Church in America (ELCA) synods in Wisconsin |
| Family Research Institute of Wisconsin | 1986 | 2.0 | 100 | Contributions come from public at-large (no membership) |
| Wisconsin Jewish Conference | 1987 | 0.5 | 100 | Jewish communities across Wisconsin |
| Pro-Life Wisconsin | 1992 | 4.0 | 100 | Membership |
| Lutheran Social Services of Wisconsin and Upper Michigan Government Relations Office | 1994 | 1.25 | 100 | Lutheran Social Services and its sponsoring congregations |
| Wisconsin Capitol Watch | 2000 | 1.0 | 100 | Membership (formerly affiliated with the Family Research Institute) |
| Wisconsin Interfaith IMPACT | 2001 | 0.3 | 100 | Individual members, denominations, and other religious organizations in Wisconsin (formerly a committee within the Wisconsin Council of Churches) |

Note: "Public Affairs" here refers to direct and indirect political advocacy as well as attempts to educate member organizations/individuals and the broader public.
Sources: State of Wisconsin Ethics Board (http://ethics.state.wi.us) and interviews with organizational representatives.

651 organizations registered 758 lobbyists with the Wisconsin State Ethics Board.[10] But the top ten organized interests—from the Wisconsin Education Association Council (the teachers' union) to Aurora Health Care—accounted for some 20 percent of all lobbying expenditures. Although four religious advocacy organizations—Pro-Life Wisconsin, the Lutheran Office for Public Policy, Wisconsin Catholic Conference, and Lutheran Social Services—spent more time and money lobbying than the average organization in Wisconsin, they spent far less than the biggest-spending and most influential groups. Moreover, the majority of religious advocacy organizations spent far less time and money than the state average for lobbying organizations.

In addition, the most effective lobbies typically establish political action committees (PACs) to make campaign donations to candidates, parties, or other PACs, and they often endorse candidates for public office as well. In his survey of interest group politics in Wisconsin, Ronald Hedlund writes, "The Wisconsin Education Association Council (WEAC) is generally reputed to be one of the most effective special interest groups, if not the most effective, in the state." Not surprisingly, in addition to the million-plus dollars it spent on lobbying annually, WEAC PAC also spent $156,000 on state elections in the 2002 election cycle, making it one of the top campaign contributors in the state.[11] As organizations exempt from federal income tax under section 501(c)(3) of the Internal Revenue Code, churches are prohibited from engaging in this sort of political campaign activity. Consequently, as a Catholic lobbyist in another state told me, "We lobby with one arm tied behind our backs."

Of the dozen or so organizations in this study, only Pro-Life Wisconsin has established a PAC, the Pro-Life Wisconsin Victory Fund. According to the Wisconsin Democracy Campaign, in the 2001–2002 election cycle, the Victory Fund made direct contributions of $4,600 to candidates for governor, lieutenant governor, attorney general, and/or the legislature. In that same period, Planned Parenthood Advocates of Wisconsin made contributions of $8,338. Of course, the contributions of both these PACs were dwarfed by those of PACs representing the teachers' union ($156,000) and realtors ($126,500). According to Matt Sande of Pro-Life Wisconsin, the potential votes garnered by the Victory Fund's *endorsements* are more important to candidates than the small amount of money provided, as the Republicans who Pro-Life Wisconsin tends to endorse get plenty of money through business and other PACs.

Other religious groups have considered forming PACs, but the Victory Fund to date remains the only one active in Wisconsin. Marvin Munyon, founder of the Family Research Institute and now director of and lobbyist for Wisconsin Capitol Watch, recently attempted to organize a pro-family PAC, but ideological differences and economic difficulties with the funders prevented it. Michael

**Table 7.2. Top Ten Lobbying Organizations in Wisconsin and Religious Lobbying Organizations Compared, January 2003–December 2003**

| Organization | Total Lobbying Expenditures | No. Registered Lobbyists | No. Hours Communicating |
|---|---|---|---|
| Wisconsin Education Association Council | $1,083,487 | 17 | 1,914 |
| Wisconsin Manufacturers and Commerce | 639,925 | 11 | 1,178 |
| Wisconsin Independent Businesses | 512,692 | 2 | 474 |
| Wisconsin Merchants Federation | 465,314 | 3 | 171 |
| Wisconsin Counties Association | 462,814 | 9 | 1,856 |
| Wisconsin Hospital Association | 424,664 | 12 | 596 |
| Wisconsin Energy Corporation | 393,438 | 18 | 572 |
| Forest County Potawatomi Community | 374,276 | 8 | 137 |
| Wisconsin Farm Bureau Federation | 337,025 | 3 | 905 |
| Aurora Health Care | 315,957 | 8 | 466 |
| Pro-Life Wisconsin | 91,771 | 2 | 263 |
| Lutheran Office for Public Policy | 71,019 | 1 | 162 |
| Wisconsin Catholic Conference | 63,762 | 3 | 113 |
| Lutheran Social Services | 47,569 | 3 | 131 |
| STATE AVERAGE | Mean: $40,000 | — | Median: 141 |
| Wisconsin Jewish Conference | 9,605 | 1 | 7 |
| Christian Science Committee on Publication | 4,616 | 1 | 31 |
| Wisconsin Council of Churches | 4,568 | 1 | 17 |
| Interfaith Conference of Greater Milwaukee | 3,188 | 2 | 22 |
| Milwaukee Jewish Council for Community Relations | 2,834 | 2 | 24 |
| Wisconsin Capitol Watch | 1,633 | 1 | 30 |
| Archdiocese of Milwaukee | 1,213 | 1 | 3 |
| Family Research Institute of Wisconsin | 634 | 1 | 13 |
| Total (651 organizations) | $26.2 million | 758 | 248,000 |

Source: State of Wisconsin Ethics Board (http://ethics.state.wi.us).

Blumenfeld of the Wisconsin Jewish Conference recalls a conversation among his board some years ago about the possibility of forming a PAC, but the idea was quickly dismissed. Indeed, most denominationally based religious groups assiduously avoid the partisanship inherent in electoral politics.

A final political resource that religious advocacy organizations have at their disposal is grassroots mobilization. In the mid-1990s, there was considerable grassroots mobilization around two key issues: welfare reform and same-sex marriage. Religious individuals and groups that were not previously mobilized at the state level became activated during this time. Groups such as the Milwaukee Innercity Congregations Allied for Hope, the Coming Out/Coming Together Coalition, and Wisconsin Christians United regularly participated in the public policy process on these issues. However, as welfare reform became a fait accompli and same-sex marriage receded from the scene (for the time being), these groups returned to their local roots and activities. Established religious lobbies like the Wisconsin Catholic Conference and Wisconsin Council of Churches would like to be able to activate the grassroots when necessary to help influence legislators, but this is difficult in practice. Not only are individuals busy and not familiar with the issues, but appeals to the grassroots also highlight the *diversity* of opinion among individuals who claim a particular religious affiliation. More than once I have heard the refrain from legislators in Wisconsin, "The Catholics in my district don't [fill in the blank: oppose capital punishment, oppose abortion, favor increasing the minimum wage, and so on]." One could substitute Lutheran, Presbyterian, Methodist, or other traditions for Catholic to the same effect. In the end, all religious lobbies would like to have grassroots support as part of their political capital, but none has completely succeeded in realizing this aspiration.

Thus, if political advocacy is conceptualized as a "three-legged stool"—(1) direct advocacy, (2) engagement in civil society (public education and cultivating grassroots activism), and (3) electioneering—religious organizations are confined largely to the first two legs. Especially when the legislature is in session, the majority of the work of religious advocacy organizations is dedicated to direct advocacy. Thus, without minimizing the importance of the others, this chapter focuses its attention on this particular leg.

## MOTIVATION

Political scientist Daniel Hofrenning contends that a prophetic vision of religious lobbyists in Washington, D.C., affects everything they do, from defining goals to choosing tactics to measuring effectiveness. Religious lobbyists, according to Hofrenning, "offer a principled and moralistic vision. Unlike most other lobbyists, they seek nothing less than the transformation of American politics to a higher moral plane." Obviously, religious lobbyists in contemporary America are not themselves prophets, but they share with the Old Testament prophets a proclivity for moral exhortations critiquing the status quo and advancing a vision of a new society.[12]

Without question, most religious advocates with whom I spoke conform to Hofrenning's model of the prophetic politics of religious lobbyists. Religious advocacy doesn't exist solely to achieve political victories, narrowly understood (for example, the passage of a particular piece of legislation), nor do religious advocates represent special interests, narrowly understood. The comments of the following two religious advocates, representing different religious traditions, are typical of this:

> *Michael Blumenfeld, executive director, Wisconsin Jewish Conference*: In my view it's not only appropriate, it's a responsibility for some [religious] organizations to be involved in political discourse and be involved in advocacy. [In the Jewish tradition] there is the concept of *tikkun olam*. The idea of responsibility, literally some people say perfecting the world, repairing the world. It's an obligation to make it a better place for everybody. That sounds corny, but I think that's a driving factor in a lot of this.
>
> *Rev. Dr. Jerry Folk, former executive director, Wisconsin Council of Churches*: The goal that we have is to contribute to the renewal of society, to the renewal of democratic society, to contribute to the well-being of all the members of society, and to contribute to a healthy relationship between the human species and the rest of the environment on which human well-being is dependent. There is a saying by a second century bishop by the name of Irenaeus of Lyons. He said that the glory of God is a human being fully alive. And so our purpose in working in what many people call politics — that is, broadly speaking, on an agenda to try to make the world a better place — is to help create the conditions that enable every human being to be fully alive. I don't think that when you are starving you can be as fully alive as God wants you to be. Or when you are suffering from ignorance and disease, and don't have access to healing or knowledge, you can't be as fully alive as God wants you to be. So our whole goal is to say, if you're going to change this, change it in a way that allows more people to be fully alive.

One interviewee, Jonalu Johnstone, the minister at James Reeb Unitarian-Universalist congregation in Madison who was active in the Coming Out/Coming Together Coalition in the late-1990s, even volunteered the word "prophetic" without prompting in the following exchange:

> *Yamane*: Do you feel like you were a political person from the start?
> *Johnstone*: Well, yeah, that's probably true. And I don't know if I'd use the word political. I think I would probably tend more toward using the word *prophetic*.

> I think that the prophetic part of the mystery is a very important one. I think the prophetic voice is an important one. I think that when we have a strong sense of what is right and wrong, it needs to be said and it needs to be said publicly and strongly.

Hofrenning's characterization of the outlook of religious lobbyists in the nation's capital as "prophetic" applies to religious advocates in Wisconsin as well.

Beyond this ultimate motivation for political involvement, religious advocacy organizations most resemble public interest groups. According to Jeffrey Berry, "A public interest group is one that seeks a collective good, the achievement of which will not selectively and materially benefit the members or activists of the organization."[13] To be sure, some lobbying effort by religious advocates is directed at protecting both material and ideal self-interest. Clearly, Lutheran Social Services hires lobbyists to defend the material interests of its human services institutions. The mission of the Christian Science Committee on Publication "is to correct impositions on the public with regard to Christian Science" and ensure that Christian Scientists' "sincerely held religious beliefs" are not compromised by any legislation or administrative rule in the state. In 2003, the Wisconsin Catholic Conference, Wisconsin Jewish Conference, and Wisconsin Council of Churches were intimately involved in the crafting of legislation to add clergy to the list of mandatory reporters of child sexual abuse. In doing so, they had to act to protect both the material and the ideal interests of the judicatories (and, by extension, congregations) they represent.

Still, much of the work of these organizations is aimed at promoting basic (if often contested) values concerning religious freedom, human rights, social justice, and the common good. This can be seen in an examination of their organizational goals. For example, according to the Evangelical Lutheran Church in America, state advocacy offices like the Lutheran Office for Public Policy in Wisconsin "represent the church in advocating at the state government level with and on behalf of those without economic or political power." And the Wisconsin Council of Churches "engages in conversation with policy makers and governmental agencies with the purpose of furthering the Common Good of the human community."

Given the publicly spirited approach of these religious advocacy organizations, to characterize their representatives as "lobbyists" could be seen as an insult (given popular perceptions of political influence peddlers). But if lobbyists are those who "deliberate[ly] attempt to influence political decisions through various forms of public advocacy," then the description fits. They are lobbyists, then, but not in the basest sense of the term. One reason people dislike lobbyists is that they are seen as willing to represent any interest on any issue as long as they get paid. As one lobbyist commented in a book on the ethics of lobbying, "The lobbyist is simply a hired gun. Lobbyists have no principles. Lobbyists have no positions. You ask someone what do you think about this and he'll say I don't know, I don't have a client. We're sort of agnostics here. A client retains us and that's fine, but if someone who didn't like that client retained us, well, that would be fine too."[14] Those who represent religious organizations in the legislative arena are emphatically not hired guns. Like other advocates for the public interest, they represent values that they as individuals hold deeply. This is especially apparent among those who purposely moved from representing secular to religious interests. Says Kathy Markeland, reflecting on the difference between lobbying for the Wisconsin Counties Association and the Wisconsin Catholic Conference, "What's fundamentally different for me is being able to feel more connected to the things I'm advocating for. This is more than a job for me. The positions that I'm taking on the issues that we're working on are things that are closer to my heart, and that's been an important and very big change." Matthew Sande left the Wisconsin Hospital Association to become legislative affairs director for Pro-Life Wisconsin because he thought, "What will I say when I meet my maker and he asks, 'What did you do to help protect the unborn? How did you use your knowledge and expertise?'"

Of course, a prophetic motivation does not translate simply or directly into a particular legislative program. The issues that religious advocacy organizations in Wisconsin address span the entire political spectrum. Groups based in mainline Protestant religious traditions, like the Lutheran Office for Public Policy and Wisconsin Council of Churches, focus largely on issues of "social justice." For example, the Lutheran Office for Public Policy describes its lobbying interest as "advocating justice for disempowered people and responsible care of creation." It lists the following issues as its specific interests: "hunger, nutrition programs; health care (mental health parity, drug costs, coverage for all uninsured); corrections (terms, treatment, education, aftercare); low income concerns; welfare reform; environmental stewardship, death penalty, gambling expansion, rights of immigrants, rural-farm issues, economic justice for low income people, and fair taxation." Groups based more in evangelical Protestant religious traditions, like Wisconsin Capitol Watch and the Family Research Institute, tend to focus more on "social regulatory" issues. For example, the Family Research Institute declares an interest in "any legislation or rules that will impact Wisconsin families, including but not necessarily limited to education, taxes/spending, social services/child-protection agencies, marriage, abortion, physician-assisted suicide, human embryonic stem cell research, cloning and gambling." Finally, as suggested by the late Joseph Cardinal Bernardin's "seamless garment," the Wisconsin Catholic Conference's advocacy engages issues that span the political spectrum. It lobbies with "conservative" organizations on education, family, and lifestyle issues and with "liberal" organizations on economic and social welfare issues.

This configuration of groups that differ by religious tradition results in a division of labor of sorts among religious advocacy organizations. There is a religiously based pro-life movement, but there is no religiously based pro-choice movement (for example, there is no Wisconsin chapter of the Religious Coalition for Abortion Rights). On the other hand, there is a religiously based anti–death penalty movement, but there is no religiously based pro–death penalty movement. The Family Research Institute has come out strongly against same-sex marriage, but no religious lobby has come out in favor of it. The Catholic Conference and other organizations favor an increase in the minimum wage, but there is no religiously based opposition to that. Rarely do two religious lobbies directly square off in the legislative arena in Wisconsin. In fact, they often work in coalition with one another, even to the extent of issuing joint letters. When there is a divergence of opinion on an issue, they typically either agree to disagree or keep the disagreement "backstage."

Although they have forward-looking legislative agendas, like many groups, religious advocacy organizations are driven in their day-to-day work by the "tyranny of the in-box." This was never more evident than in the 2003–2004 legislative session, when legislation was introduced to add clergy to the list of mandatory reporters of child sexual abuse and extend the statute of limitations for bringing criminal charges or seeking civil damages for abuse. As this sort of legislation began spreading across the country in the wake of the sexual abuse scandal in the Catholic Church that broke early in 2002, it was not totally unexpected.[15] But neither was it part of any group's legislative agenda. Still, seven of the twelve established religious lobbies in Wisconsin spent some time on this legislation. For six of them, it was either the first (Christian Science Committee, Council of Churches, Catholic Conference, Jewish Conference) or the second (Milwaukee Jewish Council for Community Relations, Wisconsin Capitol Watch) most time-consuming issue they lobbied between January 2003 and July 2004.[16] Only Wisconsin Capitol Watch opposed the legislation, seeing it as an undue impingement on the religious freedom of churches. In the end, Scott Anderson of the Council of Churches, Michael Blumenfeld of the Jewish Conference, and John Huebscher of the Catholic Conference issued a joint letter to members of the legislature supporting the legislation that eventually passed in the senate by 33 to 0 and the assembly by 99 to 0 and was signed by the governor at a public ceremony. Other issues—like legislation that would allow the carrying of concealed weapons (possibly even in churches) and a "Taxpayer Bill of Rights"—were similarly irritating to religious groups, even though the outcomes on these bills were favorable. So religious advocacy organizations continue to form and pursue their proactive agendas even while recognizing, with Robert Burns, that "the best-laid schemes o' mice an' men gang aft agley" (go often awry).

Beyond engaging particular issues, the question of how to translate their prophetic motivation into concrete political *practices* is one of the greatest challenges religious advocates face. For example, the prophetic desire for the radical transformation of the world to a higher plane runs up against the slow, incremental process of legislative "sausage-making." The prophetic temptation to advance positions as nonnegotiable confronts the imperative to compromise in policymaking. The prophetic belief in the ultimate truth of the faith defies the religious and cultural pluralism characteristic of American society and reflected in our secular liberal political institutions. And so on. The next section, then, takes up the question of religious advocacy organizations' political practices.

## PRACTICES

In his pioneering work, Allen Hertzke observes that religious lobbying organizations in Washington, D.C., often are reluctant or ill equipped to engage in the "detail work," the "microprocess," which is central to the legislative process. He distinguishes between advocacy, which consists for the most part of "*witnessing*"—that is, groups "making known their positions without really engaging the legislative process in a specific way"—and "*classic insider lobbying*"—that is, "activities designed to affect precise policy outcomes, including: drafting bill language, offering amendments, forging coalitions behind the scenes, negotiating with opponents over compromise provisions, and providing useful facts and arguments to members during legislative debates." Hertzke finds that, "with a few exceptions, there is an overall weakness at the detail level" in the work of the Washington religious lobbyists. Hofrenning, too, cites as a weakness of religious lobbying the fact that "religious lobbyists spend much of their time articulating broad moral principles; they usually leave the details to others." The "prophetic temptation," then, a pull toward purity and away from strategy and mundanity in the legislative arena, serves to undermine the effectiveness of religious advocacy.[17]

At least in Wisconsin, these statements do not ring true. Most religious advocates effectively channel their prophetic motivation into the legislative sausage-making process. Again, the experiences of those who have lobbied for both secular and religious organizations are instructive. According to Kathy Markeland of the Catholic Conference, "In terms of the day-to-day need to follow, understand, and analyze legislation, put together testimony, and appear at hearings, it's the same as at the Counties Association." Matt Sande relates a similar sentiment in comparing his work for the Wisconsin Hospital Association to Pro-Life Wisconsin: "What I do across the street [at the capitol] is no different. I call on legislators to explain our positions and try to address concerns they may have. I try to advance the good legislation and stop the bad legislation. It's no different in that respect." Michael Blumenfeld is the director of the Wisconsin Jewish Conference, but he is also a contract lobbyist with his own firm, Michael Blumenfeld and Associates, LLC, which represents interests such as Adoption Resources of Wisconsin, Elder Care of Dane County, United Cerebral Palsy of Wisconsin, and others. According to Blumenfeld, "I basically go about my work the same way," whether he is representing the Jewish Conference or his other clients. Although there are times when religious advocacy organizations will get involved in an issue because they feel compelled to give "witness" to some position they think will otherwise not be heard, this does not come at the expense of "classic insider lobbying."

It is widely recognized among political scientists studying lobbying that, next to money, *information* is the great resource of interest groups. As Lester Milbrath explained in his 1959 book *The Washington Lobbyists*, "Communication is the only means of influencing or changing a perception; the lobbying process, therefore, is totally a communicative process." As society has grown more complex and state legislatures more professionalized, the importance of interest groups in supplying legislators with *technical expertise* in the policymaking process—especially providing *information* about the consequences of legislative decisions—has also grown. Two political scientists who directed a study of interest group activity in all fifty state legislatures have concluded that, as "a consequence of the increasing complexity of issues and the movement towards a more technological society," the "new breed [of lobbyist] is a purveyor of technical information."[18] Especially in Wisconsin, with its extraordinarily strict lobbying laws, "the major currency lobbyists peddle today is information."[19]

Thus, the type and quality of information lobbyists provide is central to their credibility and hence effectiveness. As much as any religious group active in the Wisconsin statehouse, the Wisconsin Catholic Conference recognizes this. Executive Director Huebscher stresses, "I think there is a temptation or tendency to view religious groups as idealistic do-gooders who don't understand the 'real world.' Which is why being thoughtful and informed and being able to come in with data and analysis is so important to me. To quickly disabuse them of the fact that we don't know what we're talking about." Providing quality information to legislators is a vehicle for the Catholic Conference to achieve its ends by solidifying its legitimacy as a political actor in the eyes of legislators. This can be seen clearly in the Conference's testimony before the legislature. For example, on a bill that would require certain employers receiving state grants to pay their employees a "living wage," the Catholic Conference testimony begins by explaining the position of the Catholic Church on a living wage, mentioning in turn Pope John Paul II's encyclical letter on work and the U.S. Catholic Bishops' long-standing support of a living wage. It then invokes data from the Bureau of Labor Statistics that point to the large number of Wisconsinites who make less than a living wage and would not benefit from the legislation. Similarly, on a proposal to expand the ability of employers to discriminate in hiring a worker on the basis of the worker's conviction record, the Catholic Conference testimony begins by noting the rootedness of its opposition to the legislation in Catholic social teaching. Then the testimony presents data from the Department of Corrections and the Uniform Crime Reporting Program documenting the potentially adverse impact of the legislation. In both cases, it was not sufficient for the Catholic Conference to argue its position solely on the basis of Catholic social teaching. Some analysis of the impact of the legislation needed to be presented as well. This pattern is not limited to the Catholic Conference. According to the former director of communication for Pro-Life Wisconsin, Greg Chesmore, when testifying before the legislature, "obviously you want to make sure that you have good sources, that you have documentation of the things that you say, specifics. When you're dealing with public policy you can't just look at it from a faith perspective."

Conservative Christians have often been criticized for pursuing an uncompromising approach to politics and for an alleged tendency toward "Bible thumping" in public. Marvin Munyon—a born-again Christian, former head of the evangelical-dominated Family Research Institute, and currently director of Wisconsin Capitol Watch—is painfully aware not only of this stereotype but also of the ineffectiveness of forceful invocations of biblical authority before the legislature. As he put it when asked why his materials on same-sex marriage included definitions of marriage from dictionaries and state statutes but not from religious sources,

I'm not ashamed of anything in the Bible. I come from a very strong Christian background, but I find that in the public policy arena, that isn't always the argument that is most effective. I think we need to be factual. I try not to be highly emotional and that type of thing, but put things out there that are clear that people can understand and I think those things [dictionary definitions of marriage] are pretty easy for people to understand regardless of where they are on the issue.

Despite the fact that the overwhelming majority of legislators profess to be Christian, Munyon recognizes that the presentation of issues in public before the legislature is different than the way an issue might be treated in a more private setting, such as a church. The failure of some of his colleagues and constituents in the evangelical Christian community to recognize this is a source of some frustration to Munyon, as he expresses in the following passage:

> Well, unfortunately the religious community has a difficult time, I believe, of expressing themselves in the public arena. For instance, at these hearings, you know legislators are not there to have somebody come in and open the Bible and start reading Bible verses to them. They're dealing with a specific issue and they want to know something about that issue. I try to tell people that a public hearing is not the podium of your church; it's not a place to preach to these people. We need to approach them, and certainly you can use your Christian background to [ground] where you're coming from, but it's not a Sunday morning church service. And I've heard people, sad to say, tell legislators if you vote for this bill, you're going to go to hell or whatever. That is unfortunate because that's counterproductive in my way of thinking.

The need to refrain from confronting legislators with excessively strong invocations of religious authority (for example, in the form of scripture) is felt not only by religious "conservatives." Religious "liberals," like Marcus White, associate director of the Interfaith Conference of Greater Milwaukee, also tread lightly when bringing religion into the public arena. "Preaching," in the negative sense commonly associated with the term in our secularized society, is to be avoided regardless of your position on the theological continuum. According to White, "When you talk with legislators and when you represent a religious institution, you want to be careful about throwing around God. You don't want to seem heavy-handed, and I think there are legislators who can get turned off by that because they feel like you're preaching to them. And so we would be careful about that, just how it's heard by some folks."

Despite their best efforts, in the same way that they can't compete in the political money game, religious advocacy organizations also find themselves at a deficit with respect to information as political currency. Especially on complex issues such as welfare reform, biotechnology, and health care, religious advocates struggle to put out policy analysis in the same breadth, depth, and volume as more narrowly focused outfits like the Wisconsin Council on

Children and Families or more well-heeled groups like Wisconsin Manufacturers and Commerce. This fact makes work in coalitions that combine religious and secular interest groups—seen especially on the death penalty, health care, and welfare reform—all the more important. The major religious advocacy organizations in Wisconsin welcome these coalitions, even if they are not always formalized because of differences between the groups on other issues.

In the end, at the same time they want to be taken seriously as a source of "useful information," there is also a recognition that some issues are so complex that they can be engaged only on the level of principle. The Catholic Conference's Huebscher explains,

> When you get into the issue, for example, of access to health insurance, there are some people who don't want to talk about anything but a single payer system. Whereas I think that the Church would say, there's a universal human right to health care, yet we respect the complexities of the issue enough *not* to prescribe a specific means of doing that. We know we don't have the expertise to do it, but we do know that we have a Gospel mandate to do it, and the resources exist for us to do it.

Groups the size of religious advocacy organizations must be aware of their limited resources and expend their political capital wisely. Doing so allows them a modicum of success—their understanding of which I treat in the final section.

## SUCCESS

In order to be effective in securing legislative outcomes, religious groups must engage in the practical affairs of insider lobbying; however, few religious advocates I had contact with would be satisfied only with securing discrete legislative victories. The temptation for lobbying to become an end in itself is one that many religious lobbyists feel a constant need to resist. For example, one Wisconsin lobbyist looked at her organizational counterparts in Washington, D.C. as a cautionary example against becoming too concerned with being a "player" in the political game. Thus, although discrete legislative outcomes are a concern of religious advocacy organizations, they are not always the primary concern. In fact, three measures of success are operative for religious advocates: (1) having credibility in the eyes of legislators, (2) securing discrete political and legislative victories, and, most important, (3) being faithful to their calling as religious organizations.

## Credibility

Political legitimacy can be defined roughly as the right to speak, be heard, and be taken seriously in the political process. Political advocates themselves prefer the term *credibility*. Credibility in the legislative process is built up slowly over time. As Huebscher puts it, "When I meet with a legislator, [the strategic objective] is to either establish or continue to cement their view of the Conference as an agency that provides thoughtful, useful information. So that even if they're disinclined to go with us on the issue of the moment that they will see in us someone that they would want to hear from again. And that they would find it useful to hear from again because what we say would be thoughtful, informed, and helpful to them as they make a decision on an issue." In fact, as religious lobbying in Madison has expanded and matured, legislators have come to take these groups seriously, some quite so.

This can be seen in the results of a survey of Wisconsin state legislators I conducted in the mid-1990s. When legislators were asked, "As a general principle, which one of the following four statements best approximates your view of the proper role of religious groups and organizations in the legislative process?" 83.9 percent responded that it is *proper* for religious groups and organizations to be involved, though they should be treated the same as other groups and organizations. The second most common response (12.9 percent) was not only that it is proper for religious groups and organizations to be involved but also that, on certain issues, the legislative process should not proceed without their input. Only 1.6 percent of respondents answered that it is *improper* for religious groups and organizations to be involved in the legislative process, the same proportion that indicated that the legislative process should *never* proceed without input from religious groups and organizations. Clearly, legislators generally have no principled objection to the involvement of religious advocacy organizations in the political process, and a number welcome it.

To move beyond the level of principle and better understand the concrete relationships between legislators and religious advocates, legislators were also asked to "name up to five of the most important groups or organizations which *you find it useful to consult with* in your capacity as a legislator on three important issues considered in the 1995–1996 biennium: abortion, capital punishment, and welfare reform."[20] Groups were then assigned points, depending on the position in which they were named by legislators. For example, the first group named for each issue was assigned five points, the second group named was assigned four points, and so on, until the fifth group named was assigned one point. These points were then totaled for each group on each issue to yield a ranking of the groups most important in being consulted by legislators. This ranking is given in table 7.3.

**Table 7.3. Top Ten Groups Consulted by Legislators, by Issue (Asterisk = Religious Organization)**

| Rank | Abortion<br>Group (Points) | Capital Punishment<br>Group (Points) | Welfare Reform<br>Group (Points) |
|---|---|---|---|
| 1 | Planned Parenthood (122) | State Bar of Wisconsin (44) | Wisconsin Counties Association (38) |
| 2 | Wisconsin Right to Life (98) | *Wisconsin Catholic Conference (32) | Wisconsin Council on Children and Families (35) |
| 3 | State Medical Society (40) | Wisconsin Association of Trial Lawyers (14) | Department of Health and Human Services (31) |
| 4 | *Pro-Life Wisconsin (24) | Wisconsin Right to Life (13) | *Wisconsin Catholic Conference (19) |
| 5 | *Wisconsin Catholic Conference (21) | League of Women Voters (9) | AFSCME Council 40 (13) |
| 6 | National Abortion Rights Action League (12) | *Lutheran Office for Public Policy (8) | University of Wisconsin Institute for Research on Poverty (12) |
| 7 | League of Women Voters (9) | Wisconsin District Attorneys Association (8) | NAACP (10) |
| 8 | Wisconsin Citizens Concerned for Life (5) | NAACP (5) | AFT-Technical Colleges (9) |
| 9 | Legislative Reference Bureau (4) | Wisconsin Chiefs of Police (5) | Legal Action of Wisconsin (9) |
| 10 | National Organization of Women (4) | Wisconsin Coalition Against the Death Penalty (5) | AFL-CIO (8) |
| | National Women's Political Caucus (4) | Wisconsin Professional Police Association (5) | *Wisconsin Council of Churches (8) |
| | Pro-Choice Wisconsin (4) | | |
| | State Bar of Wisconsin (4) | | |

Source: Wisconsin State Legislator Survey, 1996.

Table 7.3 demonstrates very clearly that, although they rank below secular interest groups on each issue, some religious groups are taken very seriously in the public policy process in the Wisconsin statehouse. The Wisconsin Catholic Conference is clearly the most widely consulted religious advocacy organization, the only one to rank in the top ten on all three issues. Pro-Life Wisconsin, an issue-specific organization and the only religious organization to sponsor a PAC, is the highest ranked on abortion. The Lutheran Office for Public Policy ranked sixth on capital punishment, and the Wisconsin Council of Churches tied for tenth on welfare reform.

A seat at the table is a mark of success in itself. But it is also a prerequisite for concrete legislative success. Most of the religious advocacy organizations active in Wisconsin want a seat at the table but aren't satisfied with that as an end in itself.

### Victory

Groups differ in how much they embrace political influence as a measure of success, though all mention legislative victory as an important indicator. The longer a group has been involved in public advocacy and the more professionalized it becomes, the most important legislative victory seems to be.

In hiring Scott Anderson in March 2003, the Wisconsin Council of Churches' board wanted to raise its profile in the public policy arena. Unlike his predecessor, Jerry Folk, Anderson comes with major public policy experience, having served as associate and executive director of the California Council of Churches for twelve years. He has a master's degree in public policy and administration and was a registered lobbyist in California. By May 2003, he had registered as a lobbyist for the Council of Churches in Wisconsin, something Folk had purposely avoided during his tenure. In the press release announcing his hiring, Anderson echoed Folk's prophetic vision (quoted earlier in this chapter) for the Council of Churches' involvement in public life: "As a life-long Christian and Presbyterian, the counter-cultural character of God challenges me. God's justice, which in scripture is focused on the marginalized in society, is rarely embraced by the world. From poverty to economic inequality, from environmental degradation to the growing specter of violence both at home and around the world, the prophetic call 'to do justice, love mercy, and walk humbly with our God' (Micah 6:8) gives shape to the church's missional imperative in the 21st century."[21] But when it comes to assessing "success" in his advocacy work, Anderson states clearly, "The bottom line is, does a bill pass or fail? That's the ultimate measure of success. In this business, given the kinds of issues we take positions on, we fail a lot more than we succeed. That's just part of the landscape. But [in the 2003–2004 biennium] we succeeded on clergy sexual misconduct. We succeeded on killing the concealed carry bill. We succeeded on killing TABOR last week. We were part of a coalition; it wasn't our doing alone. But I feel pretty good about that."

### Faithfulness

Perhaps all interest groups expect to "win some, lose some." But the prophetic vision of religious advocacy organizations relativizes both the wins and the losses. It puts their political advocacy and understanding of success in a broader—indeed, an ultimate—context. As William Beckman put it before the demise of the Wisconsin Christian Coalition,

> I read the last chapter. I know who wins. Meanwhile, back at the ranch, we have been advised to be diligent and continue in His ways. We are going to have victories; we are going to have losses. I kid the wife all the time that when I get the grass cut and it's looking good, I have a feeling of accomplishment. Whereas this [work for the Christian Coalition] is an ongoing effort. So you can't have that sense of completion per se. We know what we are trying to accomplish, but as far as having some feeling of accomplishment, I am not so much worried about that. As a Christian, my relationship to my Lord is more important than whether I feel I have accomplished anything in the eyes of my fellow man.

Marvin Munyon, the dean of the evangelical advocates, says, "Because I do come from a strong Christian background, I feel that it's not my place to always win. And I think that many times my calling has been to be faithful, to stand and proclaim the truth. And if I do that, I don't always have to win to be the winner." This view is reflected in the official literature of the Family Research Institute, which Munyon founded in 1986:

> Although not a perfect correlation, FRI sees itself as similar to the Old Testament prophets—declaring the truth to the culture. However, unlike many political organizations, FRI's primary purpose is not to win every battle. It believes the battle belongs to the Lord. This allows FRI to pursue integrity and character first, setting an example to those who are watching. FRI does try to influence the culture, but not at the price of its integrity and character. So, sometimes it wins and sometimes it loses, just like the Old Testament prophets. By maintaining this philosophy, FRI believes it will always win in the long run.[22]

Still, for those whose daily lives are consumed by public policy work, there is a temptation to view political ends as being the bottom line. Sharon

Schmeling served as associate director of the Wisconsin Catholic Conference in the 1990s. She commented at the time,

> I think it's very easy in the political process to get so focused on trying to get money for programs, trying to get vouchers for parents, or trying to create a welfare system that is better than the one most policymakers want to create. It's really easy to forget that we're trying to spread the gospel of love and redemption and forgiveness. And if you don't keep your mind focused on that primary purpose of the church, you can just become a lobbyist who happened to work for a nonprofit organization that happened to be religious that wanted to get things or change structures—just like the business lobby or the teachers' union.

Speaking also from a Catholic perspective, Greg Chesmore of Pro-Life Wisconsin invokes Mother Teresa, who

> said once that God does not call us to be successful. He calls us to be faithful. It's not about winning all kinds of victories or having a seat at the table. Ultimately, it comes down to, are we being faithful to what we know in our heart is true: that God is the author of human life. You know, Christ did not call us to be politically popular. He called us to remain faithful to the truth that He gave us. That's our driving force here. If we can do that, then regardless of our political record, we believe we're successful.

## CONCLUSION

No one, least of all religious lobbyists themselves, would characterize religious advocacy organizations in Wisconsin as major players in the political game. In Wisconsin, as in every state, the teachers' union and manufacturers' association (and similar organized interests) are the 800-pound gorillas of the legislative process. Still, the heavily Catholic and Lutheran culture of the state, the Progressive political heritage associated with it, and the professionalization of state government allow religious advocacy organizations to occupy a significant niche in the lobbying community at the Wisconsin statehouse.

## NOTES

1. Robert C. Nesbit, *Wisconsin: A History*, 2nd ed. (Madison: University of Wisconsin Press, 1989).

2. Leon Epstein, *Politics in Wisconsin* (Madison: University of Wisconsin Press, 1958), 20.

3. Nesbit, *Wisconsin*, 539.

4. This and the following demographic data are from Paul Voss, Daniel Veroff, and David Long, "Wisconsin's People: A Portrait of Wisconsin's Population on the Threshold of the 21st Century," in *State of Wisconsin 2003–2004 Blue Book* (Madison: Wisconsin Legislature Joint Committee on Legislative Organization, 2003), 101–74; Economic Research Service, U.S. Department of Agriculture, www.ers.usda .gov; Bureau of Labor Statistics, U.S. Department of Labor, www.bls.gov; U.S. Census Bureau, U.S. Department of Commerce, www.census.gov.

5. Stephen Tordella, "Religion in Wisconsin: Preferences, Practices and Ethnic Composition," University of Wisconsin-Madison Applied Population Laboratory Population Series Report 70-13 (1979), 1.

6. See *Religious Congregations and Membership in the United States 2000* (Nashville: Glenmary Research Center, 2002).

7. Daniel Elazar, *American Federalism: A View from the States*, 2nd ed. (New York: Thomas Y. Crowell, 1972); Jean Reith Schroedel, *Is the Fetus a Person? A Comparison of Policies across the Fifty States* (Ithaca, N.Y.: Cornell University Press, 2000); Robert Erickson, Gerald Wright, and John McIver, *Statehouse Democracy: Public Opinion and Policy in the American States* (Cambridge: Cambridge University Press, 1993).

8. Peverill Squire, "Legislative Professionalization and Membership Diversity in State Legislatures," *Legislative Studies Quarterly* 17 (1992): 69–72; Nesbit, *Wisconsin*, 553; Ronald Hrebenar and Clive Thomas, "Interest Group Activity in the States," in *Politics in the American States: A Comparative Analysis*, 7th ed., ed. Virginia Gray, Russell Hanson, and Herbert Jacob (Washington, D.C.: Congressional Quarterly Press, 1999), 113–43; Ronald Hedlund, "Wisconsin: Pressure Politics and a Lingering Progressive Tradition," in *Interest Group Politics in the Midwestern States*, ed. Ronald Hrebenar and Clive Thomas (Ames: Iowa State University Press, 1993), 305–44; Cynthia Opheim, "Explaining the Differences in State Lobbying Regulation," *Western Political Quarterly* 44 (June 1991): 409; Virginia Gray and David Lowery, *The Population Ecology of Interest Representation: Lobbying Communities in the American States* (Ann Arbor: University of Michigan Press, 1996), 212.

9. Hrebenar and Thomas, "Interest Group Activity in the States."

10. Wisconsin Ethics Board, "2003 Lobbying Report" (available online at http:// ethics.state.wi.us).

11. Ronald Hedlund, "Wisconsin," 316. Contribution figure from Wisconsin Democracy Campaign, "2001–2002 Committee Contributions to Candidates and LCCs," www.wisdc.org/WEB_PAC_Alpha2002.html.

12. Daniel Hofrenning, *In Washington but Not of It: The Prophetic Politics of Religious Lobbyists* (Philadelphia: Temple University Press, 1995), 6, 93.

13. Jeffrey Berry, *Lobbying for the People* (Princeton, N.J.: Princeton University Press, 1977), 7.

14. Woodstock Theological Center, *The Ethics of Lobbying: Organized Interests, Political Power, and the Common Good* (Washington, D.C.: Georgetown University Press, 2002), 24, 7–8.

15. David Yamane, *The Catholic Church in State Politics* (Lanham, Md.: Rowman & Littlefield, 2005).

16. Thanks to Annika Brophy for her research assistance on this point.

17. Allen Hertzke, *Representing God in Washington* (Knoxville: University of Tennessee Press, 1988), 70, 75–76; Hofrenning, *In Washington but Not of It*, 181.

18. Clive Thomas and Ronald Hrebenar, "Comparative Interest Group Politics in the American West," *Journal of State Government*, September/October 1986, 134.

19. Dennis Dresang and James Gosling, *Politics and Policy in American States and Communities* (Boston: Allyn and Bacon, 1996), 160.

20. Though it does not replicate their meticulous study, these survey questions were inspired by Edward O. Laumann and David Knoke's book *The Organizational State: Social Choice in National Policy Domains* (Madison: University of Wisconsin Press, 1987), which employs network analytic techniques to model interest group activity and influence in the U.S. Congress.

21. Wisconsin Council of Churches' website, www.wichurches.org/introducing .html.

22. From the FRI's website, www.fri-wi.org/About_FRI/FRI_Information/FRI's Focus.htm.

# 8

## Religious Interest Group Activity in Utah State Government

*David B. Magleby*

Despite its role in the history and founding of Utah, the Church of Jesus Christ of Latter-day Saints (hereafter LDS Church) is infrequently involved in policy disputes and rarely lobbies the state legislature. Whether this is the result of the fact that elected officials generally share the values and perspectives of the LDS Church and therefore lobbying is not necessary or the result of a philosophical distancing between church and state, the fact remains that the LDS Church does not have a substantial lobbying presence in Utah.

This finding is consistent with the observations about religion and politics in America made by Alexis de Tocqueville in 1831. Writing about religion more generally, Tocqueville said, "One cannot therefore say that in the United States religion influences the laws or political opinions in detail, but it does direct mores, and by regulating domestic life it helps to regulate the state."[1] The LDS Church is important to understanding politics and public policy in Utah but more in the Tocquevillian sense of defining the values, mores, and political culture of the state than in lobbying policymakers. This is not to say that religion is not important to understanding the politics of the United States or Utah. Indeed, as Tocqueville said,

> While the law allows the American people to do everything, there are things which religion prevents them from imagining and forbids them to dare. Religion, which never intervenes directly in the government of American society, should therefore be considered as the first of their political institutions, for although it did not give them the taste for liberty, it singularly facilitates their use thereof.[2]

Thus, as I will demonstrate, in Utah the LDS Church is an important political institution without an active lobbying effort in state government. There have been, as will be explained, exceptions to this more passive approach to policy advocacy, but they are the exceptions.

There are only a few registered religious lobbyists who represent churches in Utah. Of the 527 registered lobbyists, the LDS Church has five, and the Catholic Church has one.[3] The LDS Church has long relied on a Salt Lake City law firm, Kirton and McConkie, as well as church employees working in its public affairs department for its lobbyists. The Catholic Church is represented by Dolores Rowland. Church leaders from the Episcopal, Jewish, and other churches occasionally serve as advocates in the policy process but not as registered lobbyists. Religious groups and churches may seek to influence public policy without using registered lobbyists. This happens regularly at all levels of government and includes nonprofit groups organized under section 501(c)3 of the tax code.

Compared to other professional lobbyists, church lobbyists in Utah are not as high profile or active as those representing business, labor, education, or other interests. Episcopal Bishop Carolyn Tanner Irish observed that corporate, labor, and other lobbyists far outnumber religious lobbyists in state government. She continues, "This is a terrible problem in our governance."[4] In 1983, legislators and lobbyists were asked to rank interest groups in terms of influence. The lobbyists ranked the LDS Church as the tenth most influential group, well behind the education lobby, which ranked first, and legislators didn't rank the church—or churches more generally—as having influence.[5] This is not surprising, given the heavy focus of state government on taxes, education, crime, corrections, and economic growth. On these issues, churches rarely become involved in Utah. This pattern differentiates Utah from other states and may be explained by the long-standing commitment of the LDS Church to public education and the large school-age population, meaning that support for private or parochial schools has been minimal.

In this chapter, I examine the role and success of religious lobbyists in Utah. To put that in context, I first discuss the religious culture of the state and its effects on state and local politics. I then examine the most important issues in the state and the extent to which religious lobbying is relevant to them. To explore in more detail the activity of religious lobbyists in Utah politics, I examine the following policy areas: liquor laws, concealed weapons in churches, and a ban on same sex-marriage. The chapter uses data collected over the past two decades in the KBYU-Utah Colleges Exit Poll as well as interviews conducted over the past several years for a longer book I am writing on Utah politics and government. For this chapter, I conducted an additional set of elite interviews.[6]

## THIS IS THE RIGHT PLACE

Utah's unique founding and political development provide an important context for the workings of state and local government today. Persecution had driven the church from Missouri and Ohio, and in 1844 the church's founder, Joseph Smith Jr., was killed by a mob in Carthage, Illinois. LDS Church members were forced to flee their headquarters in Nauvoo, Illinois, in 1846, migrating west to Utah.

Over the course of forty years, until the transcontinental railroad was completed, 100,000 Latter-day Saints typically walked the thousand miles from near Omaha, Nebraska, to the Salt Lake valley, bringing what few things they could in a wagon or handcart.[7] Many of these pioneers were new converts to the church from the eastern United States and Europe. They shared a common commitment to find a place where they could practice their religion in peace. When their leader arrived in what was an isolated and desolate place, he stated, "This is the Right Place." Despite later proposals to relocate to California or another less harsh environment, the Mormons remained and pursued an aggressive colonization process that within ten years stretched from Fort Limhi at the bottom of Idaho's panhandle to San Bernardino in southern California.[8] Over the first thirty years the Mormons were in Utah, they established more than 300 settlements in present-day Utah, Idaho, Wyoming, Arizona, Nevada, California, and Hawaii.[9]

While they achieved isolation, they did not achieve peace. Only a decade after their arriving in Utah, the federal government sent 2,500 troops to the territory. One concern was the close connection between the LDS Church and Utah government. Brigham Young, Joseph Smith Jr.'s successor as prophet and church president, for example, was the territorial governor from 1850 to 1857. President James Buchanan wanted to appoint new government officials in Utah, particularly a new governor to replace Brigham Young, and he felt that he would need to back his appointments with force.[10] The presence of federal troops in Utah reinforced an antigovernment sentiment born of the lack of government protection from past persecution. Between 1846, when the advance party of pioneers first arrived in Utah, and fifty years later, when Utah became a state, there were substantial tensions between the church and its members in Utah and the federal government. Many of these tensions centered on the practice of polygamy by the Mormons, a practice banned in federal legislation by the Morrill Act in 1862 and later abandoned by the church.

Non-Mormons came to Utah for reasons other than religion and have always been in the minority. Some came for mining, others with the railroad. The non-Mormons, or gentiles, as Mormons have sometimes called them,[11] have often worked amicably with the Mormons. But there have always been tensions and political conflicts.

As early as 1849, the Territory of Deseret, as Utah was originally named, petitioned for statehood.[12] At least five constitutional conventions and separate applications for statehood took place over a nearly fifty-year period.[13] During this protracted process toward the end of the nineteenth century, pressure was brought on the state to become "Americanized."[14] Public schools, a two-party system, and a constitution with clear boundaries between church and state were the kinds of "Americanization" steps taken. The most notable concession was the church's ban on polygamy. With the church's assets and leaders under siege, prophet and church President Wilford Woodruff in 1890 issued the "Manifesto," advising "the Latter-day Saints to refrain from contracting any marriage forbidden by the law of the land."[15] Utah was made a state in 1896.

In an effort to avoid either national party becoming an anti-Mormon party in Utah, church members were encouraged to be active in both major parties. Prominent Latter-day Saints remain in both parties, but in the past half century, the membership has become disproportionately Republican.

Until as recently as the Eisenhower administration, church leaders also served in government. Apostle Reed Smoot, a Republican, served both as one of the twelve apostles and as U.S. senator from Utah for thirty years. Another church leader, B. H. Roberts, a Democrat, was denied his seat in the U.S. House of Representatives because of his views and practices concerning polygamy.[16] No church leader has served in government since Ezra Taft Benson, an apostle at the time, who served as secretary of agriculture in the Eisenhower administration.

Earlier in Utah history, the church endorsed political candidates, often unsuccessfully. And some candidates clearly sought to imply a church endorsement.[17] As both the church and Utah have grown, the relationship has changed. The church, now a global church with more members outside of North America than in North America, is no longer primarily a Utah or an intermountain West church. Its policy concerns and membership are international and increasingly diverse. Utah has also changed and in many ways now more closely resembles other intermountain West states.

Important cultural differences remain in Utah. Liquor continues to be a source of friction, as I will explain later. Utah's moral conservatism combines with a strong hostility to government, especially the federal government. For much of the rest of the intermountain region, conservatism lacks the strong moral orientation found in Utah. The tendency of LDS families to have more children means that public schools are crowded and even more pressed for funds than in other states. But other parts of Utah's conservatism, including hostility to taxes and the role of government generally, are not different from conservatism in Wyoming, Idaho, Arizona, or Montana.

The concern with morality in such matters as liquor, pornography, abortion, and marriage is related to the religious beliefs and values of members of the LDS Church. As Dani Eyer of the American Civil Liberties Union (ACLU) said, "A lot of what happens in the legislature is a result of culture."[18]

## RELIGION AND POLITICS IN UTAH TODAY

Utah is the most religiously homogeneous state, with an estimated 70 percent of its population members of the LDS Church, surpassing predominantly Catholic states like Rhode Island (64 percent) and Massachusetts (49 percent).[19] Three states have half or more of their population in evangelical or mainline Protestant churches: Alabama (55 percent), Oklahoma (55 percent), and Arkansas (51 percent).[20]

The Utah public also exhibits the highest level of religiosity of any American state.[21] In the nomenclature of Utah, people with high levels of religiosity self-classify as "active," and less observant persons who attend church less frequently or for other reasons often describe themselves as "inactive." "Active" is therefore similar to such labels for religiosity as "practicing." In Utah, even non-Mormons have adopted the distinctively Mormon euphemism for religiosity. An active member of the LDS Church would attend church most Sundays; pay 10 percent of income (tithe); adhere to the "Word of Wisdom," which prohibits alcohol, tobacco, harmful drugs, tea, and coffee; and serve in some capacity in the church. The church has a lay ministry; local ecclesiastical leaders rotate periodically and serve without compensation. About half of Utah voters classify themselves as very active members of the LDS Church. There are also relatively few nonadherents in the state.[22]

The predominance of one faith and the high levels of religiosity make Utah an interesting state in which to examine religious group representation in state government. It also means that the political culture of the state reflects the attitudes, mores, and values of this group, as de Tocqueville would have predicted. Church-state tensions had been a part of the history of the Latter-day Saints before they came to Utah, and they continue today. As with other groups that are presumed to be powerful, the LDS Church tends to be less involved and vocal than some assume. Just as in another celebrated case of presumed control, Yale University was in fact not actively involved in the governance of New Haven, Connecticut.[23] Speaking of the LDS Church more generally, journalists Robert Gottlieb and Peter Wiley said, "We knew that the church had become in recent years a powerful institution, with its ability to influence events, to move large amounts of capital, to help elect candidates, and to orchestrate antifeminist campaigns."[24] Some have even called Utah a theocracy.[25] But as documented in this chapter, the LDS Church rarely lobbies state government and, in the words of several key players, is largely "invisible." The dominant organized religion in Utah thus chooses to largely remove itself from policymaking, just as Yale did in New Haven.[26]

Elected officials at all levels in the state tend to be even more disproportionately members of the LDS Church than the general population. No official record is kept of religion of public officials, but published reports put the proportion of LDS state legislators at more than 90 percent.[27] Something approaching that proportion would likely be the case in many city and county governments in the state.[28]

A notable exception to the tendency of Utah public officials to be disproportionately LDS more than the general population is Salt Lake City, where the church has its headquarters and its best-known temple and tabernacle are located. Salt Lake City has had a non-LDS mayor for more than twenty years, and the demographics of the city are more diverse, approximately 45 percent of the population of Salt Lake City being LDS.[29] The church–state tensions in Salt Lake City are more visible and contentious, especially in recent years.[30]

The pervasive influence of the LDS Church on the culture of Utah extends to its economy. The headquarters of the world's twelve million Mormons is Salt Lake City, and the church employs an estimated 9,000 workers in Salt Lake City, not including employees of church-owned businesses.[31] Statewide, the Department of Workforce Services estimates the LDS Church employs 29,500 people, including employees of Brigham Young University.[32] Owned and operated by the LDS Church, Brigham Young University has 32,000 students, with approximately 24 percent of the student body being from Utah.[33] The church has long been an owner of television and radio stations, in part to facilitate broadcast of its semiannual general conferences. For many years, the most popular evening newscast has come from LDS Church–owned KSL-TV. The church also owns a Salt Lake City newspaper, *The Deseret Morning News*.

## A REPUBLICAN STATE AND REGION

Over the past three decades, Utah, like much of the intermountain West, has become strongly Republican. For three decades, Utah has led the nation in its share of the vote going to the Republican nominee. Since 1972, Utah has voted 63 percent Republican, and when the 1992 election with Ross Perot on the ballot is removed, the average climbs to 66 percent.

States in this region have similar economies, are large public-lands states, and, as noted, share a long-standing hostility toward the federal government. The rhetoric and personal style of Ronald Reagan were especially popular in Utah and the region. Some scholars have declared Utah as "the most conservative and the most Republican state in the union."[34] As noted, voting data continue to substantiate this point.

Republicans enjoy a greater-than-two-to-one edge in party identification among Utah voters.[35] The Utah Republican Party is even more religiously homogeneous than the state as a whole. Over the past twenty years, 87 percent of Utah Republican voters have been LDS. Utah Democrats in the same period were also disproportionately LDS, with 58 percent of that faith.[36]

The Utah Republican Party effectively has labeled the Democratic Party as liberal, especially on such moral issues as abortion and gay marriage. Political editor of the *Deseret Morning News*, Bob Bernick, observes that "Utah Democrats have long differentiated themselves from National Democrats."[37] The nexus between the GOP and LDS Church in the minds of some has fostered an attitude that an active Mormon could not be a Democrat. This is not the church's position. Before every election, the LDS Church has local leaders read a letter that says, "We reaffirm the Church's long-standing policy of political neutrality. The Church does not endorse any political party, political platform, or candidate."[38]

The Democratic Party, in part in reaction to the perception that the Republican Party in Utah is the "Mormon" party, has become the party of everyone else in Utah. As table 8.1 demonstrates, Democrats compose at least a plurality of all other religious groups. Catholics are nearly as Democratic in Utah as Mormons are Republican. Protestants are more evenly divided with 44 percent being Democrats and 39 percent Republican, if independent leaning voters are included as partisans.

The GOP has had veto-proof majorities in the state legislature since 1996.[39] This is not to say there are many attempts to override gubernatorial vetoes since Republicans held the governorship for the past twenty years. Democrats have been competitive in one of the three congressional districts. That continued prospect was made more tenuous given the 2002 partisan gerrymandering done by the Republican state legislature with the governor's blessing.[40] Democrats in the legislature have long complained about the closed GOP party caucuses, where they say important decisions are made. Joe Hatch, Democratic Salt Lake City councilman, said of closed party caucuses, "They create hard feelings, they shut out the public, they close the door on good ideas."[41] In important respects, the politics of Utah now resemble the politics of the once-solid South, except the dominant party in Utah is the Republican Party.[42]

**Table 8.1.   Religion and Party Identification in Utah, 1982–2002**

|                              | Democrat | Independent | Republican | Other | Don't Know |
|------------------------------|----------|-------------|------------|-------|------------|
| Protestant                   | 44.4%    | 12.9%       | 39.3%      | 2.2%  | 1.1%       |
| Catholic                     | 61.3     | 7.6         | 24.4       | 3.8   | 2.9        |
| LDS/Mormon, very active      | 10.2     | 7.7         | 77.4       | 2.4   | 2.3        |
| LDS/Mormon, somewhat active  | 21.8     | 13.1        | 57.1       | 3.5   | 4.4        |
| LDS/Mormon, not very active  | 33.5     | 14.4        | 46.7       | 3.1   | 2.3        |
| LDS/Mormon, not active       | 45.0     | 14.0        | 31.1       | 2.9   | 7.0        |
| Jewish                       | 40.9     | 13.6        | 29.6       | 13.6  | 2.3        |
| Other                        | 59.2     | 12.7        | 22.1       | 4.8   | 1.2        |
| No preference                | 58.6     | 13.0        | 20.3       | 6.1   | 2.1        |
| Prefer not to say            | 43.6     | 14.0        | 14.0       | 6.0   | 5.0        |

Note: Percentages are merged data for the twenty-year period 1982–2002.
Source: Utah Colleges Exit Poll (www.exitpoll.byu.edu).

For religious interest groups and their lobbyists, this partisan/religious divide has consequences. The name of the game is access to and influence in the Republican Party, especially its closed caucus. With the LDS Church not playing an active role and the agenda of other religious lobbyists being more in line with the Democratic Party agenda, religious lobbyists have only limited direct influence. However, the LDS Church indirectly influences the GOP caucus because so many of these legislators are active members of the faith. Other lobbyists work hard to cultivate good relations with the Republicans, especially their legislative leadership.

## ISSUES THE PUBLIC CARES ABOUT

For more than twenty years, students from throughout Utah have conducted a statewide exit poll of Utah general election voters. The KBYU-Utah Colleges Exit Poll has provided accurate and detailed information on the voting intentions of Utah voters as well as their views of issues of public controversy. In that poll, we have asked voters the following question: "What do you think are the most important issues facing Utah?"[43] Table 8.2 provides the data on the most important problems over the six years for which we have data.

It is striking how infrequently Utah voters select from a list of issues ones that relate directly to the religious interest groups. Public education and population growth are the two issues most consistently seen by Utah voters as the

**Table 8.2.  Most Important Issues Facing Utah, 1996–2002**

|  | *1996* | *1998* | *2000* | *2002* |
|---|---|---|---|---|
| Gangs/crime | 34.1% | 43.1% | 03.5% | 03.4% |
| Population growth | 37.6 | 26.6 | 32.8 | 29.2 |
| Public education | 14.4 | 9.4 | 42.2 | 36.4 |
| Transportation | 7.8 | 4.5 | 4.5 | 2.4 |
| Pollution | 1.1 | N/A | 2.0 | N/A |
| Olympics | 0.6 | 4.9 | 1.2 | N/A |
| Federal lands | 1.8 | N/A | N/A | N/A |
| Rising crime rates | 2.5 | N/A | N/A | N/A |
| Increasing teen pregnancy | 0.2 | N/A | N/A | N/A |
| Environment/wilderness | N/A | 8.9 | N/A | 1.3 |
| Nuclear waste | N/A | N/A | 13.8 | 24.6 |
| Taxes | N/A | N/A | N/A | 2.6 |

Note: N/A means this issue category was not included in the question that year.
Source: KBYU-Utah Colleges Exit Poll (www.exitpoll.byu.edu).

most important issues facing Utah. Some issues see an increase in voter concern, as nuclear waste did in 2000 and especially in 2002. Other issues wane in importance, for example, with crime and gangs between 1996 and 1998 and 2000 and 2002.

Even an issue as visible and contentious as gay marriage has not become a frequently cited "most important problem" in national surveys. Pollsters and policymakers have frequently cited the fact that the public has not been more engaged on this issue.[44] While the pubic does not identify church–state relations as one of the most important problems, controversies in Utah's history have shed light on these dimensions.

## Liquor by the Drink

An issue on which the LDS Church has taken a clear and consistent policy position is the regulation of liquor. On this issue, the public has not always supported the church position, but more recently the widely shared perception is that the public and officeholders alike favor a policy of limited access. Local mores, in a de Tocqueville sense, have been tested by such external mores as the international Olympic community, and despite these tests and pressures, the local mores and values continue in force.

Not unlike other states, Utah has long been divided over how to regulate the sale of alcohol. What may come as a surprise is the fact that Utah was the thirty-sixth and deciding state to repeal Prohibition by ratifying the Eighteenth Amendment in a 1933 referendum. The stakes in the Utah referendum were high. LDS Church President Hebert J. Grant strongly urged church members to vote to retain prohibition. Clearly, enough Mormons did not heed the counsel of their prophet to defeat the referendum repealing Prohibition.

For active Mormons, the consumption of alcohol is forbidden, and concerns about access and availability are not a priority except insofar as they might encourage consumption or be available to minors. Utah liquor laws are seen by many non-LDS as restrictive and "archaic."[45] To some non-Mormons, the issue is seen as the majority trying to impose its morality on the minority by restrictive laws. Other states have laws that are just as restrictive—and arguably more restrictive—than Utah's. For example, West Virginia allows the advertising of alcohol prices but not brands, and Texas has fifty-three dry counties, while Utah has none.[46] Such comparisons do not diffuse the symbolic potency of the issue in Utah.

The issue of alcohol regulation was also put to the voters in 1968 when Utah voters considered a referendum to allow liquor by the drink. At the time, Utah law did not allow restaurants or bars to serve wine, cocktails, or mixed drinks. Those who wanted a drink brought their own wine or liquor to the restaurant and ordered setups, or mixers. LDS Church President David O. McKay issued a statement urging voters to reject liquor by the drink. In this referendum, unlike the 1933 vote on Prohibition, Utah voters cast an anti–liquor liberalization vote. The 1968 vote was the last attempt to set liquor policy at the ballot box.

Utah liquor law has been liberalized since the 1968 liquor-by-the-drink referendum. These changes have followed a pattern that involves advance work by the regulatory agency over alcohol and the state legislature and vetting to key interest groups like the LDS Church, the travel and tourism industry, and the restaurant association. Utah law now allows for private clubs where for a nominal fee persons could join and in which liquor by the drink is served.[47] The law has also created new special licenses that allow hotels, convention centers, and so on to serve alcohol when catering special events.[48]

The state agency charged with enforcing Utah's liquor, the Department of Alcohol Beverage Control (DABC), consists of five commissioners.[49] Who is appointed to this agency has itself been the subject of some dispute. Disgruntled liquor drinkers and people who feel the LDS Church has too much sway in the state will often complain that a majority of commissioners are nondrinking members of the LDS Church.

As part of the effort to secure the Winter Olympic Games and even after the bid had been awarded, groups advocating further liberalization of Utah's liquor laws called for more "hospitable" liquor laws. Salt Lake City Mayor Rocky Anderson was the most prominent leader in this attempt, saying, "We are not going to move into the 20th century—let alone the 21st—without updating our liquor laws."[50] The LDS Church issued a statement about changing the liquor laws in the period before the Olympics, saying that "the Church opposes the liberalization of Utah's state or local alcohol regulatory laws to accommodate the 2002 Winter Olympics. Such an action would have an on-going effect on the citizenry of Utah long after the Olympics are over. Utah's long-standing alcohol laws to protect the public health, safety, and welfare should not be eroded to appease short-term Olympic visitors to our state."[51] Mayors from eleven different Wasatch Front cities also opposed Anderson's attempt to liberalize the laws.[52] Neither the state legislature nor the agency charged with regulating alcohol changed the liquor laws in advance of the Olympics.

Later, in 2003, the legislature modified Utah liquor laws.[53] The law was changed to make it more difficult for minors to purchase alcohol, some administrative housekeeping changes for the DABC were made, and cities were allowed more freedom to regulate drinking establishments within certain proximity of schools or churches.[54] The process of arriving at this set of changes illustrates an approach that fostered communication and compromise early on and thereby minimized the chances of opposition from groups, including religious groups, later on. Participants in this process were the DABC, the hospitality industry, and the LDS Church. LDS Church lobbyist Jerry Fenn described the process as follows: "While there are some aspects of the comprehensive legislation which may be considered as liberalizing, and which standing alone the church may oppose, there has been an attempt in this bill to balance the interests of those who responsibly consume alcohol on the one hand and, on the other, the interests of state regulation and control, including protection of citizens, many of whom do not consume alcohol."[55] The hospitality industry lobbyist who had pushed for the changes defended the involvement of the church, saying that it "reflects the culture of the state."[56] This recent round of changes then reflects an open process in which a range of groups participated and in which there was compromise.

Over time, what has been the role of religious lobbies on the alcohol issue? Aside from the role of the LDS Church both in actively working to defeat the 1968 liquor-by-the-drink vote and in working with coalitions of interest groups to propose changes to the law, these groups have typically not included other faith-based groups.

While generally conservative, the LDS Church is not always so. It has not taken a position on stem cell research, for example. Research by others on the role of religious groups on Utah drug laws provides insights into how nonreligious groups seek to partner with religious groups or at least co-opt them. Utah, in 1971, was one of the first states that reduced the penalty for first-offense possession of marijuana to a misdemeanor.[57] Those pushing the lesser penalty for marijuana possession included the Utah Bar Association and the

Citizen Advisory Committee on Drugs, which was composed of prominent Utah citizens.[58] Galliher and Basilick report that the LDS Church opposed high mandatory sentences, though they held no position on the specific 1971 bill that lowered the mandatory sentences.[59] Proponents of the legislation persuaded legislators that harsh penalties for drug possession would hurt young people, especially first-time offenders. As noted, the legislation passed.

## Concealed Weapons in Churches and Schools

Utah, like other intermountain states, has long been a state with an organized and powerful gun lobby. Politicians of both parties seek the endorsement of the National Rifle Association and the Utah Shooting Sports Council. The most visible gun-related issue to arise in many years is whether individuals with a license can be allowed to carry concealed weapons without restriction except in large airports, prisons, jails, and courtrooms.[60]

In 1995, the legislature passed a statute that allowed licensed individuals to carry concealed weapons anywhere "without restriction" except in specific designated places or on private property. The "without restriction" language included churches and schools, a provision that was reinforced with legislation in 2003. After a protracted dispute with the University of Utah, the legislature in 2004 passed legislation stating that only the legislature can set policy regarding guns on public property and that public schools and universities are public property.

Utah churches, including the LDS Church, are unified in their opposition to allowing concealed weapons in churches. This, then, is another issue where the LDS Church and conservatives part ways and where the church position is likely not welcomed in the GOP legislative caucus. The leadership of the LDS Church issued the following statement: "Churches are dedicated for the worship of God and as havens from the cares and concerns of the world. The carrying of lethal weapons, concealed or otherwise, within their walls is inappropriate, except as required by officers of the law."[61] This was again reaffirmed in 1999 when two of the LDS Church's general authorities, Apostle Russell Ballard and Seventy Alexander Morrison, reaffirmed the opposition, saying that "guns—even legally concealed firearms—do not belong in schools or houses of worship."[62]

Not only was the Catholic Church in Utah opposed to weapons in its own buildings, but it also unsuccessfully attempted to put an initiative on the ballot that would ban guns from schools and churches. Catholic lobbyist Dolores Rowland observed that the Catholic bishops spoke out against gun violence in 1975 in part because of all the gang deaths and suicides. Rowland observed that the Catholic Church and other churches, but not the LDS Church, gathered signatures for an initiative that would have banned guns from schools and churches. She volunteered, "The LDS took too cautious a role in gathering signatures, though they did allow us to use prior statements made in light of incidents such as the shooting at their genealogy library. I was heartbroken they didn't get more involved."[63] The initiative failed to gather enough signatures to qualify for the ballot, and Rowland points to some intimidation from the gun lobby toward the PTA and the hospitals association as reasons for the demise of the initiative.

The legislature in 1999 changed the law on concealed weapons in churches, allowing them to ban guns, but only if they posted a sign saying such weapons were not permitted.[64] Both the Catholic Church and the LDS Church refused to post the signs. Apostle Ballard expressed an opinion on the gun ban when he said, "Isn't it an awful thing that we are in a time in society where you have to put up a sign in a church stating that you have to leave your guns out."[65] The chief legislative sponsor of the 1995 legislation lifting restrictions on concealed weapons in churches and schools, Senator Michael Waddoups, who is LDS, responded to the LDS perspective by saying, "If that is the policy, then it's important that it apply to all members [including bishops and other local leaders] and not just the congregation members."[66]

In part to make a statement about how much they opposed the new law, the Episcopal Church posted such signs saying guns were banned in their church.[67] Episcopal Bishop Irish, referring to the sign in a press release, said, "I hope it embarrasses the legislature," and later described the tactic as "our way of mocking the state legislature."[68]

At least partially in response to the strong opposition of several churches to the signage requirement if churches wanted to ban concealed weapons, the legislature passed SB 108 in 2003. This legislation says that "churches can use methods other than signage to tell visitors and members they can't bring a gun to church."[69] The LDS Church in 2004 formally announced that "it will impose a gun ban in its hundreds of houses of worship throughout Utah, invoking provisions of the new state law that allows for criminal prosecution of violators."[70]

The battle over concealed weapons in churches and schools is an example of an issue on which churches, including the LDS Church, did not get their way. Rather than achieve the outright ban it desired, it initially faced a burdensome signage requirement that was inconsistent with the welcoming ethos of churches. Only belatedly did the legislature compromise and allow churches to use means other than signs to convey the message that concealed weapons are not allowed to those who attend church.

What has been the role of religious lobbies on the concealed weapon's issue? The concealed weapons controversy served to unify religious leaders in

**Table 8.3.    Religion and Views on whether Concealed Weapons Should Be Banned from Utah Churches and Schools, 2002**

|  | Strongly Agree | Agree | Disagree | Strongly Disagree | Don't Know |
|---|---|---|---|---|---|
| LDS, very active | 49.5% | 20.4% | 15.6% | 11.2% | 3.3% |
| LDS, somewhat active | 55.6 | 14.4 | 11.1 | 14.4 | 4.4 |
| LDS, not very active | 37.8 | 16.2 | 18.9 | 21.6 | 5.4 |
| LDS, not active | 50.0 | 28.1 | 12.5 | 3.1 | 6.3 |
| Non-LDS | 63.4 | 18.2 | 6.9 | 9.6 | 2.0 |

Source: KBYU-Utah Colleges Exit Poll (www.exitpoll.byu.edu).

Utah. It also is an example of a high-profile issue on which the state legislature acted in ways contrary to the wishes of churches, including the LDS Church. Overall, 63 percent of Utah voters favored banning guns in churches and schools. As table 8.3 shows, majorities of all religious groups favored a ban on guns in churches and schools, including more than two-thirds of all very active and somewhat active Latter-day Saints. Large majorities of Republican voters also favor banning guns from churches and schools. When asked what this issue teaches us about the legislature defying the united wishes of churches in Utah, Bishop Irish of the Episcopal Church responded that "it shows us the legislature is in the pocket of the National Rifle Association."[71]

## Ban on Gay Marriage

Utah, like many other states, in the wake of the Massachusetts Supreme Court decision legalizing gay marriage,[72] considered legislation and a possible state constitutional amendment on marriage. The 2004 legislature initially passed legislation defining marriage as between "a man and a woman" and blocking Utah from having to recognize gay marriages performed in other states. At the end of the legislative session, a proposed constitutional amendment to put the gay marriage ban into Utah's constitution was passed and placed on the 2004 Utah general election ballot. The measure goes beyond defining marriage to limit the rights of nonmarried couples and families. The proposed amendment carried in the state senate by only one vote.

After the legislative session, the LDS Church made a formal announcement supporting constitutional amendments defining marriage at both the state and the federal level, without endorsing any particular proposed amendment.[73] All three candidates for attorney general (Republican, Democrat, and Libertarian) came out against the amendment. Interestingly, the Republican

**Table 8.4.    Religion and Views on whether Utah Should Allow Same-Sex Marriages, 2002**

|                  | Strongly Agree | Agree | Disagree | Strongly Disagree | Don't Know |
|------------------|----------------|-------|----------|-------------------|------------|
| Very active      | 4.3%           | 2.2%  | 4.3%     | 88.5%             | 0.8%       |
| Somewhat active  | 3.2            | 2.1   | 3.2      | 89.4              | 2.1        |
| Not very active  | 0              | 16.0  | 4.0      | 80.0              | 0          |
| Not active       | 3.2            | 12.9  | 41.9     | 35.5              | 6.5        |
| Non-LDS          | 14.6           | 29.5  | 17.0     | 31.9              | 7.0        |

Source: KBYU-Utah Colleges Exit Poll (www.exitpoll.byu.edu).

incumbent attorney general cited conversations with unnamed LDS Church leaders as part of his decision to oppose the amendment.[74]

The Catholic Church worked closely with the LDS Church and others on California's Proposition 22. That initiative stated that "only marriage between a man and a woman is valid or recognized in California."[75] Catholics have joined Mormons in similar efforts in other states but opposed the 2004 Utah constitutional amendment because of a provision that limits the rights of domestic partners and others. In Utah, the Catholics were not consulted in the drafting of the initiative and thus would "not support it as written."[76]

Gay marriage is an example of an issue in which churches in Utah do not have the same position. While the Catholics and Mormons support defining marriage as between a man and a woman, the Episcopal and Jewish congregations have different perspectives. Jim Isaacson, president of the United Jewish Federation of Utah, stated, "Orthodox Jews think homosexuality should be shunned. . . . As you move more towards conservative and reform movement they are more accepting. One of the [Utah] rabbis in reform and conservative ranks is an active lesbian with a partner."[77]

## ADVOCACY AVOIDANCE: THE LIMITED LOBBYING ROLE OF THE LDS CHURCH

Churches as organized lobbyists in Utah government have a very limited presence, including the LDS Church. The Catholic Church in Utah, as in many other states, is the most active and visible advocate for organized religion. It is ironic that it is the Catholic Church that is the most visible and vocal voice for organized religion in Utah, the bastion of the LDS Church.

The conclusion that the LDS Church plays only a very limited role in lobbying policymakers will be surprising to some given the role the LDS Church played in founding the state. But as noted, it is consistent with the long-standing view that churches influence policy first and foremost by teaching values and mores and in the culture. Despite the LDS Church's limited presence and hesitation to become involved in issues, state government is widely seen as seeking to enact policies consistent with LDS values. The reason for this is the widely shared perspectives on many issues in the Utah polity, and the single most important influence on values in Utah is the LDS Church. Jim Isaacson of the United Jewish Federation of Utah sees the influence of the LDS Church in Utah as natural. He said, "It's a natural evolution where there is a predominant faith so the majority of candidates and voters are from one faith."[78] As Ron Hrebenar, a University of Utah political scientist, has argued, "When a legislator has served as a bishop or stake president [lay leader] in the church, he knows well the policy preferences of his church."[79] Hrebenar also concludes that the LDS Church exercises "influence without flexing a muscle."[80]

These conclusions are consistent with those of earlier studies of the role of churches in Utah politics. Frank Jonas, writing about the period from the late 1800s through the mid-1960s, concluded,

> The Mormon church does have both potential and real influence in politics, but for success at the polls or in the legislature, much depends on the circumstances in a particular situation and on its own choice of tactics. In every instance since the early days, when the Church has made its position public in the press or elsewhere in print and its leaders have endorsed candidates or propositions, it has lost its cause at the polls. When it has used its organization and institutional structure, and has worked on the "inside" of these to achieve its purposes in politics, it has been more successful.[81]

In recent years, the LDS Church's publicly announced positions on liquor and gambling referenda have prevailed.[82]

For the LDS Church, nonpartisanship and the rare taking of stands on issues means it rarely lobbies state government. Dani Eyer, executive director of the ACLU of Utah, a group known to be critical of the church on occasion, said of the LDS Church, "They're not keen on direct lobbying."[83] Other lobbyists and elected officials I interviewed drew similar conclusions. Current Utah Governor Olene Walker indicates that she has received only one or two contacts in her twenty-four years in public life and that they were not on pressing or major matters.[84] Walker's report of very limited contact from the church is consistent with other interviews I have done with former Governor Rampton as well as former Salt Lake City Mayor Ted Wilson.

Former Democratic and non-LDS state legislator and current lobbyist Frank Pignanelli sees the LDS church as "unreasonably cautious. They are so scared to say anything. Every once in a while we'd meet with the Church. We never said, 'Please don't say anything,' it was always, 'Can't you say more?'"[85] The caution, Pignanelli believes, stems from a desire "not to be seen as controlling."[86]

Dolores Rowland, the government liaison for the Catholic Diocese and the director of the Peace and Justice Campaign for the Catholic Church, is widely perceived to be the most visible and active religious lobbyist in Utah. She believes the LDS Church is "determined not to interfere" and describes its presence as advocate as largely "invisible; I don't even know the name of their lobbyist."[87] Rowland, it should be noted, works the legislature virtually every day it is in session. Other full-time lobbyists also observed that they rarely see LDS lobbyists and would be hard-pressed to name them. Sue Ferry, who represents many corporate clients, said, "In all my years I have seldom seen the Mormon Church lobby the legislature."[88] Episcopal Bishop Irish comes to similar conclusions, saying of the LDS Church that "they rarely speak out in a public way."[89] Utah Governor Olene Walker describes the LDS Church as "low key, low profile."[90] Ironically, the disengagement of the LDS Church in lobbying has enlarged the influence of "people like Dolores Rowland, who can speak out on a lot of issues because the LDS Church is so quiet."[91] Another industry lobbyist, Sue Ferry, sees the Catholics as the most active of the religious lobbyists. "They are there every day," Ferry reports.[92]

Despite the church's reluctance to flex its muscles, legislators recognize the power of the church's position. Former legislator Pignanelli reports that, on occasion, legislators falsely evoke the name of the church as supporting a piece of legislation. According to Pignanelli, "Someone would stand up and say, 'I talked to the [LDS] church and they told me . . .' Nine times out of ten the church didn't say that. I would sometimes call the church right after things like that were said. A minute later the guy who had been on the floor would get a call, and his face would turn white."[93]

The limited institutional role played by the LDS Church does not diminish perceptions among some that the church "controls" Utah politics. There have long been examples to the contrary. Writing about Utah politics roughly forty years ago, Frank Jonas said, "The alleged control by the Mormon Church was still a myth, if by control it is meant that, in order to gain its ends, all its leaders have to do is snap their fingers and pass the word along."[94] Thus, the notion of a heavy role of the LDS Church in policymaking has long been disputed. In addition, the history of the founding of Utah and its relationship with the federal government planted antigovernment attitudes that persist today.

The United Jewish Federation of Utah also lobbies very little. This is the case because the two synagogues or Jewish congregations in Utah have somewhat different views on some issues. Occasionally, on matters like considering moving Election Day to a Saturday, the group has spoken out to sensitize legislators on the importance of the Jewish Sabbath to its members.

## CONCLUSION: POLITICAL CULTURE AND
## INTEREST GROUP ACTIVITY

Given the religious homogeneity and visibility of the LDS Church in Utah, the conclusion of this study that the LDS Church is largely invisible as lobbyists in state government may be surprising. The uniform perspective of those interviewed, including some who have been critical of the church, is that the church is only infrequently involved as an advocate in the legislature or state government generally. In contrast, the Catholic Church has a broad advocacy agenda, and the Episcopal Church has identified those "without a voice" who need an advocate. Bishop Irish identified Latinos and the environment as two priorities for advocacy by the church.

Lobbyists and officeholders agree that the reasons for this aversion to advocacy by the LDS Church stem from its desire not to be seen as controlling or dominating public policy. This leads to an irony in Utah politics: the continuing impression that the LDS Church runs Utah and the reality that instead it is very cautious.

One explanation for the lack of engagement in advocacy is that the LDS Church does not need to speak out because policymakers already know the church's position on many issues and share the culture and values of the church. Dolores Rowland, the Catholic lobbyist, observed that the predominantly LDS state legislature makes her advocacy of the sanctity of life easier because Mormons and Catholics have similar views of abortion. She contrasted other Catholic lobbyists in other states who must invest much of their time on the abortion issue. In Utah, the values and culture of the legislature mean that Rowland does not need to focus much attention on abortion, allowing her to more aggressively pursue social justice issues. Rowland said, "I feel fortunate being in Utah because the LDS church has such a strong position on abortion. I am grateful that I don't have to devote resources because we have the luxury of the LDS church being antiabortion. We can take for granted that the Utah state legislature will not weaken abortion laws."[95] The attitudes and values of the legislators and other officials also mean the LDS Church does not need to lobby them on many matters, according to Sue Ferry, a prominent industry lobbyist.[96]

The influence of religious beliefs and values on policymakers makes the relationships between church and state "so subtle here," says Dani Eyer, executive director of the ACLU of Utah. At the same time, Eyer defends the rights of LDS citizens when people call to complain about the liquor laws. She responds, "The church has a right to lobby just as much as any other interest group."[97] Catholic lobbyist Rowland observes that "I think honestly the LDS church is determined not to interfere, but the fact remains that the legislature is predominantly LDS and people have a right to bring their own views and relationships to the table."[98]

Lobbyists for churches in Utah thus play a limited role, and the largest denomination is rarely involved. Religious values, however, pervade the Utah culture and are a part of the life experience of elected officials. On questions where those values are directly related, policymakers have little need for lobbying to know where the churches stand. On most policy questions that are not central to religious values, the churches are not often involved and rarely important.

## NOTES

I gratefully acknowledge the assistance of Emily McClintock, Chad Pugh, Paul Russell, and Dustin Slade in preparing this chapter. Don Norton provided helpful comments on an earlier draft of the chapter, as did the editors of this volume. The exit poll data reported in part in this chapter resulted from the wonderful collaboration with nine Utah colleges and universities and now thousands of undergraduate students.

1. Alexis de Tocqueville, *Democracy in America*, ed. J. P. Mayer, trans. George Lawrence (Garden City, N.Y.: Doubleday, Anchor Books, 1969), 291.

2. Tocqueville, *Democracy in America*, 292. For an explication of the views of de Tocqueville on religion and politics, see Ralph Hancock, "The Uses and Hazards of Christianity in Tocqueville's Attempt to Save Democratic Souls," in *Interpreting Tocqueville's Democracy in America*, ed. Ken Masugi (Savage, Md.: Rowman & Littlefield, 1991), 348–93.

3. www.governor.state.ut.us/lt_gover/lobby.htm.

4. Carolyn Tanner Irish, bishop of the Episcopal Diocese of Utah, phone interview by David Magleby, Salt Lake City, Utah, August 25, 2004.

5. Ronald J. Hrebenar, Melanee Cherry, and Kathanne Greene, "Utah: Church and Corporate Power in the Nation's Most Conservative State," in *Interest Group Politics in the American West*, ed. Ronald J. Hrebenar and Clive S. Thomas (Salt Lake City: University of Utah Press, 1987), 119.

6. The elite interviews I conducted for this research included Governor Olene Walker; Carolyn Tanner Irish, bishop of the Episcopal Diocese of Utah; Frank Pignanelli, lobbyist and former Democratic leader in the State House of Representatives; Sue Ferry, Utah lobbyist; Dani Eyer, executive director, ACLU of Utah; Dolores Rowland, director of Peace and Justice Campaign; Jim Isaacson, president, United Jewish Federation of Utah; and Bob Bernick, political editor, *Deseret Morning News*. The LDS Church declined my request for an interview.

7. Leonard J. Arrington and Davis Bitton, *The Mormon Experience: A History of the Latter-day Saints* (New York: Knopf, 1979), 108.

8. Richard D. Poll, Thomas G. Alexander, Eugene E. Campbell, and David E. Miller, *Utah's History* (Logan: Utah State University Press, 1989), 133, 730.

9. Poll et al., *Utah's History*, 133.

10. Poll et al., *Utah's History*, 165; Scott Nielson, "Albert Sidney Johnston," in *Utah History Encyclopedia*, ed. Allan Kent Powell (Salt Lake City: University of Utah Press, 1994), 287.

11. Daniel J. Elazar, *American Federalism* (New York: Crowell, 1972), 196.

12. Ken Verdoia and Richard Firmage, *Utah: The Struggle for Statehood* (Salt Lake City: University of Utah Press, 1996), 30.

13. Verdoia and Firmage, *Utah: The Struggle for Statehood*, 190–96.

14. Poll et al., *Utah's History*, 387–95.

15. Doctrine and Covenants, Official Declaration—1, Found at the end of Doctrine and Covenants.

16. Verdoia and Firmage, *Utah: The Struggle for Statehood*, 185.

17. Gary James Bergera, "'A Sad and Expensive Experience': Ernest L. Wilkinson's 1964 Bid for the U.S. Senate," *Utah Historical Quarterly* 61, no. 4 (1993): 304–24.

18. Dani Eyer, director of the Utah Chapter of the ACLU, interview by David Magleby, Salt Lake City, Utah, August 20, 2004.

19. "Three States Contain Third of U.S. Catholics," *Washington Post*, January 22, 2000, B8.

20. American Religion Data Archive, www.arda.tm.

21. Paul Brace, Kellie Sims-Butler, Kevin Arceneaux, and Martin Johnson, "Public Opinion in the American States: New Perspectives Using National Survey Data," *American Journal of Political Science* 46, no. 1 (January 2002): 176.

22. American Religion Data Archive, www.arda.tm.

23. Raymond E. Wolfinger, *The Politics of Progress* (Englewood Cliffs, N.J.: Prentice Hall, 1974), 28.

24. Robert Gottlieb and Peter Wiley, *American Saints: The Rise of Mormon Power* (Toronto: General Publishing, 1984), 11.

25. Julie Cart, "Olympic Spotlight: The Mormon Church Wields the Clout in Utah, but during the Games It's Going for a Lighter Touch," *Los Angeles Times*, February 2, 2002, B1.

26. Wolfinger, *The Politics of Progress*, 28.

27. Travis Reed, "Utah G.O.P. Isn't Part of Religious Right," *Deseret Morning News*, August 29, 2004, A7.

28. Neither the Utah League of Cities nor the Utah Association of Counties keeps data on the religion of elected city or county officials.

29. Heather May, "Is Downtown Becoming Another Vatican? Future Look, Feel of Downtown Divides Residents," *Salt Lake Tribune*, February 15, 2004, A15.

30. The tensions between the LDS Church and Salt Lake City came to a head in the dispute over the purchase of one block of Main Street to create a private plaza adjoining the LDS Temple. The idea for the sale of the block street came from Mayor Deedee Corradini, who faced a budget shortfall. The purchase price was $8.1 million.

31. Dan Harrie, "State Continues to Keep Church Off Staffing List," *Salt Lake Tribune*, January 14, 2003, A1.

32. Harrie, "State Continues to Keep Church Off Staffing List," A1.

33. Brigham Young University, *About BYU: Demographics*, http://unicomm.byu .edu/about/factfile/demo.aspx?lms=9, September 14, 2004.

34. Hrebenar et al., "Utah," 114.

35. KBYU-Utah Colleges Exit Polls, 1982–2002, www.exitpoll.byu.edu.

36. KBYU-Utah Colleges Exit Poll, 1982–2002, www.exitpoll.byu.edu.

37. Bob Bernick, political editor, *Deseret Morning News*, interview by David Magleby, Salt Lake City, Utah, September 20, 2004.

38. The Church of Jesus Christ of Latter-day Saints, "The First Presidency Reaffirms Political Neutrality," *The Church of Jesus Christ of Latter-day Saints Newsroom*, www.lds.org/newsroom/showrelease/0,15503,4044-1-2947,00.html, September 10, 2004.

39. U.S. Bureau of the Census, *Statistical Abstract of the United States, 2003* (Washington, D.C.: U.S. Government Printing Office, 2003), 266; and U.S. Bureau of the Census, *Statistical Abstract of the United States, 2001* (Washington, D.C.: U.S. Government Printing Office, 2001), 248.

40. The Republican-dominated state legislature redrew all three congressional districts following the 2000 census so that each included a piece of the urban Salt Lake area as well as rural parts of the state. Utah's second district grew from 250 square miles covering the Salt Lake area to 50,000 square miles, leaving Jim Matheson, the only Democrat in the Utah congressional delegation, with a higher percentage of Republicans in his constituency. For an editorial denouncing this redistricting, see "The Gerrymander Scandal," *Wall Street Journal*, November 7, 2001, A22. The 2000 redistricting was typically more incumbent protection than partisan. Two notable exceptions were Utah for the Republicans and Georgia for the Republicans. See also Kelly D. Patterson, "When Redistricting Means Never Having to Say You're Sorry: Utah's Second District," in *The Last Hurrah: Soft Money and Issue Advocacy in the 2002 Congressional Elections*, ed. David B. Magleby and J. Quin Monson (Washington, D.C.: Brookings Institution Press, 2004), 241–57.

41. Thomas Burr, "S.L. County Demos Push Caucus Law; GOP Open to Discussion, Opposes an Outright Ban," *Salt Lake Tribune*, January 22, 2003, D3.

42. See V. O. Key, *Southern Politics in State and Nation* (New York: Knopf, 1949).

43. In earlier KBYU-Utah College Exit Polls, the question was worded somewhat differently. For example, "What was the most important issue that helped you decide how you voted today?" or "What is the most important issue generally?" For purposes of comparability, I have used only the data from the 1996–2002 period.

44. Pew Research Center for People and the Press, "California, Kobe and Gay Marriages Spark Little Public Interest," http://people-press.org/reports/print .php3?PageID=734, August 14, 2003; Caryle Murphy, "Activists Urge Bush, Kerry to Focus on Poor in U.S.," *Washington Post*, May 22, 2004, B9.

45. See Jay Baltezore, "Thirsty for a Booze Debate? Drink Up; Liquor Issue: Utah Can't Get Its Fill," *Salt Lake Tribune*, December 7, 1997, A1.

46. Joe Baird, "Liquor Laws a Bit Quirky All Over U.S.," *Salt Lake Tribune*, August 5, 2001, A12.

47. In 2003, the legislature made is easier for out-of-town visitors to patronize Utah's private clubs. They pay a temporary membership fee that allows them to patronize the

private clubs for up to three weeks, and it allows up to eight people to enter on one membership.

48. Jerry D. Spangler, Bob Bernick Jr., and Amy Joi Bryson, "Liquor-Law Changes Loom," *Deseret News*, 24 January 2003, sec. A, p. 1.

49. Utah Department of Alcohol Beverage Control, www.alcbev.state.ut.us.

50. Glen Warchol, "Mayor Clarifies 'Misconception'; Change Liquor Laws Permanently, Not Just for Olympics, Anderson Stresses," *Salt Lake Tribune*, October 13, 2000, A10.

51. Warchol, "Mayor Clarifies 'Misconception,'" A10.

52. Mark Eddington, "Anderson's Alcohol Bis Is All Wet, Foes Claim; Alcohol Law Proposal Finds Few Supporters," *Salt Lake Tribune*, November 8, 2000, D1.

53. Mike Gorrell, "New Regulations Bog Down Alcohol Control Department; Paperwork Piling Up; Staff Rushing to Update Computer Systems with Changes to Liquor Laws," *Salt Lake Tribune*, March 29, 2003, B9.

54. Glen Warchol, "Liquor Law Changes Measured, Says DABC; Three Major Parties Helped Shape Revamp; Liquor Law Changes Fair, Says DABC," *Salt Lake Tribune*, February 3, 2003, A1.

55. Josh Loftin, "Liquor Bill Gets Mixed Reaction," *Deseret News*, February 13, 2003, B01.

56. Warchol, "Liquor Law Changes Measured, Says DABC," A1.

57. John F. Galliher and Linda Basilick, "Utah's Liberal Drug Laws: Structural Foundations and Triggering Events," *Social Problems* 26, no. 3 (February 1979): 288.

58. Galliher and Basilick, "Utah's Liberal Drug Laws," 295.

59. Galliher and Basilick, "Utah's Liberal Drug Laws," 293.

60. Kirsten Steward, "Campus Guns a Step Closer; Senate Endorses Broad Access by Permit Holders; Bill Heads to House; Guns-in-Schools Bill Passes," *Salt Lake Tribune*, February 19, 2003, A1.

61. "The First Presidency of the Church of Jesus Christ of Latter-day Saints to Area Presidencies, Area Authority Seventies, Temple Presidents, Stake Presidents, Bishops, and Branch Presidents in Utah," www.lds.org/newsroom/files/Firearms_First_Presidency_Letter.pdf, 16 January 2004.

62. Dan Harrie, "LDS Leaders Toughen Stand on Guns and Violence," *Salt Lake Tribune*, May 16, 1999, A1.

63. Dolores Rowland, registered lobbyist for the Catholic Diocese of Salt Lake, interview by David Magleby, Salt Lake City, Utah, August 23, 2004.

64. Bob Mims, "State Struggles to Determine Where Weapons Are Welcome," *Salt Lake Tribune*, August 29, 1999, A1.

65. "Church Leaders Say Guns Should Be Kept Out of Schools, Churches," *Associated Press State and Local Wire*, May 16, 1999.

66. Harrie, "LDS Leaders Toughen Stand on Guns and Violence," A1.

67. Carrie A. Moore, Bob Bernick Jr., and Jennifer Toomer-Cook, "Clergy Say Violence Now Societal Problem," *Deseret News*, April 24, 1999, E1; Irish, interview.

68. Irish, interview.

69. Bob Bernick Jr. and Jennifer Toomer-Cook, "Leavitt to Sign Bill on Weapons," *Deseret News*, March 19, 2003, A1.

70. Dan Harrie, Kirsten Stewart, and Peggy Fletcher Stack, "LDS: No Guns in Church: First Presidency Letter Says Firearms in Houses of Worship 'Inappropriate,' Vows to Enforce the Ban," *Salt Lake Tribune*, January 24, 2004, A1.

71. Irish, interview.

72. *Hillary Goodridge & others v. Department of Public Health & another*, 440 Mass. 309 (2003).

73. Deborah Bulkeley, "LDS Church Supports Gay-Marriage Bans," *Deseret Morning News*, July 8, 2004, A1.

74. Deborah Bulkeley, "Shurtleff Checked with LDS Official," *Deseret Morning News*, August 25, 2004.

75. University of California Hastings College of the Law, "Full Text of California Initiative," *Hastings Law Library*, http://holmes.uchastings.edu/cgi-bin/starfinder/ 24026/calinits.txt, 2004.

76. Rowland, interview.

77. Jim Isaacson, president of United Jewish Federation of Utah, interview by David B. Magleby, August 18, 2004.

78. Isaacson, interview.

79. Hrebenar et al., "Utah," 115.

80. Hrebenar et al., "Utah," 114–15.

81. Frank H. Jonas, "Utah: The Different State," in *Politics in the American West*, ed. Frank H. Jonas (Salt Lake City: University of Utah Press, 1969), 337–38.

82. Utah voted on liquor by the drink in 1968 and on pari-mutuel gambling in 1992. In both campaigns, the church took a position, and in both instances that position prevailed.

83. Eyer, interview.

84. Olene Walker, governor of Utah, phone interview by David Magleby, Salt Lake City, Utah, August 19, 2004.

85. Frank Pignanelli, lobbyist and former Democratic leader in the state house of representatives, phone interview by David Magleby, Salt Lake City, Utah, August 19, 2004.

86. Pignanelli, interview.

87. Rowland, interview.

88. Sue Ferry, Utah lobbyist, phone interview by David Magleby, August 23, 2004.

89. Irish, interview.

90. Walker, interview.

91. Pignanelli, interview.

92. Ferry, interview.

93. Pignanelli, interview.

94. Frank H. Jonas, "Mormons and Politics: Utah," in *Democracy in the Fifty States*, ed. Charles Press and Oliver P. Williams (Chicago: Rand McNally, 1966), 228.

95. Rowland, interview.

96. Ferry, interview.

97. Eyer, interview.

98. Rowland, interview.

# 9

## The Lively World of California's Religion and Politics

*Edward L. Cleary*

Despite its image of ever-changing youth, California is not a new state or a raw government. With more than 150 years of history as a state, California has achieved a high degree of sophistication in its structures and progressive practices. However, California does not reflect the high degree of localism of the Northeast colonies. Township meetings and local autonomy count for much less in the state than in, say, New Hampshire or Vermont. In California, virtually all power flows from the state. This gives the state a unitary system. Cities, school districts, and the rest of lower-level governmental entities receive their power to act from the state. Citizens in California feel dependency to a large and powerful state as Vermonters may not.

Religion has had an important place in state history, beginning with its iconic Catholic mission churches, its later Protestant imprint, and now its wide religious diversity. How religion and politics meet at the state capitol is the focus of this chapter. The chapter emphasizes that the major issue facing the religious interest groups has been the maintenance of programs for the poor and the marginal within California's budget.

The following sections begin with an appraisal of state government and interest groups at the state capitol. This is followed by an analysis of the somewhat unique situation of religious groups in the state. Next the evolution of the current religious lobby is taken up. This is followed by the special focus of this volume: the issues that the religious lobby and other religious groups are pressing on state government. Finally, the underlying ideologies—the theologies of the public square that are especially vibrant in the state—are examined.

## GOVERNING CALIFORNIA

In contrast to the attention given California governors (such as Ronald Reagan) for the past decades, the executive office itself is fragmented, power being shared by several officers and a strong civil service.[1] The legislature is relatively strong in the state. State agencies have unusual strength. Progressivism marks the state's political culture, as it has for a relatively long time. Thus, the hallmarks of California's early twentieth-century Progressivism—professionalism and grassroots policy initiatives (as recall election and propositions)—characterize California's state government.[2]

Viewing all states, Peverill Squire, Keith E. Hamm, and Garry F. Moncrief ranked California first for the professionalism of its legislature.[3] The 120 members of the senate and assembly are among the highest paid in the country. California legislators are expected to work full time at their jobs. The legislative calendar is much more lengthy than most other states. This is the legislators' full-time work, in contrast to many other states where legislators are not well paid and meet only occasionally. (Rhode Island legislators do not even have their own statehouse offices.)

California was the first state in the nation to professionalize its legislature, going full time in 1966. It also greatly increased salaries, added competent professional staff, and improved facilities. Political scientists approve of this as highly rational, given the size of the budget and the complexity of issues legislators face. Nonetheless, many Californians are not impressed by having a complex organization that matches modern needs; they want less government. Some would return to the days of part-time legislators if they could. Many Californians distrust government,[4] which is one of the major themes of California's politics. Further, there is an objective basis for this low opinion of state government and the state legislature. When political scientists look at governmental performance among the most populous states, California shares with one other state the lowest, C-minus grade.[5]

It has been harder for politicians to make a life out of politics in California since term limits began in 1990, but the politicians as a professional class figured out other ways to stay on in politics. They move from the assembly to the senate (almost never the other way) or move back or on to local politics. Willie Brown went from a historically long string of elections as speaker of the house to two terms as mayor of San Francisco. Current senators use the upper house as the base for running for mayor of Los Angeles or of other cities.

The capitol building, the senate and assembly, and the relatively abundant staff impress visitors as highly efficient, well-organized, and welcoming institutions. Visitors walk through metal detectors at entry, without having to show an ID. They attend committee meetings and full chamber meetings. Information about location of meetings, themes, and printed copies of resolutions are posted on monitors, on websites, and on tables of committee meetings. Qualified experts or lobbyists wishing to speak at committee meetings just need to sign up ahead of time. Four closed-circuit television channels carry committee and legislative sessions to subscribers within approximately a one-mile radius of the statehouse.

This legislative transparency mirrors the second major characteristic of California politics: openness of the political system as shown in policy initiatives outside the legislature. California has become famous for seemingly endless and sometimes trivial use of initiatives and referenda. Signs urging "yes" votes on propositions make ugly, even scenic, views of the state at election time. This experiment in direct democracy pushed by Progressives in 1911 has often turned into a brokered business for special interests. Well-worded propositions are needed. So are signatures. Close to half a million signatures are required for placing initiatives on the ballot.[6] Thus, propositions are big business. The large staffs of Kimball Petition Management and American Petition Consultants, for example, help gather signatures, raise money, and produce ads.

As political analysts have noted, the initiatives process has empowered special interests at the expense of representative democracy.[7] Despite this lateral challenge to the legislature for making laws, Matthew Cahn and associates believe that "the legislative authority of our elected representatives continues to provide the foundation and framework of California's democratic system."[8]

## Interest Groups in the State Capital

If state legislatures—at least the one in California—have a bad name, lobbyists are believed to be even worse.[9] California lobbyists deserved their notoriety because of their representation of predatory railroad and logging interests through the 1960s. These lobbyists spent their time mostly fighting against restrictions. Their tactics included parties, brothels, and other entertainments in the days when legislators were mostly male, part time, and living out of sight of their families and constituents. Artie Samish, the consummate lobbyist, was called by *Collier's* magazine in 1949 the secret boss of California.

A great deal has changed, as California led the way among American states away from patronage politics and toward professionalization. California's politics cannot be understood without its version of Progressivism.[10] Over time, these reform forces made California's government modern in terms of civil service and bureaucratic organization. However, this early twentieth-century movement took decades before finally putting strong limits on interest group influence in the state by imposing strong regulations of lobbying.

The change became clear by 1995, when legendary lobbyist Clay Jackson was serving two years in prison.

In place of the old-boys' informal lobbying tactics and their lack of financial accountability, California's legislature has produced a thick rule book for lobbyists, with registration, accounting, and transparency requirements. More than a thousand lobbyists and 350 firms go through the process of registering themselves as lobbyists and of reporting expenditures. For the two-year 1999–2000 legislative session, they spent some $344 million.[11] Lobbyists and lobbying firms represented a large range of interests, typically topped by local and county government and reaching down to lodging and restaurant interests.[12] Being a registered lobbyist is an established status, with rights and privileges that include easy access to addressing committees. The number of California lobbyists stands in the middle of ranking by numbers among the states.

Among political scientists studying states, California's lobbying corps is characterized by professionalization. Lobbyists tend to be highly qualified by education and experience. They are generally paid well enough to belong to the middle-middle class. The culture of lobbying in California changed notably after 1974 with the Political Reform Act, which largely ended the era of entertainment, and Proposition 112 further curtailed gifts, parties, and trips. Long hours at noon or after work at the Derby Club or other places in Sacramento have been replaced by going home at 5:30 P.M. and making it out to the Sacramento Kings basketball or Sacramento River Cats baseball games where legislators and lobbyists may spot one another with their families. "Living in Sacramento now is a lot like living in Oak Park, Illinois (a large family-centered village)—politicians, lobbyists, and state employees—fitting in to a community," said Libby Sholes, a key lobbyist for California Impact, the lobbying arm of the California Council of Churches.[13]

Within the larger universe of interest groups at state capitals, California's interest groups are reckoned to have a relatively strong impact. Experts studying state politics depict California's interest groups as dominant/complementary.[14] Interest groups as a whole have shown strong and consistent influence on policymaking but also work with political parties and the executive. The millions of dollars expended in lobbying at Sacramento appear to be well spent in terms of effectiveness.

## CALIFORNIA'S RELIGIONS

Religious diversity, marked by an unusual brand of theatricality and peculiarity, has been evident since the early twentieth century.[15] While the Azuza

Street Church in Los Angeles is seen as a birthplace of American Pentecostalism, the movement spread mostly in remote areas of Kansas and the Southeast. What California did was allow Pentecostalism to move onstage from the margins of society. One has only to go to the Echo Park district of Los Angeles to view the dramatic setting of Angelus Temple. There one of the icons of California religion, Aimee Semple McPherson, reshaped a branch of American Pentecostalism. McPherson was the most famous woman in religion in the 1920s and 1930s, theatrical in temperament, and founder of the Foursquare Gospel International Church, a religion embraced by small entrepreneurial types and spread throughout several parts of the world.

California is more likely to have an open and Hollywood look to some of its religions. Thus, Robert Schuller is another icon of Californian religion. His Crystal Cathedral and televised services could not be more transparent. Located in Garden Grove, the Crystal Cathedral is near Disneyland and is thought to mirror Walt Disney Corporation's creation when in fact Crystal Cathedral began in the drive-in theater format. Schuller took the hard edges off midwestern Protestantism (never show the cross with Jesus crucified) and created one of the great megachurches with a televised outreach. The church building itself is an architectural gem created by Frank Gehry. Variations of Schuller's religion can be viewed among many of 14,000 congregations throughout the state: Christian without denominational identification.

To be sure, plenty of nontraditional Christian or spiritual groups have sprung up in California. One only has to pick up the free city or regional magazines to find meetings for creation spirituality, Eastern meditation, and myriad other groups. Famous and deadly cults, as Jim Jones and other suicidal groups, gained headlines some time ago. But truly esoteric and secretive sects tend to seek out mountain or southwestern states.

## Historical Displacement and Diversity

On the surface, the California Catholic Church appears to have had an easy existence for most of its 250 years in the territory.[16] When Californians organized to become a state in the mid-1800s, they did so on Catholic Church property in Benicia, near Oakland. A Dominican priest was among those who cast a vote in the state legislature for approving California's entry into union with the United States in 1850. Saints' names appear on cities, towns, and highways throughout the state. The number one religious icon for the state, said Senators Diane Feinstein and Barbara Boxer, is its twenty-one Catholic missions. They proposed that federal monies would go to preserve the incomparable state symbol.

The Catholic Church thus was historically part of the state scenery. However, Catholic numbers in the 1840s were relatively small. Mexicans numbered as few as 7,000 before purchase of California from Mexico and annexation as a state. Mexicans were poorly organized politically, weak administrators, and not much of a religious force with which to be reckoned. Protestants were encouraged to go to California to provide California the Protestant qualities it needed to be part of Protestant America. For years, the Catholic Church did little to call outside attention to itself. However, Catholicism was growing throughout the state throughout the late nineteenth and early twentieth centuries. Today, ten million Catholics are ministered to by more than 3,500 priests. Supplementing priests are some 25,000 lay ministers.

While at one time less numerous than Catholics in the state, Protestants made a strong imprint on the state. Some may have assumed, as Samuel Huntington and many others have, that America is essentially Protestant and would cease being America if not Protestant.[17] In this view, Mexicans pose a direct threat to the true nature of America. Further, a strong secular spirit infused California writers, newspapers, and universities. Symbolic of the shift toward the secular, University of Southern California and Occidental University, among other institutions, moved from being sectarian Protestant to the category of "no religious identification."

To a great extent, the intellectual life of the state, as mirrored in its writers and universities, was dominated by persons writing or acting from a Protestant or secular, not Catholic, background. Members of the super-wealthy elite, Stanford University's founders, Leland and Jane Stanford, are described by Stanford University as "deeply religious but not committed to any denomination." "Their view of denomination" meant Protestant, not Catholic. Only within the past ten years have Catholics, the largest religious group on campus, been allowed to worship at Stanford's Memorial Church. In describing America's power elite, William Domoff chose as the major symbol for the U.S. power elite a California-based organization, the Bohemian Club, a largely male and vaguely Protestant establishment of 2,500 persons.[18]

Only three historical Protestant churches—Presbyterian, United Methodist, and Missouri Synod Lutherans—are numbered among the ten largest faith groups in California, in seventh, eighth, and tenth places, respectively. The largest, the Presbyterians, fifty times smaller than the Catholic Church in the state, has about 230,000 members. The world of Protestantism in California, however, is much wider than denominational Protestant churches. Some 11 percent of Californians describe themselves as Christian,[19] in ways already noted about Pastor Schuller. Their estimated 3.7 million outnumber conventional Protestants. Southern Baptists are fourth in the state with 471,000 members; Assemblies of God, a classical Pentecostal church, is fifth with

310,000 members.[20] The latter churches are growing in membership. The historically older Protestant groups are not.[21]

Jews as a group represent the second-largest religious institutional group in the state. That their 3 percent places them in second place indicates both the extreme fragmentation of Protestants and the strong presence of Jews in contrast to their weak numbers in many states. Jews organize themselves in federations, located primarily in the San Francisco Bay and Los Angeles–Orange County areas. Jewish Social Services are very active providers of health and other social services but are only one of a myriad of agencies under Jewish sponsorship. Through the years, Jewish agencies have also focused on ties with Israel and with fostering education in public schools to counter hate and discrimination. Jewish affiliation showed an 8 percent increase from 1990 to 2001.

Non-Christian or nontraditional Christian groups fill out the top ten list of religious groups in California. Mormons are in third position among the state's religions with about half a million (and declining from 1990 to 2001) and Muslims in sixth position with a quarter million (in 2000 but probably rapidly growing). Seventh Day Adventist, with slightly less than 200,000, are in ninth place.

In sum, first, California's religious landscape is highly diverse. Even more, it is divided into small, almost unworkable fractions of national denominations and sects. Second, the dominant religious element among California's elite members was Protestant. Its educational institutions, newspapers, and wealth showed this. Third, Catholicism, as evidenced in recent governors and 30 percent membership in the state, has now become a major influence in the state. Fourth, large numbers of Californians are religious without belonging to a specific congregation, and almost 20 percent of its inhabitants say they have no religion (also typical of northwestern states). Fifth, despite widespread fragmentation, a solid core of organized religion gives structural backbone to the state's religions.

Elazar's often-cited typology of state religious contexts described California's dominant culture as moralistic and individualistic.[22] This culture, with its drive toward individual moralizing and the privatization of religion, is being contested by the Mexicanization of many Catholic and some Protestant congregations, characterized by a preference for a communitarian, not individualistic, religion.[23] Further, rapidly growing numbers of Filipino and Vietnamese religious practitioners make clear that there is not a unitary California religious culture. One of the signs of this acceptance of this religious diversity was the Catholic Church's successful drive to have a statue of Cesar Chavez, the Mexican American farmworker organizer, unveiled near the state capitol despite the resistance of agribusiness leaders.

## CALIFORNIA'S RELIGIONS AND ITS LOBBIES

However much religious diversity thrives or not in California, little diversity is evident in Sacramento's religious lobby. No Pentecostal or Muslim groups maintain a presence there, and the evangelical presence has been weak or nonexistent. Instead, mainline Protestant traditions, Jewish federations, and Catholics were represented in Sacramento. This mirrors the institutional side of religion in California. Organizationally, California is very much a Catholic, Protestant, and Jewish state where parishes and congregations anchor the state's religion. These religious groups present their policy issues actively and, to a relatively high degree, effectively at the state capital.

The religious Right made a new drive to establish a political presence in the state. In late 2003, Focus on the Family, a parachurch group founded by James Dobson, established the California Family Council. Dobson, the noted radio personality heard on some 6,000 broadcast facilities worldwide, began his radio ministry to families in Arcadia, California. He moved from a position at the University of Southern California's School of Medicine to build a large international headquarters in Colorado. Dobson's Focus on the Family group started California Family Council with a small staff that is highly experienced in legislative affairs. Southern Baptists, through its Committee on Moral Concerns (considered a service to its pastors), has become part of California Family Council. It is too early to assess the Council's impact on policy or elections.[24]

### History of Religious Lobbying

The religious lobby evolved just as lobbying was evolving away from an entertainment and old-boys' network of some fifty lobbyists in Sacramento to a highly professional corps. The following account is based on interviews and observation at Sacramento over three years and also on documentary histories of the religious lobby. The first religious interest group grew from a California Quaker group, the Berkeley Friends. In 1952, they opened an office for policy advocacy, first in San Francisco, then moved to Sacramento. They believe themselves to be the first public interest group in the state. At first, they were concerned about civil liberties under assault during the Cold War era. Berkeley Friends, expressing the values of Quakers, evolved into the present-day Friends Committee on Legislation (FCL). The board of directors of FCL is overwhelmingly Quaker. The three staff members are not Quaker but share the same values. The priority issues pursued by FCL have been diffuse. It was especially interested in the plight of farmworkers, and it moved on to other issues as other religious lobbyists joined in advocacy for farmworkers. The organization turned to emphasizing a peace economy in California rather than its dependence on defense dollars being spent in California. Currently, FCL, in coordination with similar groups in other states, has centered much of its energies on criminal justice.

In viewing the criminal justice system, Jim Lindburg, the legislative advocate for FCL, believes California took two wrong turns in the 1970s. The state began a frenzied prison building spree, constructing twenty-two of its thirty-three prison facilities in twenty years (in contrast to previous decades when college campuses went up at a unprecedented rate). Also, California's policy in 1977 stated that imprisonment for punishment was punitive. Lindburg and his allies have been pushing the state, with some success, to move toward rehabilitation rather than only punitive punishment for prisoners. In Lindburg's opinion, Quakers are drawn to this effort because they see in every individual something of God and a person capable of change. Others agree; 70 percent of FCL's budget comes from non-Friends contributors.

The second group historically to organize to influence state policy grew into the California Council of Churches. This umbrella group includes a wide spectrum of mainline Protestant churches (such as Episcopal, Presbyterian, and United Methodist), some black Protestant churches, three Orthodox groups but also diverse groups, a splinter Mormon group, a Swedenborgian group, Metropolitan Community Churches (largely gay and lesbian), and the Church Women United group. In all, it represents 1.5 million members and over 4,000 congregations. Rick Schlosser, executive director of the California Council of Churches, describes the goals of the Council as advocating for justice, peacemaking, and the well-being of the powerless. For tax purposes, so that the church group can have a political advocacy wing, the California Council created California Church Impact.

The Evangelical Lutheran Church also has a relatively long history in Sacramento. ECLA, an intermediate-size church group within the California Council, chose to maintain its own Lutheran Office of Public Policy. Mark Carlson, its executive director, explained that the church feared its distinctive voice would be lost among many others. Carlson represents the policy interests of the leadership of three Lutheran synods in the state. Further, he represents national Lutheran public policy, receiving two-thirds of funding for his office from the national church. Even more than Catholics (who receive no national funding), Lutherans in California coordinate more closely their policy positions with colleagues in other states, especially with those in national offices in Chicago and Washington. Carlson helps write national policy statements; other Sacramento religious lobbyists typically do not. Lutherans appear to exercise more care about doctrine and uniformity of positions than many other groups.[25]

The Catholic bishops began organizing themselves statewide in the 1970s. The Church now maintains two legally separate entities at Sacramento: the California Catholic Conference and Catholic Charities. Each has an executive director and a separate board of directors and pursue somewhat different agendas. Both represent huge constituencies. In the case of Catholic Charities, its twelve diocesan units stand to lose or gain millions of dollars through state agency budget appropriations. In 2002, Catholic Charities received 50 percent of its $187 million expenditures through local, state, and federal funding.

The strength of the California Catholic Conference derives, in part, from its claim to represent Catholic institutions.[26] In a word, the Catholic Church forms the largest bloc in important state sectors. It is the largest private provider of health care, social services, and education in the state. Twelve diocesan Catholic Charities agencies annually serve more than one million persons. These clients come from diverse ethnicities, statuses, and religious backgrounds. Fifty Catholic hospitals serve five million patients a year. Catholic universities and other schools educate almost 300,000 students.

The language of advocacy used by the California Catholic Conference to define its mission employs universal, not sectarian, description. It professes to be about preferential care for the weak and vulnerable, human life, the rights of workers, food and income security for "our low-income neighbors," and the environment. None of these issues, as such, are specifically "Catholic," although some may disagree.

The Church's presence in the state—that is, in its parishes and human resources—is formidable. Its 1,067 parishes in twelve dioceses cover every corner of the state.[27] The *New Historical Atlas of Religion in America*[28] shows a pervasive Catholic presence. In all but one county, the Catholic Church is the largest denomination. In the single exception, Trinity County, the Church is the second-largest denomination. (Fragmentation of the other churches, not overall percentage, helps explain this dominance.)[29]

Politicians can quickly grasp the universal reach of such an institution. Its 3,592 priests and twenty-nine bishops offer upper- and middle-management strength, to say nothing of thousands of women religious and laypersons employed by Church institutions and presumably loyal to Church interests. It is not as if these institutions are owned, financed, and controlled by the Church as corporations, with bishops as directors. Rather, the institutions, often owned and directly controlled by religious orders or independent directors, form only a very loose federation of schools and hospitals who recognize the bishops as having a measure of authority over them. What is not always acknowledged is the wide measure of freedom from episcopal oversight and supervision enjoyed by Catholic institutions. Not many Catholic colleges or universities have complied with bishops' requests for theology faculty to obtain the so-called *mandatum*.[30] The support of many Catholic institutions for the California Catholic Conference is strong but voluntary.

An independent religious lobby, Jericho for Justice, has been operating since 1987 in Sacramento. It has no exact counterpart anywhere in the United States. Jericho was created by Sister Sheila Walsh and is directed by Sister Simone Campbell; both sisters are members of a small international Catholic religious congregation, the Sisters of Social Service. Simone Campbell has her feet in both secular and spiritual worlds. She lobbies as an accomplished lawyer who maintains a prayer-support network. She recruited mostly retired nuns in the Bay Area to adopt each one of the 120 legislators. The nuns have pictures of their adopted legislators and pray for her or him every day. Likewise, the legislators have pictures of the sisters who are praying for them. Despite its singularity, Jericho, in the person of its previous and present lobbyists, is well accepted as a major player in the religious lobby.

Two other groups form part of the religious lobby. The Universalist Unitarian church revived its position of religious lobbyist in the spring of 2004. The Jewish Political Action Committee (JPAC) completes the core religious lobby. While the other religious interest groups employ in-house lobbyists, JPAC (Jewish Political Action Committee), the Jewish lobby, engages a professional firm, Governmental Advocates, to represent them.

These eight groups are the main religious interest groups in Sacramento. With the exception of Jericho, they are maintained by church organizations or federations. This core group making up California's religious lobby is well defined and relatively stable. The corps of lobbyists know one another well, form coalitions when possible, disagree without rancor, and sponsor jointly important common events. A wider perspective on religious interest groups will taken up later when grassroots faith-based organizations are considered.

The credentials and professional experience of California's religious lobbyists are impressive by any standards. Rick Schlosser (California Church Impact) earned a doctorate at Graduate Theological Union, Berkeley; Elizabeth Sholes (also California Church Impact) pursued doctoral studies in colonial American history; Al Hernandez (California Catholic Conference) gained a master's degree in urban planning and a law degree at the University of California, Berkeley; Sister Simone Campbell (Jericho) is also a lawyer; Rick Mockler (California Catholic Charities) has graduate degrees in theology and administration; and other religious lobbyists have pursued advanced studies, as in environmental or religious studies.

One of the striking changes from an earlier generation of lobbyists at the state capital is lay presence in place of clergy. None of the ten employees of the California Conference is clergy; only two of ten staff at the California

Council of Churches are ordained clergy, and Sister Simone Campbell is a vowed Catholic religious sister; the rest are laity.

## Coalitions and Their Limitations

The most public face of the religious interest groups in recent years is the California Interfaith Coalition (CIC). The CIC and its history, in many ways, tell the core of the story of the religious lobby. The CIC began in 1990 as the Coalition for a Just Budget. In a word, the strongest thrust of the religious lobby has been to maintain programs that benefit the weak and vulnerable of the state. The organization's name changed in 1993 to the California Interfaith Coalition. The member groups that make up the coalition are the eight religious interest groups mentioned earlier. Together, the groups monitor state budget negotiations, follow legislation, and act as advocates on issues such as immigration, criminal justice, welfare reform, housing, and health care.

The most publicized event of CIC is the annual Legislative Issues Briefing Day. Hundreds of persons from across the state attend. This occurs in March, the important point in the Sacramento calendar, when legislation previously proposed by legislators has moved through vetting for legal language and other refinements and then moves to committee and full-session debates. Participants in the Briefing Day hear senators, assembly members, or state government officials describe key bills before the legislature and meet with their legislators at the capitol. In the parade of Legislative Days at Sacramento, many other interest groups, such as Landscape Management, Community Technology, and others, make the same trip to Sacramento, forming a ritual as regular as demonstrations on the north lawn of the capitol. Despite the repetition of Lobby Days, religious lobby members regard their Legislative Issues Day as effective in reinforcing the image of CIC as an organization that in some way speaks for millions of Californians and alerts legislators to issues that religious groups believe important.

The CIC fulfills only a limited purpose. In many ways, it does not promote some issues that some religious lobbies believe are most important to them in state policymaking and implementation.[31] Thus, Catholic Lobby Day, held separately from CIC events, shows more clearly specific policy priorities of the California Catholic Conference. In 2004, 900 Catholics, almost all of them lay, came to Sacramento. In their visits with state legislators, they reinforced the CIC's opposition to budget cuts that they said "would hurt the most vulnerable among us." However, they also took up other issues, such as compassionate release of prisoners, opposition to gender-neutral marriage, and higher-education cuts.

JPAC participates in a few joint activities with other religious groups. Its lobbyist from Governmental Associates seldom interacts with other religious lobbyists. The JPAC lobbyist appears at legislative committee to testify on behalf of interests JPAC thinks important. JPAC acts as the voice of California's federated Jewish communities and receives funding from regional federations within the state. A major event for JPAC occurs when about 150 Californians go to Sacramento for a day of preparation and for Jewish Lobby Day itself. In 2004, JPAC chose to emphasize three issues—issues that indicate the thrust of Jewish interests at the state capital. First was expression of strong opposition to proposed weakening of the state's support for adult day care and other senior programs. Second was a plea to reopen California's trade office in Israel. Third was a plea that the state attorney general and the state insurance commissioner find legal means of ensuring that insurance companies that do business in California pay all Holocaust-era insurance claims.[32]

Except for the JPAC lobbyist, the lobbyists who make up CIC tend to divide up labor on issues according to personal competency and according to local histories of the religious groups. The lobbyist for the Friends, Jim Lindburg, takes the lead on criminal justice issues. He and Ned Dolesji from the California Catholic Conference especially aim at eliminating the death penalty. The Lutheran representative monitors and mobilizes on environmental issues. Libby Sholes from California Impact and Linda Wanner from the Catholic Conference emphasize welfare, children, and women's policies. Al Hernandez from the Catholic Conference and Sister Simone Campbell from Jericho focus much of their energies on the general shape of the budget.

## POLICY ISSUES

### Choice of Issues

What is most characteristic of the established religious lobby is that it is reactive. Issues that may be closest to the hearts and minds of Catholic and Protestant leaders are not necessarily those in a given year for legislators. Abortion, which was a hot-button issue for national politicians in 2004, is not currently an issue on the table in California.[33] In sum, religious lobbyists largely choose issues to concentrate on from the long list of bills that make their way through committees to the senate and assembly floors.

This reactive mode has important consequences. First, registered lobbyists believe that one has to be in Sacramento to truly affect policy. Second, Muslims, evangelicals, and other groups may be deluding themselves into thinking they have influence in the public sphere if they are not making themselves felt in Sacramento. Third, abundant opportunities for theological reflection and religious activism exist in the issues debated at Sacramento. Fourth, contextual theology, based on a method of see–judge–act, is especially well suited to state legislative and executive politics. Theological reflection is more fully treated later in this chapter.

## Major Issues

The major issue facing the religious lobby has been sustaining programs for the poor and marginal in California's budget. Following the economic downturn in Silicon Valley and the great energy payout debacle, the budget fell into a perilous state from a heady surplus. This crisis was increased by severe reduction of devolution of revenues from federal programs since California receives about 20 percent of its revenues from federal programs.

Within California, declines in revenues from major taxes began in May and June 2001. A shortfall was easily absorbed by a $9 billion surplus from the prior fiscal year. By 2002, California had an operating shortfall of $13 billion. As an expert at the Urban Institute wrote, "California relied on a myriad of one-time solutions to close the budget gaps for FY 2002–2004."[34] California delayed program expansions and cost-of-living increases and made many administrative cuts and funding shifts. It did this to avoid cutting cash assistance, work supports, or job placement or training. California was very much a reflection of New Deal politics. It had managed for some fifty years to create and maintain programs that benefit the poor and the marginal. These appeared to be in great jeopardy with a new and muscular Republican governor who threatened to greatly reduce the budget.

The core issues for the religious lobby can be summarized as maintaining within the state budget the established programs for the weak and the vulnerable. This was the focal point of the Lobby Day 2004 for the CIC. It also was the centerpiece for Catholic Lobby Day. Each drew important numbers to Sacramento. In addition, the California Council of Churches and Catholic Charities cooperated in sponsoring projects in child care and energy assistance.[35] Al Hernandez, the lead lobbyist for the Catholic Conference, Elizabeth Sholes from Church Impact, Sister Simone Campbell from Jericho, and other religious lobbyists were elated that their efforts had helped maintain these programs.

In effect, they reinforced the key persons in the budget process, the leaders in the senate and assembly. Political commentator Peter Schrag pointed out that Senate President Pro Tem John Burton succeeded "in protecting California's poor, sick, blind, and disabled from some of the most devastating cuts that [Governor] Schwarzenegger proposed in his original budget."

Schrag described as Burton's legacy his passion to protect the poor and the sick.[36] The same description fits the religious lobbyists who spent hours with Burton and other influential legislators, especially those on the budget committees.

Those concerned about the condition of the poor were fearful that callous governors and legislators would address California's budget shortfall by cutting out or drastically revising programs for the poor.[37] While Democrats held control of the governor's chair and the two houses through 2003, a large measure of programs for the poor were maintained. Once Gray Davis (Democrat) was recalled from office and Arnold Schwarzenegger (Republican) was in charge in 2004 to create a new budget, the full implications of California's fiscal condition became clear. The state would soon go into bankruptcy unless something drastic was done. Part of the fundamental solution, economists believed, was increasing taxes. Schwarzenegger, the Republican "Governator" (as buttons sold in the state capital proclaim him), vowed never to do that. So it was believed that relief programs like CalWorks and TANF would be drastically cut. Religious lobbyists thought of CalWorks and TANF as centerpieces of the state programs for the poor. The main political leaders in the senate and assembly held to their promise that the budget would continue to take care of those on welfare, albeit in somewhat reduced terms. Schwarzenegger pulled together a bipartisan group of advisers, and he himself worked one unusual deal after the other. In the end, he delivered a budget of about $100 billion, a budget that looked little different from those of Gray Davis.

## Key Allies: Policy Centers

Lobbying and religious advocacy depend on *information*. This is the key commodity lobbyists are able to provide legislators and, to a lesser extent, executive branch officers. Provision of information by outsiders has become increasingly important because of term limits. In the California assembly, members may have three terms for a total of six years in a lifetime. The limits for senators is two terms for a total of eight years in a lifetime.[38] The assembly and the senate thus lost a large measure of institutional memory. Legislatures repeat mistakes and compound errors when veteran legislators are not part of crucial debates. Term limits shifted influence over policy formation to veteran legislative staff members and to lobbyists who know more about the history of issues than new legislators, thus enhancing the role of the religious lobbyists.[39]

The making of the budget is the essential political enterprise in California, with its more than $100 billion in expenditures. A bewildering maze of laws

mandating or limiting state expenditures has grown in California. Schwarzenegger, with his carefully chosen aides, many of whom have been Sacramento insiders, tried the strategy of claiming to know budget regulations and implications that outsiders could not know. He and they were immediately countered
by expert information and counterinterpretations from crucial policy institutes
that have grown up in the state.

In its efforts to protect key programs for the poor in the budget, religious
lobbyists have a partner in the California Budget Project (CBP). This highly
competent and well-staffed policy enterprise began as an effort to aid legislators and the public in understanding the great legal and fiscal complexities
that California's budgets have become. The CBP began about ten years ago
as the brainchild of Jean M. Ross. From her work as consultant to the assembly and her education in city and regional planning at the University of California, Berkeley, she pulled together a group of nine persons and funds from
various foundations to make sense of state policy issues, primarily those
within the state budget. The group has special interest in policies that affect
low- and middle-income families. The CBP's presence in Sacramento came
at a critical time when hardly any outsider could counter one or another as-
sertions by legislators or statehouse advisers. Other centers, such as the California Institute for Federal Policy Research and the Public Policy Institute of
California, have aided in policy analysis.[40]

The budget for the past four years has been put together with a bewildering
array of deals between cities and the state, counties and the state, and unions
(especially prison guards and teachers). Governors Davis and Schwarzenegger
acted like a pair of magicians who kept the budget close to $100 billion with-
out raising taxes. Religious lobbyists could not follow the implications of the
deals without CBP's description and analysis.

Aiding the religious lobby's analytical capacities has been a remarkable
center at the University of Southern California, the Center for Religion and
Civic Culture, which has been carrying on academic studies, often with a
practical bent of evaluation and improvement of California religious activism, interfaith coalitions, and various faith-based initiatives. The center's
members have faced the critical questions that the Clinton administration's
Charitable Choice and Bush's policies of faith-based initiatives have posed.

### Other Issues

Other issues of concern to the religious lobbyists in 2004 were those of compassionate release for some prisoners, minimum wage, and similar social justice concerns. However, one issue—a hot-button one—divided the religious
lobby, especially the Catholic Conference, from the California Church Im-

pact. The Catholic lobby, as it has at the national level, clearly opposed granting marital status to same-sex couples. Recognition of same-sex marriage was heartfelt and exceptionally important to Rick Schlosser, the executive secretary of the California Council of Churches. Schlosser came to the Council from a leading organization of gay and lesbian Christians. He is pastor to one of Berkeley's Metropolitan Church Congregations and was recently married to his own gay partner.

Thus, a main California issue in the summer of 2004 was responding to President Bush's plan to amend the U.S. Constitution to ban marriage between same-sex couples. California's assembly opposed the Bush initiative on a straight party vote, 44 to 28. The Democrats who won the vote had the support of Hispanic Democrats (presumably Catholic), an indication of a major problem for the Catholic Church. In a word, Hispanic legislators have grown increasingly independent from Catholic influences on social-moral issues, such as abortion and same-sex marriage. One Catholic lobbyist said, "Hispanics, many of whom are from a foreign background, probably would have voted against same-sex marriage back in Latin America; in California they vote against the Church's position. They see this falling in with the Democrats as being modern and enlightened."[41]

A major question that did not become an issue on the floor of the legislature was the priests' scandal. To head off a public debate about possible legislation that could act as a corrective to the Church's alleged cover-up of priestly misconduct, the California Catholic Conference sent a lobbyist to each of the 120 legislators with a full account of which priests in their district were charged, what the nature of the accusations was, and what measures the Church had taken. These measures were enough to convince legislators that no new laws or legislative debate were needed.

### From Grassroots to State Advocacy

A new development in the California religious lobby has been the move from grassroots activity to state advocacy in 2001. When the two legendary large-scale community organizing groups, PICO and ACORN, established offices in Sacramento, they were well known in the state and nationally. The Pacific Institute for Community Organizations, better known as PICO, started in the Bay Area in 1972 and now includes more than a million persons. The Association of Community Organizations for Reform Now, commonly referred to as ACORN, also has a large membership. Both advanced from community problems to state politics. PICO believes it achieved considerable gains in health care and education; in 2004, ACORN was just beginning to help shape legislation to benefit low-income families.[42] PICO was a faith-based organization

long before George W. Bush became president. ACORN is more secular but
has received support from such religious organizations as the national Catholic
bishops' Campaign for Human Development.[43]

Emphasis is given here to PICO because of its greater ties to organized religion. Growing as it has from Catholic, black and white social Christianity, and
Hispanic cultural ties, PICO is not dependent on any one denominational tradition. The organization has grown to include hundreds of thousands of persons
in many states. Begun in the Bay Area more than thirty years ago by a Jesuit
priest, John Baumann, PICO grew from having significant clout at Oakland's
city hall to possessing deep and wide roots in California. It now represents
some 400,000 families in seventy cities. When PICO took the next step and organized the PICO California Project, it began in May 2000 with 3,000 Californians uniting at Sacramento to demand greater funding for health care for the
poor. Their efforts led to $50 million in additional funding for community
health services. This was the first of many new efforts to influence state policy
and practice. Two years later, the organization drew 4,000 community leaders
to Sacramento for a statewide town hall meeting. PICO California anchored its
efforts with a Sacramento office and three staff persons. None are registered
lobbyists, but they and colleagues from member organizations around the state
have lobbied on specific issues for four years with impressive victories.[44]

Similarly, ACORN has a Sacramento office and has become active in lobbying for specific issues, such as affordable housing for the poor in the metropolitan sprawl of California. The Center for Religion and Civic Culture sees
the evolution of both community-based groups into state politics as major
steps in civic participation and democracy and in the articulation of social
movements and the state.[45]

The existence of large movement advocacy does not guarantee impact on
policy or practice. The relation between grassroots organizations and actual
influence is a major question in American and comparative politics. New social movements, as those in Latin America, were presumed to be foundations
of democratization. Yet the ties were more alleged than proven. Skeptics point
to repeated co-optation of social movements by the state. Nor does the fact
that a lobby promoted a policy mean that its adoption was caused by the
lobby's activities. However, some influence seems incontestable: PICO,
through 3,000 activists appearing in Sacramento, put a $30 million project on
the legislative agenda that was not there before PICO's activity.

## Theologies of the Public Square

All the lobbyists, registered or not, consider the formulation of a public theology crucial for their work. A public theology that has been developing

gradually in the United States in the past thirty years drives the efforts of the California Catholic Conference. While formulated largely in the United States and emphasizing active citizenship, this theology derives from 110 years of worldwide Catholic social teaching. This public theology resembles contemporary Latin American social theology, an inductive theology that begins with a reflection on the context. In place of the key Latin American theme of option for the poor, it addressed the defense of the weak and the vulnerable.

The United States Conference of Catholic Bishops (USCCB) provides ideological/theological resources. The chief person for providing intellectual resources has been Father J. Bryan Hehir, professor of the practice of religion and public life at Harvard Divinity School. He was crucial for articulating a public theology for Catholics in the United States and for the USCCB and state conferences.[46] The most succinct statements of the American bishops' view can be seen in *Political Responsibility* (1976)[47] and *Faithful Citizenship: Civic Responsibility for a New Millennium* (1999).[48]

Father John Coleman of Loyola Marymount University at Los Angeles similarly aided the California Catholic Conference.[49] In addition to Coleman, California Catholicism has a strong backbone in its public intellectuals, such as Kevin Starr, Richard Rodriguez, Allen Figueroa Deck, John E. Coons, and John T. Noonan Jr. Coons and Noonan, whose books are widely circulated, have added considerable historical and legal depth to aspects of private and Catholic education in democracy and of religious freedom.

The statements of the Evangelical Lutheran Church in their formally structured arguments are probably closest to the Catholic Church's theology of political involvement. As noted, unlike other religious lobbies, the national body—in this case, the National Office of Lutheran Social Concerns—provides a large part of funding for the California Office, which, in turn, gives great emphasis to the doctrinal backing for its political involvement and for the specific stands it takes on issues. While the California Council of Churches does not have a comparable social doctrine since it represents a wide spectrum of churches, from Presbyterian to independent Mormon, the Council emphatically offers a vision of social Christianity. Further, the Council has a much more vigorous educational program for parishes and groups statewide than the California Catholic Conference.

To an extent, the fusion of theologies and activism can best be seen in PICO. The organization was beginning to stagnate until it sought greater collaboration with churches. This closer collaboration provided a religious culture and a primary shared language. Leaders allowed themselves to use their own theological training and religious commitments to tie themselves to their participants' diverse faith commitments. Further, with PICO in Oakland, the organization had easy access to the theological and scriptural resources of a faculty with 200 members at the Graduate Theological Union in neighboring Berkeley. With many African American church clergy and members, PICO also employed scriptural interpretations and pulpit oratory of the African American tradition.[50] This is a tradition that fueled the drive for civil rights under Martin Luther King Jr. Another strong theological resource has been provided by Allen Figueroa Deck, his colleagues, and disciples through Latino theology and its emphasis on community and struggling for social justice.

Theological fuel has been important for religious activism of the lobbyists and the grassroots participants in movements. However, several religious lobbyists and leaders of the grassroots movements were skeptical of the Bush White House's faith-based initiatives. Simone Campbell, director of Jericho, sees faith-based initiatives as bad for religion and bad for politics. John Baumann of PICO believes there may be reason for poor and independent churches to take funds from these sources for the short term. He is skeptical of long-term relations with government programs. Not all agree, and some programs eagerly receive help for the homeless or the addicted from Bush's religious-oriented programs.

## CONCLUSION

Clear ideas and theological rationales are called for to avoid fundamentalist, intemperate extremes. California's vaunted universities and theological schools, in union with its activists, have provided a well-articulated view of the role of religious values in politics. Notable, too, is the apparent change in Fuller Seminary, thought to be the paragon of noncritical, apolitical Protestant fundamentalism. Fuller's ties with the University of Southern California's Center for Religion and Civic Culture indicate a shift toward full engagement in the discussion of faith and politics.

Further, the implications of what is going on in the state are being watched and copied in Central America. Bishop Alvaro Ramazzini of San Marcos, Guatemala, attended a training session of PICO in California in 2004. This was a prelude to a program to spread PICO's views of grassroots organizing and of building civil society in Central America and Panama at the invitation of Ramazzini and Cardinal Oscar Rodríguez of Honduras.

In sum, one may say, in general terms, that observers believe California's religious interest groups have a moderate impact on policymaking. However, in the author's view, religious lobbyists have had a major impact on legislation and implementation over the past two decades, sometimes at crucial times. Further, large-scale grassroots organizations, with a broad religious base, are reaching increasingly into state politics.

## NOTES

1. Brian P. Janiskee and Ken Masugi, *Democracy in California: Politics and Government in the Golden State* (Lanham, Md.: Rowman & Littlefield, 2003), 75.

2. California government and politics are widely explored: six college-level books have had five to fifteen editions. Bernard L. Hyink and David H. Provost's *Politics and Government in California* (New York: Longman, 2001) is its 15th edition. New works are entering the field: Brian P. Janiskee and Ken Masugi, *Democracy in California: Politics and Government in the Golden State* (Lanham, Md.: Rowman & Littlefield, 2003), and Matthew Alan Cahn et al., *Rethinking California: Politics and Policy in the Golden State* (Upper Saddle River, N.J.: Prentice Hall, 2001), 74–79. See also Peter Schrag, *Paradise Lost: California's Experience, America's Future* (New York: New Press, 1997), 188–256, and especially Mark Baldassare, *California in the New Millennium: The Changing Social and Political Landscape* (Berkeley: University of California Press, 2000).

3. Peverill Squire, Keith E. Hamm, and Gary F. Moncrief, "Legislative Politics in the States," in *Politics in the American States: A Comparative Analysis*, 8th ed., ed. Virginia Gray and Russell L. Hanson (Washington, D.C.: Congressional Quarterly Press, 2004), 158.

4. Mark Baldassare treats distrust in government at length in *California in the New Millennium*, esp. 42–49. Legislative gridlock, by which the governor and legislature have been unable to meet the June 30 deadline for passage of the state budget nine of eleven years from 1993 to 2004, contributed strongly to negative views of state government.

5. *Governing* periodical gave California one of the lowest grades for government performance in the most populous states in its February 1999 issue, 33.

6. Over 690,000 valid signatures are required for constitutional change and over 430,000 for statutory initiative. See Cahn et al., *Rethinking California*, 76.

7. Cahn et al., *Rethinking California*, 74–79. See also Schrag, *Paradise Lost*, 188–256.

8. Cahn et al., *Rethinking California*.

9. Research on lobbying and interest groups is very developed. For lobbying in the states, with reference to California, see Alan Rosenthal, *The Third House: Lobbyists and Lobbying in the States* (Washington, D.C.: Congressional Quarterly Press, 2001), esp. the first edition (1993). See also Jay Michael, Dan Walters, and Dan Weintraub, *The Third House: Lobbyists, Money, and Power in Sacramento* (Berkeley, Calif.: Public Policy Press, 2002); Jennifer Wolak, David Lowery, and Virginia Gray, "California Dreaming: Replicating the ESA Model, Unusual Cases, and Comparative State Political Analysis," *State Politics and Policy Quarterly* 1, no. 3 (2001): 255–72; Robert L. Giovati, "Busy Signals: Underrepresentation of Lobbyists Advancing Conservative

Interests in California," *California Political Review* 14, no. 6 (2003): 25–30; and Fair Political Practices Commission, *Lobbying Disclosure Information Manual* (Sacramento, Calif.: Fair Political Practices Commission, 1998). A large body of oral histories of California lobbyists has been published through the Oral History Program of California State University, Sacramento.

10. Among other works see Kevin Starr, *Inventing the Dream: California through the Progressive Era* (New York: Oxford University Press, 1985), and Spencer Olin, *California's Prodigal Sons: Hiram Johnson and the Progressives, 1911–1917* (Berkeley: University of California Press, 1985).

11. Secretary of State Bill Jones, *Lobbying Expenditures and the Top 100 Lobbying Firms* (Sacramento, Calif.: Secretary of State's Office, 2001).

12. Governmental advocates (state and municipal) were pushed from the top of the list by a large temporary increase in lobbying that was caused by utilities and insurance companies having to defend their interests in connection with proceedings against them, especially in 1999 and 2000.

13. Interview with Elizabeth Sholes, May 27, 2004.

14. See Clive S. Thomas and Ronald J. Hrebenar's compilation and description of states in Gray and Hanson, *Politics in the American States*, 122.

15. Study of California's religions has been well served by religious research centers, especially at the University of California, Santa Barbara, and University of Southern California. The Capps Center at UCSB has a selected bibliography at their website. Among recent works, see Ferenc Morto Szasz, *Religion in the Modern American West* (Tucson: University of Arizona Press, 2000), and Ava Fran Kahn and Marc Dollinger, *California Jews* (Waltham, Mass.: Brandeis University Press, 2003).

16. Kay Alexander presents a useful bibliographical essay in her *California Catholicism* (Santa Barbara, Calif.: Fithian Press, 1993). To this should be added Allen Figueroa Deck, *The Second Wave: Hispanic Ministry and the Evangelization of Culture* (New York: Paulist Press, 1987), and his "A Latino Practical Theology: Mapping the Road Ahead," *Theological Studies* 65, no. 2 (June 2004): 275–97.

17. Samuel Huntington, "The Hispanic Challenge," *Foreign Policy*, March/April 2004, 30–45.

18. G. William Domoff, *The Bohenian Grove and Other Retreats: A Study in Ruling-Class Cohesiveness* (New York: Harper and Row, 1974). While the 2,500 men who are members are mostly from California, many others are national and international power elite members.

19. American Religious Identification Study, available at www.gc.cuny.edu.

20. Statistics for denominational faith groups are from *Religious Congregations and Membership in the United States: 2000* (Nashville: Glenmary Research Center, 2002), cited at www.cappscenter.ucsb.edu.

21. Increases and decreases in adherents are noted at www.thearda.com study site.

22. Daniel J. Elazar, *American Federalism: A View from the States* (New York: Crowell, 1966).

23. See Alan Figueroa Deck's description of Latino-Anglo disparities in his "A Latino Practical Theology: Mapping the Road Ahead," *Theological Studies* 65, no. 2 (June 2004): 275–97.

24. Based on communications from Karen Holgate, director of legislative affairs of California Family Council, which referred voters to *Voter Guides* provided by Christian Coalition of California.

25. See the fullness and range of statements by the Lutheran Office of Public Policy at its website. One should also note that, while mainline Lutheran church bodies are members of the World Council of Churches, Lutherans also maintain the Lutheran World Federation.

26. Studies of the California Catholic Conference include Edward L. Cleary, "Religion at the Statehouse: The California Catholic Conference," *Journal of Church and State* 45, no. 1 (winter 2003): 41–58, and mention in William Bole's "What Do State Conferences Do," in *American Catholics and Civic Engagement: A Distinctive Voice*, ed. Margaret O'Brien Steinfels (Lanham, Md.: Rowman & Littlefield, 2004), esp. 95–99 and 103–6; Edward Dolesji, executive director of California Catholic Conference, "The Limits of Coalitions and Compromises: The California State Conference," in Steinfels, *American Catholics*, 110–25.

27. Catholic parishes are estimated nationally to have about ten times as many members as typical Protestant church congregations. See Bryan T. Froehle and Mary L. Gautier, *Catholicism USA: A Portrait of the Catholic Church in the United States* (Maryknoll, N.Y.: Orbis, 2000), 51.

28. Edwin Scott Gaustad and Philip L. Barlow, *New Historical Atlas of Religion in America* (New York: Oxford University Press, 2000).

29. Gaustad and Barlow, *New Historical Atlas of Religion in America*, 319, 321.

30. *National Catholic Register* carried a series on articles on the *mandatum* (approval of the resident bishop to teach theology at Catholics college and universities) in the summer of 2004.

31. Edward Dolesji, executive director of California Catholic Conference, has an extended reflection in "The Limits of Coalitions and Compromises: The California State Conference," in Steinfels, *American Catholics*, 110–25.

32. From *The Jewish Journal*'s website. In 2003, the three issues presented to legislators were avoiding Medi-Cal cuts, condemning the Arab League's boycott of Israel, and training of teachers in prevention of hate crimes.

33. California's former governor, Gray Davis, a Catholic convert, was informed indirectly by the bishop of Sacramento that communion would be denied him at a particular parish because of his stance on pro-abortion. Davis simply went to another parish. For a view of the abortion issue before 2004, see Michael Russo, "California: A Political Landscape for Choice and Conflict," in *Abortion Politics in the American States*, ed. Mary C. Segers and Timothy A. Byrnes (Armonk, N.Y.: M. E. Sharpe, 1995).

34. Kenneth Finegold et al., *Social Program Spending and State Fiscal Crises* (Washington, D.C.: Urban Institute, 2003), 24.

35. Projects described as a Faith-Based Child Care Capacity Building Project and California Interfaith Energy Assistance Project.

36. Peter Schrag, "As the Governor Baloons, Legislature Goes Pfffft," *Sacramento Bee*, June 23, 2004.

37. See, for example, President Pro Tem John Burton's interview with sfpolitics.com.

38. Term limit law took effect for the assembly in 1996 and for the senate in 1998. See www.termlimits.org.

39. See, for example, Charles M. Price, "Advocacy in the Age of Term Limits: Lobbying after Proposition 140," *California Journal* 24, no. 10 (1993): 31–34.

40. See Policy Resources at www.cpb.org.

41. Anonymous interview, May 24, 2004.

42. Craig McGarvey, *Civic Participation and the Promise of Democracy* (2004), draft available from the Center for Religion and Civic Culture at www.usc.edu/schools/college/crcc/private/docs/publications/CivicParticipation.pdf.

43. Several academic studies have been made of ACORN, including Daniel M. Russell's doctoral dissertation at the University of Massachusetts at Amherst, 1986.

44. See "Issue and Victories" (although not updated after 2002) at their website www.picocalifornia.org.

45. McGarvey, *Civic Participation*.

46. For a description of Hehir's career and his thought, see William J. Gould, "Father J. Bryan Hehir: Policy Analyst and Theologian of Dialogue," in *Religious Leaders and Faith-Based Politics: Ten Profiles*, ed. Jo Renee Formicola and Hubert Morken (Lanham, Md.: Rowman & Littlefield, 2001), 197–223.

47. Full title: *Political Responsibility: Reflections in an Election Year*. See document and commentary in *Renewing the Earth: Catholic Documents on Peace, Justice, and Liberation*, ed. David J. O'Brien and Thomas A. Shannon (Garden City, N.Y.: Doubleday, 1977), 411–20 and 527–37.

48. *Faithful Citizenship: Civic Responsibility for a New Millennium* (Washington, D.C.: United States Catholic Conference, Administrative Board, 1999).

49. For a view of Coleman's theology, see his "The Common Good and Catholic Social Thought," in Steinfels, *American Catholics*, 3–18; John Coleman, ed., *Public Discipleship and Modern Citizenship* (Urbana: University of Illinois Press, 1998); "Development of Church Social Teaching," *Origins* 11 (June 4, 1981): 41; and *An American Strategic Theology* (Ramsey, N.Y.: Paulist Press, 1982).

50. Richard L. Wood, "History and Development of PICO," in *Faith in Action: Religion, Race, and Democratic Organizing in America* (Chicago: University of Chicago Press, 2002), 291–97.

# 10

## Conclusion: Themes in Religious Advocacy

### Kevin R. den Dulk and Allen D. Hertzke

To conclude this book, we turn to a discussion of themes that emerge from the case studies. These themes, of course, do not exhaust the possibilities, especially given the rich diversity in the states. But we think they will help readers draw their own lessons from the chapters contained in this book.

### ALIVE AND ACTIVE

The first theme that emerges from these chapters is that religious advocacy is alive and active at the statehouses. In every state surveyed, diverse groups weigh in on a wide variety of concerns. These concerns include not only such hot-button issues as abortion and same-sex marriage but also education policy, health care, social welfare funding, crime, the death penalty, the environment, the state budget, and even (in a few cases) foreign policy. And religious groups do make an impact—often modest to be sure—but nonetheless tangibly, as numerous examples in the chapters show.

But is this religious political effort distinctive? Or are the tactics and values of religious groups and lobbyists indistinguishable from their secular counterparts? Based on the sample of states surveyed here, we believe that state-level religious advocacy is distinct. It is different from many other forms of advocacy because religious leaders represent broad moral visions rooted in their respective church traditions and teachings. As David Yamane demonstrates, religious advocates often see themselves as offering a prophetic witness, seeking to transform or renew society in conformity to biblical values. Thus, a Jewish lobbyist sees his responsibility as nothing less than *tikkun olam*, or repairing the world. Variations on this theme are echoed by representatives of mainline Protestants, evangelicals, and the Catholic Church. We hear them saying that faith demands that they defend morality, fight for the common good, promote social justice, protect the weak, and "contribute to the well-being of all of the members of society."

A sense of sacred mandate suggests the distinct motivation of religious advocates. For some, this is very personal. As one pro-life lobbyist in Wisconsin remarked, "What will I say when I meet my maker and he asks, 'What did you do to help protect the unborn?'" Others, especially Catholic leaders, draw from their churches' long-standing reflection on public theology. These motivations create relatively strong connections of lobbyists and other staff to their organizations. Religious group advocates are rarely "hired guns" who work for money or prestige and are quick to leave when either runs out. They tend to have intense commitment to the cause.

This idea of political advocacy as "witnessing" to the faith, of course, does not mean that religious advocates always agree; indeed, vehement disputes occur, especially on cultural issues. In Texas, for example, Calfano, Oldmixon, and VonDoepp show that religious conservatives bring their particular interpretation of "God's guidance" in fighting battles over same-sex marriage and the teaching of evolution in public schools. In California, on the other hand, Cleary provides numerous examples of progressive "witness" on behalf of the weak and vulnerable by Catholics and mainline Protestants. In Massachusetts and Virginia, we see black church representatives joining with Catholic institutions and mainline Protestant denominations on behalf of initiatives for the homeless, the poor, and the accused.

While groups sometimes compete or oppose each other, collectively they do represent values that transcend those advanced by the economic and professional lobbies that otherwise would dominate the scene. From family policy to gambling, abortion to euthanasia, homelessness to child poverty, sentencing guidelines to treatment of prisoners, religious advocates interject faith-based arguments into the grubby world of state lobbying.

A look at a few issues illustrates this alternative witness of religious groups. In California, the lobbyist for the Quakers (Friend's Committee on Legislation) led a modestly successful coalition to advance rehabilitation versus punishment of prisoners, along with humane release policies. A coalition of mainline denominations and the Catholic Church also worked to blunt what would have otherwise been "devastating" budget cuts proposed by Governor Schwarzenegger for California's "poor, sick, blind, and disabled." The Catholic Church, with its large Hispanic population, often champions the cause of undocumented immigrants.

One of the most visible cases of groups promoting distinct issues, of course, concerns the Christian Right. Since its rise and influx into the Republican Party, the relationship between the business (or country club) wing of the Republican Party and the "moralists" has never been entirely natural or without strain. Economic conservatives certainly welcome support for candidates who advance their interests, but without the "moralists," certain issues would never have emerged onto the national and now state agenda.

We see this powerfully in such states as Virginia, Texas, and Georgia but to a degree in all the states where Christian Right mobilization occurs. Efforts to restrict abortion remain at the top of the agenda. But because of the narrow confines of Supreme Court doctrine, substantive policy victories are modest or symbolic. In Virginia, as Larson, Madland, and Wilcox show, Christian conservatives successfully backed a law that makes killing a pregnant woman a double murder and gained restrictive language in sex education curricula that might have been construed as promoting abortion. Texas also passed restrictions on abortion, but in Georgia, as Bullock documents, the Christian Right has been stymied up through the 2004 session.

Same-sex marriage is another issue that has a high profile because of traditionalist mobilization. While some states banned same-sex marriage, Virginia went beyond marriage to ban same-sex civil unions and any recognition of same-sex contracts. Michigan, through the mobilization of several religious groups, passed a state constitutional amendment of similar breadth through a 2004 ballot initiative. And Massachusetts, because of its state supreme court finding that restricting marriage to heterosexuals is contrary to the state constitution, has become ground zero in the battle over gay marriage, with religious traditionalists mounting the effort to amend the state's constitution.

Beyond issues, a final distinctive feature of religious advocacy is the approach commonly employed by the groups. As several authors note, religious groups do not "wine and dine" legislators or provide donations from political action committees; in other words, they operate without some of the tools of their secular counterparts. They rely more on moral appeals and grassroots mobilization than on classic "influence peddling" because of their religious consciousness. This approach can diminish their effectiveness, but they see the trade-off as worth the choice. As Kevin den Dulk argues for Michigan, religious faith not only provides the motive for activism but also shapes "the strategies and tactics those groups use to pursue their goals." Thus, "worldview—distinctly religious ways of explaining and evaluating the social and political world—can shape a group's strategic decision making."

David Magleby's account of Mormon lobbying in Utah illustrates this strategic distinctiveness. While its moral concerns delineate clear policy positions, the Church of Jesus Christ of Latter-day Saints (LDS Church) exercises a cautious and understated strategy to advance them. This velvet glove approach reflects the church's desire to remain above the political fray as much as possible but probably also the reality that the vast majority of legislators share Mormon values and thus need less overt lobbying to reflect church teaching.

What emerges from this review is that "representing God at the statehouse" reflects a distinctive political witness. While church groups often join in coalition with secular organizations, they do bring moral voices that, in the American religious context, carry considerable weight. And what the groups lack in money they sometimes can make up in moral legitimacy and intense commitment to the cause at the grassroots and among group leaders.

## DIVERSITY IN BOTH RELIGION AND POLITICS

In addition to the remarkable vitality and distinctiveness in religious lobbying across the states, statehouse lobbying reflects a diverse religious and political landscape. Unlike the lobbying milieu in Washington, D.C., where nearly every religious tradition is active to varying degrees, each state government attracts a unique combination of religious groups. These groups are motivated by a bewildering range of beliefs and interests, and they have widely different capacities to represent their faith in the statehouse.

Some religious traditions join a set of clear theological inclinations with ready-made leadership and financial resources. Such a combination of means and motive helps explain how American Catholicism, which has a presence through conferences in every state considered in this book, has developed a remarkable reach into American state politics. Bishops create Catholic conferences as the policy arms of the Church in particular states, and they can draw from the diocesan structure of the Church in each state as a resource. Still, levels of Catholic access and influence appear to be higher in the Northeast, Midwest, and West, where immigration patterns have resulted in disproportionately large Catholic populations.

Resources are similarly localized for other religious traditions. David Magleby's examination of the Latter-day Saints in Utah, when contrasted with profiles of the other states (most of which do not even mention a Mormon presence), demonstrates how the resource of a concentrated membership can lead to significant access (though perhaps not direct influence) in a limited area. Evangelicals, too, have concentrated numbers in a particular region—in their case the South—though there is good reason to be cautious about attributing decisive importance to their regional distribution, as we discuss later.

Yet even groups with the most highly motivated members and ample resources inevitably face obstacles within their specific political environments. As Larson, Madland, and Wilcox aptly put it in their examination of Virginia, institutions can "quiet" the voices of religious advocates. All groups must confront the peculiarities of state governments—their levels of professionalization, party competition, political culture, and so on—as well as the influence of other groups, including such traditional state powerhouses as labor, education, and business. Whether political environment mutes religious voices or provides opportunities for being heard, the state profiles in this book suggest that political context matters.

Consider, for example, the level of professionalization in a state legislature. In some states, primarily in the North and West, legislatures are appropriately called professional institutions, with relatively high pay for legislators, ample staff support, and lengthy legislative sessions. Several of these highly professionalized states—especially Michigan and California but also New Jersey, Wisconsin, and Massachusetts—are represented in this book. These states present opportunities for advocacy groups, including religious ones, by providing greater points of access. Groups can build relationships with legislators and staff members who are committed full time to their work, and longer legislative sessions allow greater time to influence legislation. Several of the chapters that examine states with professional legislatures speak specifically to the importance of networking in these states. After all, despite widespread reputations for being scoundrels or worse, lobbyists trade in useful information, and they cannot be effective if public officials do not trust the source. Building long-term relationships, which foster the norm of trust, is much easier when legislatures provide longer periods of time to make contact.

Still, groups face networking problems even in professionalized statehouses. Michigan and California, two of the most professional legislatures, are also among the twelve U.S. states with term limits. In 2004, California's state government lost nearly a quarter of its legislators to term limits; Michigan saw a remarkable 34 percent of its membership term-limited out of office, the most of any state in the nation. For groups, religious or otherwise, the loss of these legislators often means the loss of years of relationship building. On the one hand, the loss can be especially acute for groups with smaller staffs and budgets, like most of the religious organizations in this study, since they have fewer resources in state capitals to develop such relationships. But, on the other hand, many religious groups also have ready-made connections to up-and-coming legislators through their relatively large grassroots networks. As den Dulk shows in Michigan, legislative turnover as a result of the recent addition of term limits in that state has forced religious advocates to rethink their tactics and rely to a greater extent on ordinary members who may have personal or professional associations with new legislators.

The effects of institutions on religious lobbying are amplified even further in the least professionalized state legislatures, including Virginia, Texas, Georgia, and Utah. The opportunities for networking are less abundant; indeed, the possibility of simply making contact with elected officials is greatly reduced. As Larson, Madland, and Wilcox point out through the voice of a Virginia Christian Coalition staffer, lobbyists face poor odds of making contact with elected officials when a state government combines a short legislative session (in Virginia's case, no more than two months a year) with daunting legislative workloads conducted by part-time legislators who quickly leave for their regular jobs after their work is complete. For religious groups, particularly conservative evangelical groups that often use mass pressure to influence policymakers, the shortened legislative sessions make it difficult to keep up a lobbying campaign.

Party control of government also affects opportunities for statehouse lobbying. Conservative evangelicals, who have become an increasingly powerful faction within the Republican Party, often benefit when the GOP has statehouse control. The electioneering of Christian conservatives in places as varied as Michigan and Texas is illustrative. The greater the perception that there is a connection between "Christian Right" electoral efforts and GOP success, the greater the legislative access—though not necessarily success, as Georgia illustrates—of movement organizations like the Christian Coalition. Conversely, groups associated with the more liberal agendas of mainline Protestants, Jews, and Catholics do not fare as well in those states as, say, Massachusetts or California. States with deeply divided government, such as Wisconsin and Michigan (both currently have Democratic governors and GOP legislatures, reflecting relatively long histories of rough partisan parity in those states), present both opportunities ("a level playing field," as David Yamane puts it) and obstacles to the various religious traditions.

These characteristics of political institutions often reflect broader features of a state's political culture that can affect religious advocacy. Although Daniel Elazar's typology of traditionalist, moralist, and individualist state cultures does not easily correspond to the states surveyed in this book, his underlying argument that each state operates according to some basic political norms and values is a subtext running through the book profiles.[1] Texans tend to support the individualistic norms of free markets and suspicion of government on the one hand and traditionalist religious values on the other. In contrast, the state of Massachusetts identifies itself as a "commonwealth," representing a "moralistic" or positive view of government's role in creating a good society. Such cultural patterns in these and each of the other states can present openings or obstructions to religious advocacy, depending, of course, on the ideological and political commitments of religious advocates themselves.

The political culture of a state is not manifest solely in governmental institutions; it is also reflected in the countervailing influence of other lobbying groups, a key feature of a religious group's political environment. The goals of well-resourced groups, chief among them some combination of labor, business, agriculture, and education in most states, tend to dominate legislative agendas, crowding out "moralist" concerns that may be particularly important to religious believers. Such a pattern was evident even in states like Utah, where the striking concentration of the LDS Church has not necessarily resulted in Mormon lobbyists dominating the state legislative process.

## COALITIONS ARE CRUCIAL

In terms of religious group strategy, perhaps the most prominent theme that emerges from the state profiles is the decisive importance of coalition building. The fact that religious advocates are not as well heeled as other lobbyists makes work in coalitions vital. Sometimes coalitions form naturally between ideologically like-minded groups; other times, a specific issue will draw unlikely allies together. Whatever the motives, coalitions are invariably more effective than unilateral action.

The coalition partner with the broadest reach, of course, is the Catholic Church. Its breadth is not only the result of its relatively strong presence in nearly every state; it is also the only religious advocate found routinely in both liberal and conservative coalitions. This feature is nicely captured in Massachusetts, where the Catholic lobbyist one day joins with the American Civil Liberties Union to oppose the death penalty and the next opposes it on abortion.

A number of evangelical groups have coalesced around the banner of "family values" and traditional morality. They are joined with others on the basis of issue, such as with the Catholic Church on abortion and some black churches on gay marriage. Sometimes conservative religious groups join coalitions that appear to reflect more an ideological concordance than a religious one. In Virginia, for example, Christian Right organizations closely coordinate strategy with antitax groups. In Texas, such prominent religious groups as Eagle Forum and Christian Coalition joined with other conservatives to lobby against health coverage for uninsured children. The strained theological reasoning behind such a stance was indicated by the fact that the lobbying arm of the conservative Texas Baptist General Convention parted company with these groups and backed state health care accessibility.

Not all traditionalist alliances work. For some groups, traditionalist principles are absolute and therefore nonnegotiable; for others, short-term compromise and incremental policy change is a tolerable expediency. The state of
Georgia illustrates the past failure of one group, in this case Georgia Right to
Life (GRTL), to build a broad enough coalition to achieve even modest legislative success. As Bullock shows, GRTL advanced the most uncompromising position in its advocacy, more extreme than that taken by the Christian
Coalition. In the end, the inability of such pro-life allies to forge a common
strategy diluted their effectiveness.

To varying degrees, most states also have a self-identified "social justice"
coalition that includes historically mainline denominations, the Catholic
Church again, black churches, and Jewish groups. The mix varies depending
on the religious configuration in each state. In Wisconsin, the progressive
coalition is anchored by the Lutheran lobby and the Catholic Conference. The
agenda is captured by the Lutheran office's stated purpose as "advocating justice for disempowered people and responsible care of creation." In Massachusetts, large Catholic institutions join with Jewish groups and mainline
Protestants on child and elderly welfare and immigration issues. In diverse
California, the liberal coalition includes a wide spectrum of Protestants (including the largely gay and lesbian Metropolitan Community Church),
Catholic groups, Quakers, black religionists, and Jews, along with a host of
secular progressive entities.

Strange-bedfellow groupings show us the pull of coalition building most
clearly. While African Americans join fellow religious progressives and oppose much of the Christian Right agenda, on some issues they have joined
strange-bedfellow coalitions. In Virginia, Michigan, and elsewhere, we see
such unconventional alliances on backing for state educational vouchers. In
Massachusetts, black ministers joined the traditional coalition against gay
marriage. One of the more unusual alliances brought together Jewish groups
and evangelical Christians in support of the state of Israel. While foreign policy seems far removed from state politics, for Jewish lobbyists this is not the
case. We see this vividly in the case of Texas, where the Jewish Federation
sponsors trips for legislators to Israel. Evangelical support for Israel, consequently, led to the development of strong relationships between these otherwise strange bedfellows, to the point that the Federation receives major financial support from a Christian Right group. Of course, Jewish and evangelical
groups find themselves in opposite alliances on many church–state issues.

Because of its religious composition, the state of Utah presents a unique
case, with less formal alliances than elsewhere. In part this is because of
greater religious homogeneity in the state but also because the LDS Church
chooses to operate in quieter ways and thus does not formally join coalitions.

The unique Utah context does shape the work of others. The Catholic lobbyist, as Magleby notes, is able to devote more time to "social justice issues" because her "advocacy of the sanctity of life" is already shared by the Mormon population and the heavily Mormon legislature.

Occasionally, an issue will unite all religious groups. Proposals for expanded gambling in Texas, for example, sparked the ire of religious groups across the spectrum. Mainline liberal and Catholic organizations depicted state-promoted gambling as a regressive tax, while conservative evangelical groups opposed it as patently immoral.

Within coalitions there is a pattern of targeting and specialization that maximizes religious leverage on specific issues. As den Dulk argues, "Groups with fewer financial resources but targeted priorities are able to do more in concentrated areas than other groups that cast too wide a policy net." Thus, savvy groups target particular issues they judge both crucial to the cause and opportune for impact. In Michigan, this meant that the conservative Family Forum decided to focus attention in the past few years on "marriage and sex education in the schools, leaving other issues to other groups."

As groups target particular issues, a kind of specialization arises. The most obvious kind of such specialization is between broad coalitions. As Yamane shows, in most cases the work of the "social justice" coalition does not come into direct conflict with the "social regulatory" coalition. The liberal coalition's focus on hunger, nutrition, health care, corrections, welfare, and environment is not opposed by conservative groups, just mostly ignored. The liberal coalition, in turn, does not directly oppose the conservative agenda on abortion and gay marriage.

Specialization also arises *within* coalitions. In other words, while all groups in a coalition may back a particular cause, one of the groups may spearhead the effort. We see this in cases where black churches take the lead on such issues as civil rights, housing, and jobs. In Virginia, for instance, the African American leaders have focused recently on racial profiling and unequal prison sentencing as legislative priorities. In California, different liberal religious groups operate with explicit divisions of labor—Quakers on criminal justice, Lutherans on environment, and Catholics on welfare policy.

Within the traditionalist coalition, the most obvious specialization is the pro-life movement. Because of their clear focus, state right-to-life organizations often anchor coalitions against abortion, stem cell research, and euthanasia while backing laws to encourage adoption. To be sure, considerable overlap exists with pro-life churches, but issue specialization ensures that other priorities do not submerge "sanctity of life" issues.

Texas, with its formidable network of Christian Right groups, provided one of the clearest examples of specialization in conservative ranks beyond

abortion. Eagle Forum targets education policy, specifically the sex education curricula, while the American Family Association focuses on negative
messages in the mass media. As specific issues arise, moreover, the theological and strategic positions of an organization can create opportunities for
leadership. With pro-gambling forces mounting initiatives in the state, the
Christian Life Commission, the policy arm of the Baptist General Convention, took a leading role in opposing expansion of gambling. The Convention, both because of its central place in the state's religious landscape and
its biblical understanding, was a formidable adversary to gambling interests.

## THE EVOLUTION OF THE CHRISTIAN RIGHT

Although the state profiles reveal a remarkable diversity of religious expressions and many important interrelations among them, there are two religious
traditions—Catholicism and evangelical Protestantism—that emerge as particularly active across state governments. The electioneering and lobbying efforts of these traditions are themselves themes that are an integral part of the
story of state-level politics.

While evangelical political activity has ebbed and flowed over the past
century, the emergence of the "Christian Right" in the 1980s and 1990s sig-
naled a new movement into public life. From its beginning, the Christian
Right has been a moralist reaction to perceived cultural threats, from abortion
to indecency to secularism in public schools. The nature of that reaction, however, has changed over time, including its political targets. Christian conservatives' most recent efforts to "spread out and dig in"[2] suggest even greater
attention to state government than in the past.

What is the Christian Right at the state level? Who constitutes it? What are
their concerns and tactics? Political categorizations often convey too much
and too little simultaneously, and so it is with the "Christian Right." Problems
with the phrase "Christian Right" are evident especially when we consider its
applicability across the states. The singular term "Right," for example, con-
notes a monolithic ideological grouping. But as the state profiles in this book
attest, there are important religious and political differences, some subtle and
inconspicuous, others clear and explicit, that distinguish Christian conservative organizations across the states. So, too, the term "Christian" defines the
movement in distinctively religious terms. While it is certainly the case that
this political movement is fueled largely by highly committed Christians and
especially traditionalist evangelicals, there are many within the movement
profiled in these pages who would prefer "pro-family" or some other term to
focus attention on their policy goals rather than their religious motivations.

Accordingly, while we use terms such as "Christian Right," "Christian conservative," or "evangelical conservative" here, the diverse motivations, tactics, and experiences of groups across the states remind us that such characterizations are simplifications of a varied movement.

The emergence of the Christian Right as an influential movement, especially in the South and the Midwest, illustrates the familiar link between electioneering and governing. Political scientists have long recognized the key connection between legislators' policy efforts and their electoral ambitions. Interest groups know well the importance of this linkage and seek to exploit it by providing indispensable support to candidates for office. While religious conservatives were slow to learn this lesson, many eventually realized that they would have to develop organizations that were something more than mailing lists and threat letters.

This lesson was often learned through failure. In the midst of the Moral Majority's decline in the late 1980s (it finally dissolved in 1989, in part because of a lack of grassroots support), the Reverend Pat Robertson ran for the GOP presidential nomination in 1988. His campaign generated intense interest among some Christian conservative activists throughout the country, and his surprising second-place finish in Iowa buoyed his supporters. Yet his message had little appeal outside his relatively small support base, and his campaign quickly fizzled. In its wake, Christian conservative loyalists at the state level were left demoralized and, in many instances, ostracized by "mainstream" members of the Republican Party. They were perceived as uncompromising and politically naive, not to mention a thorn to more conventional and established party candidates whose agendas were economic, not moralist. Some activists, as a Robertson operative in Michigan put it, were forced into a "sackcloth and ashes" mode in which they actively sought to reintegrate into state-level political networks by making amends for Robertson's often torrid campaign.

Some of these conservatives also learned a new kind of incrementalism; rather than seeking highest elective office, Christian conservatives turned their attention to local government and began to develop electoral strategies for county- and statewide offices. They also redoubled their efforts at educating the grassroots. These strategies paid off in at least two ways: Christian conservatives helped elect officials into legislative positions, and they began developing as an established and apparently long-term faction within both the national and the state divisions of the Republican Party (something Robertson's campaign had less success accomplishing). In particular, the political mobilization of the Christian Right movement was a key reason for GOP ascendancy in the 1994 congressional elections. Christian conservatives themselves took lessons from the 1994 national elections into their own political backyards, running for everything from local school board to governor.

As a result of their various political efforts, the Christian Right began to develop a reputation as a major political player, especially in the South. Certainly, the Calfano, Oldmixon, and VonDoepp profile of Texas suggests that their reputation was well earned in some states. But while Christian conservatives had some successes in state elections (and were widely perceived as George W. Bush's kingmakers in the 2000 and 2004 elections), their influence in the governing process can be overstated. Campaigning and governing are interrelated, but they are not the same thing. To be sure, Christian Right influence remains greatest where legislators perceive that Christian conservatives form a substantial voting bloc. But legislators are cross-pressured in many ways that can present obstacles to conservative Christians even in states where their numbers are relatively large.

Indeed, the contrast of state profiles in this book yields a counterintuitive image: the size of the Christian conservative constituency in a state is not always positively correlated with its access and influence. On the one hand, while evangelicals have relatively large numbers in southern states, they have not always fared well in the legislative arena. They have no control over some of the reasons for their legislative failures: even in GOP-controlled legislatures, evangelical-associated organizations have faced the issues of intra- and interparty competition and scarce resources that confront any other group. Larson, Madland, and Wilcox's description of the mixed success of numerous Christian Right organizations and churches in Virginia is a good illustration. But the level of Christian conservative influence is often the result of strategic choices groups themselves have made as well. For example, Georgia Right to Life, while in a state with a relatively large number of evangelical conservatives, "commands a position of electoral irrelevance," as Bullock puts it, because of its uncompromising one-exception approach to the abortion issue.

On the other hand, while they are by no means monolithic or overwhelmingly powerful, Christian Right groups in states where their natural constituency is smaller have had some notable successes. One might expect that in California and Massachusetts (and to a lesser extent in Michigan and Wisconsin), Christian conservatives would enjoy less respect—or fear—in government than they do in the southern states. After all, the North and West simply have fewer right-leaning evangelicals and Catholics engaged in the political process. But it is not simply the proportion of Christian conservative voters that explains political potency; it is a legislator's perception that Christian conservatism is broadly palatable to the voting public as a whole. If conservatives mobilize the broader public on an issue, the pressure on a legislator is much greater than if those same conservatives can muster only a threatening press release or a few phone calls from their strongest loyalists. Even outside the South, Christian Right groups have been successful when they are open to compromise, spend a great deal of time and energy attending to the grassroots and mass education, and take an incrementalist approach to public policy.

This contrast of state profiles suggests that Christian conservatism can be — and is — active and influential across the United States, not simply in the "red" states that appear to lean toward the conservative side of the so-called culture wars. This finding dovetails with other studies that have suggested that the state-to-state variation in Christian Right influence is not necessarily wedded to the expected regions. Conger and Green's systematic interviews of key state-level elites found that the perception of the Christian Right's influence in individual state Republican parties had increased in five out of twelve midwestern states from 1994 to 2000, and the remaining states in that region stayed in either the moderate or the strong category (the three categories were "weak," "moderate," and "strong"). Michigan was among those states boosted from moderate to strong Christian Right influence; Wisconsin stayed in the moderate category. No midwestern state was characterized as having a "weak" Christian Right presence. While all fourteen states in the South were also described as moderate or strong, four were actually dropped from the strong to the moderate category, including Georgia. Western states tended to have a moderate Christian Right influence, including both California and Utah. The only region where there was a marked difference in the sway of the Christian Right was the Northeast, with all seven weak states, including Massachusetts, hailing from this part of the country.[3]

The overarching theme of Christian Right activity across the states is uneasy political integration. The 1994 elections taught evangelical conservatives that they could come out of the wilderness and enter the nitty-gritty of public life as influential "insiders," especially through the medium of partisan politics. Yet as Christian Right activists assimilate into the political process through state Republican parties and other avenues, they risk what often happens when movements are institutionalized, namely, the loss of a distinctive and independent critical voice in American politics. They face the question of whether they can speak as prophets and politicians at the same time.

## A DISTINCT CATHOLIC VOICE

A major Pew survey of Catholic civic engagement suggests that the community represents "a distinct voice" in American politics.[4] This theme emerges strongly in the cases represented here. In institutional structure, lobby approach, and ideological blend, the Catholic Church represents a unique presence in state capitals. Moreover, the Church's various educational and social service interests are often the direct responsibility of state governments.

As den Dulk notes, the hierarchical structure of the Catholic Church "parallels American federalism," with Catholic conferences operating at the state level, followed by dioceses and local parishes. Because of this formal structure, the Catholic Church operates with a strong institutional bearing. Bishops, even in states with relatively small Catholic populations, speak with formal authority for the Church, while their representatives lobby for official Church positions in state capitals.

But this institutional position extends beyond the formal Church structure. As a large but minority presence from the nineteenth century onward, Catholics have built an array of separate institutions with their own perspectives and interests. These include the nation's paramount parochial school system, a large hospital system, extensive charitable institutions and adoption agencies, along with diverse religious orders. Thus, Catholic institutions have keen interests in policy issues, and state policymakers generally pay attention to the leaders of these large nongovernmental entities.

A great illustration of this presence is California, where numerous semiautonomous Catholic institutions provide the largest share of private "health care, social services, and education in the state," as Ed Cleary observes. Not only do these institutions represent the employment interests of thousands of people, but their provision touches a wide array of patients, clients, and students across the state. Moreover, leaders of such institutions form a well-educated and articulate cadre of potential lobbyists.

Not surprisingly, in states with large Catholic populations, we see the institutional weight of the Catholic Church in state capitals. The Michigan Catholic Conference, for example, exercises a "breadth of regional and local coverage" that other religious denominations cannot muster. With assured funding from the state's bishops, the Conference is able to lobby on a wide range of issues. And it can use ties to the official Church for grassroots mobilization, such as sending its legislative policy newsletter to all parishes in the state.

Catholic institutional structures also facilitate lobbying where conditions are not favorable for others. As Larson, Madland, and Wilcox note, in the truncated Virginia legislative session there "is little denominational lobbying outside the Catholic Church." Even where it seems unlikely, as in Utah, this institutional presence is felt. In the Mormon heartland, Magleby concludes that the "Catholic Church is the most active and visible advocate for organized religion in Utah." Indeed, the lobbyist for the Catholic diocese is the one religious representative who works "every day" during the legislative session.

A second distinctive feature of Catholic lobbying is that it is hard to typecast in ideological terms. Catholic lobbyists join with conservative evangelicals on abortion, gay marriage, educational vouchers, and public displays of religion but turn around to back liberal Protestants and Jews on social welfare issues, food stamps, homelessness, the death penalty, and crime. As Larson, Madland, and Wilcox summarize it, Catholic lobbyists find "themselves supporting and opposing items on both agendas" of Democrats and Republicans.

This blend flows in part from Catholic social teaching, which does not fit neatly into the current ideological configurations of American politics. For one thing, the Church's stress on the government's necessary role in promoting "the common good" conflicts with the economic libertarianism now ascendant in the Republican Party. On the other hand, its doctrine of subsidiarity—that higher levels of society should support and not supplant the subsidiary ones—places it in tension with aspects of modern liberalism, especially on church–state matters. Removing obstacles for state aid to parochial schools, for example, is framed by the Church in terms of the right of parents to shape the education of their children. To subsidize only a secular public education and thus limit options for parents violates subsidiarity because the state is supplanting the key subsidiary institution of society—the family.

In terms of issues, we see a similar odd fit with the Left–Right dichotomy in American politics. The Church's teaching about society's obligation to uplift the poor results in progressive policy positions. As we see in California, Michigan, Texas, and elsewhere, the Catholic Church has lobbied for more state spending on such programs as child health care, poverty programs, job training, and education. And in one state, Texas, it has done so in opposition to several prominent Christian Right groups and Republican leaders.

Concern for working-class citizens leads the Church to lobby for increases in minimum wages, as we see in several states. This advocacy is often couched in terms of the right of a worker to a "living wage," a principle articulated over a century ago by Pope Leo XXIII and reemphasized by Pope John Paul II. In this arena, the Church finds it legislative champions primarily among Democratic legislators.

The Church also weighs in on crime, sentencing, and the death penalty. In Wisconsin, for example, the Catholic Conference representative drew on Catholic social teaching to testify against a bill that would have allowed employers to bar or terminate ex-felons from employment. In Texas, the "Catholic Church has been the most vocal opponent of the death penalty," and its lobbyist identified capital punishment as "among the key issues" addressed.

On the conservative side, wherever abortion policy is in play, the Catholic Church is there representing its pro-life stance. Only in strongly pro-choice California, where the issue is "off the table," does the Catholic Church not spend serious time lobbying to limit abortion. The Church has also defended its hospitals from provisions that would require them to perform abortions. On education policy, of course, the Church lobbies for greater state support to private religious schools, vouchers for parents, and accommodation of faith in the public schools—policies often promoted by conservatives today and embraced in varying ways by state Republican parties.

Finally, because the Church teaches that marriage is a sacrament—a sacred union of one man and one woman—it was plunged into the center of the gay marriage controversy. The issue exploded on state agendas when the Massachusetts Supreme Court struck down constitutional grounds barring homosexuals from marrying, leading to a flood of gay marriages in the commonwealth. Fears that their states might be required to recognize such marriages under the Full Faith and Credit Clause of the U.S. Constitution, legislators moved to pass legislative bans on gay marriage, while voter referenda did so in thirteen state constitutions. In all cases, the Church backed efforts to maintain the traditional definition of marriage and the privileges provided to married couples by state law. In Massachusetts, where only a constitutional amendment would override the state supreme court ruling, the Church invested heavily in the gay marriage battle. Not only did it lobby legislators, but it mailed a million letters to the state's Catholics urging them "to support traditional marriage."

Intriguingly, support for traditional marriage did not always mean opposition to certain rights of domestic partners. As Magleby notes, while Catholics worked closely with the LDS Church in efforts to ban same-sex marriage in California and other states, Utah provided a different story. Catholics were not consulted when the 2004 constitutional amendment banning same-sex marriage was drafted, and their lobbyists refused to back it because a provision would have limited the "rights of domestic partners and others."

As this section illustrates, both in institutional reach and in ideological mix, the Catholic Church brings a distinct witness to state policymaking. As we have seen, this facilitates some of the most prevalent coalitions in state lobbying today. Of course, the Catholic Church is not monolithic, and we see ideological diversity (or issue specialization) among the separate institutions and even occasionally within the official structure of the Church. This can facilitate creative coalition building. Thus, the Arlington diocese, "one of the most conservative in the nation," joins with evangelical groups to advance the church's pro-life agenda, while the more liberal Richmond diocese partners with progressive organizations on social welfare issues.

## CONCLUDING REFLECTIONS ON REPRESENTATION

The overall picture of religious interest groups across the states is that pluralism reigns. A great assortment of religious expressions are represented in the statehouses. On some issues, a religious group will compete with groups both within and outside the religious fold, but on other issues, that same group will seek common cause with its previous adversaries. In Madisonian terms, this group interaction translates into checks and balances among the various groups. Despite the relative strength of groups associated with some traditions—especially Catholicism and Evangelicalism—the state profiles suggest that, at least among religious groups, no single group dominates the state-level scene.

Religious advocacy also serves an important representative function in the states. Unlike traditional state powerhouses such as business, labor, or agriculture, the "interest" that religious groups represent is not associated primarily with economic values and objectives. Their efforts fit with a trend toward greater representation of so-called postmaterialist values and interests, especially transcendent moral values that are central features of all the religious traditions in these studies. Moreover, while some religious groups focus partly on the protection of narrow interests, most pursue a broader vision of the "public interest" or "common good" that would garner little attention in the policymaking process without religious pressure. By bringing these broader visions to the public square in the states, religious groups expand the scope of the policy agenda.

## NOTES

1. Daniel J. Elazar, *American Federalism: A View from the States*, 3rd ed. (New York: Crowell, 1972).

2. Kimberly H. Conger and John C. Green. "Spreading Out and Digging In," *Campaigns and Elections,* February 2002, 58.

3. Conger and Green, "Spreading Out and Digging In," 58.

4. Margaret O'Brien Steinfels, *A Distinctive Voice: American Catholics and Civic Engagement* (Lanham, Md.: Rowman & Littlefield, 2004).

# Index

# About the Contributors

**Charles S. Bullock III** is the Richard B. Russell Professor of Political Science and the Josiah Meigs Distinguished Teaching Professor at the University of Georgia. Among his recent books are *Runoff Elections in the United States* (coauthored with Loch Johnson), winner of the 1993 V. O. Key Award for the Best Book on Southern Politics presented by the Southern Political Science Association; *The New Politics in the Old South*, second edition (coedited and coauthored with Mark Rozell); and *Elections to Open New Seats in the U.S. House* (coauthored with Keith Gaddie).

**Brian R. Calfano** is a doctoral student in political science at the University of North Texas. His dissertation examines the role of institutional forces as constraints on clergy attitudes and behavior in mainline Protestant denominations.

**Anne Marie Cammisa** is a professor of government at Suffolk University in Boston. Her publications include *From Rhetoric to Reform? Welfare Policy in American Politics*. She researches and teaches in the areas of public policy, legislative politics, and women in politics.

**Edward L. Cleary** is professor of political science at Providence College. He has published eight books and numerous articles, focusing especially on religion and politics. His earlier study of California politics and religion, "Religion at the Statehouse," dealt with the California Catholic Conference.

**Kevin R. den Dulk** is assistant professor of political science and faculty fellow in the Honors College at Grand Valley State University. A scholar of judicial politics and the role of religion in public life, he is coauthor of *Religion* *and Politics in America* and numerous journal articles, book chapters, and reviews.

**Allen D. Hertzke** is professor of political science and director of religious studies at the University of Oklahoma. He is the author of *Freeing God's Children: The Unlikely Alliance for Global Human Rights*; *Representing God in Washington: The Role of Religious Lobbies in the American Polity*; and *Echoes of Discontent: Jesse Jackson, Pat Robertson, and the Resurgence of Populism* and coauthor of *Religion and Politics in America*, a text now in its third edition. He is a frequent news commentator who has been featured in such outlets as the *New York Times*, the *Washington Post*, the *Wall Street Journal*, and the *Weekly Standard*.

**Carin Larson** is a Ph.D. candidate at Georgetown University. She has contributed to a number of books on the subject of religious beliefs and political behavior. She is coauthor of the forthcoming book *Onward Christian Soldiers? The Religious Right in American Politics*, third edition.

**David Madland** is a government Ph.D. student at Georgetown University as well as a political adviser for labor unions and environmental organizations.

**David B. Magleby** is Distinguished Professor of Political Science at Brigham Young University. He has authored numerous articles and edited *The Other Campaign: Soft Money and Issue Advocacy in the 2000 Congressional Elections* and *Outside Money: Soft Money and Issue Advocacy in the 1998 Congressional Elections*.

**Elizabeth Anne Oldmixon** is assistant professor of political science at the University of North Texas. She has authored and coauthored numerous articles on religion and legislative politics as well as the book *Uncompromising Positions: God, Sex, and the U.S. House of Representatives*. She received her doctorate from the University of Florida and served as an APSA Congressional Fellow from 2000 to 2001.

**Mary C. Segers** is professor of political science and chair of the Political Science Department at Rutgers University's Newark campus. Her recent work has been in the religion and politics subfield. Her books include *The Catholic Church and Abortion Politics: A View from the States*, coedited with Timothy Byrnes; *Piety, Politics and Pluralism: Religion, the Courts, and the 2000 Election*; and *Faith-Based Initiatives and the Bush Administration: The Good, the Bad, and the Ugly*, coauthored with Jo Formicola and Paul Weber.

**Peter VonDoepp** is assistant professor of political science at the University of Vermont. His primary research interests are religion and politics and democratization processes in Africa. His work on these topics appears in numerous articles and book chapters.

**Clyde Wilcox** is professor of government at Georgetown University. He has written extensively on religion and politics, interest group politics, campaign finance, and gender politics.

**David Yamane** is assistant professor of sociology at Wake Forest University. He specializes in the sociology of religion, especially postwar American Catholicism, and is author most recently of *The Catholic Church in State Politics* and, with Sarah MacMillen and Kelly Culver, *Real Stories of Christian Initiation: Lessons for and from the RCIA*. He lives in North Carolina with his wife and three children.